KU-316-129

EAST SUSSEX COUNTY COUNCIL
WITHDRAWN
-9 AUG 2024
04024902

A GARDENER'S GUIDE TO

Bulbs

A GARDENER'S GUIDE TO

Bulbs

Christine Skelmersdale

THE CROWOOD PRESS

First published in 2012 by
The Crowood Press Ltd
Ramsbury, Marlborough
Wiltshire SN8 2HR

www.crowood.com

British Library Cataloguing-in-Publication Data
A catalogue record for this book is available
from the British Library.

ISBN 978 1 84797 376 4

🏆 This cup symbol has been used throughout the text to indicate the Royal Horticultural Society Award of Garden Merit

Diagrams by Charlotte Kelly

Dedication
For Roger

Acknowledgements
My thanks are due to my botanist friends, especially Kit Grey-Wilson, Martin Rix, Brian Mathew and Sharon McDonald, the International Daffodil Registrar, who so patiently answered my queries. Any mistakes, however, are all my own. I could not have written this without help from my many gardening colleagues, but special thanks are due to Jane Kimber and Jonny Clothier for their unfailing encouragement and support and for the use of some of his photographs.

For more information about the author and her work, visit her website www.broadleighbulbs.co.uk.

Typeset by Kelly-Anne Levey
Printed and bound in India by Replika Press Pvt Ltd

CONTENTS

FOREWORD

Any gardener who doesn't plant bulbs is missing out. For me they are 'firework' plants – light the blue touch-paper and stand well back – someone else having done all the work. That someone is, quite often, Christine Skelmersdale, whose bulbs have graced my garden for longer than I care to remember.

Christine is passionate about these plants, and frighteningly knowledgeable, but she is also a dab hand at passing on the information and skills that she has learned over a lifetime of growing bulbs, corms and tubers.

It always makes sense to grow plants that like your garden, its soil and situation. That way you stand the best chance of your plants doing well without either you or they having to struggle. But now and again it's good to present yourself with a challenge, and to do that you need to be armed with information from someone who has been there before you. I can't believe that there are many bulbs that Christine has not grown – and learned to cultivate to best effect – in her lifetime. That information you will find between these covers.

Just as important, you will also find details and pictures of the more obliging bulbs, from my favourite miniature narcissi, to those nodding angels the snakeshead fritillaries, crocuses and supremely elegant tulips. Each spring would be a dreary time of year without them.

But bulbs are not just for spring – carefully chosen, they will embellish your garden in every season; and that is the very premise of this book – it will widen your bulbous horizons and open your eyes to unknown treasures that are not always tricky to grow, but often unjustly neglected.

There are autumn crocuses and spectacular nerines that provide as much colour in 'the fall' as the foliage of a bright maple. Brilliant winter-flowering cyclamen are as vivid as summer bedding, and the snowdrops we all wait for signal that spring is just around the corner. But did you know that some of them flower in autumn too?

In summer there are alliums and dieramas (I've always struggled with the latter, but I'm hoping this book will improve my cultivation skills), and lilies (I love them), and mouthwatering nomocharis. Oh, and just in case you think I can only grow the easy stuff, I can boast a very happy clump of that wonderful orchid *Cypripedium x grande* (though to be honest, they seem to do very well with very little help from me).

Going through this book, I am struck by just how much (at my mature time of life) I have yet to try growing. But that's the thing about gardening – no one has ever grown everything that is available in today's plantsman's paradise. Perhaps that's why gardeners remain so enthusiastic, so passionate and so optimistic. We deal in beauty on a daily basis, and the kind of beauty we deal in is real, not imagined. Not for us the potions and creams that come with a promise so rarely fulfilled. No, we deal in beautiful reality – the reassurance that each year our plants will come up and give of their best without disappointing (provided we or the weather do not conspire to defeat them). As a group, bulbs are among the least disappointing in that respect.

And yet we can all be better gardeners by relying on the information of those more experienced than ourselves. When it comes to bulbs and other plants that possess swollen underground storage systems (the corms, the rhizomes and the tubers if we're being technical), few gardeners have a greater all-round experience than Christine Skelmersdale. Her book is destined to be one of those in my collection that falls apart through over-use. No author could be paid a greater compliment, but it is a compliment that Christine richly deserves.

Alan Titchmarsh – *gardener, author and broadcaster*

INTRODUCTION

Tulips with grape hyacinths and daffodils make the perfect spring picture.

A bulb, technically a geophyte, is a plant that produces a swollen underground storage organ. These have evolved to allow the plant to survive a period of inclement weather, usually drought. Bulbs are found in areas of the world where there is a strong seasonality in the weather, particularly those with a Mediterranean type of climate. These have cool, wet winters followed by a hot, dry summer. Woodland, where the tree canopy acts like an umbrella, has also produced its fair share of bulbs – we have only to think of the bluebell or snowdrop. Some families, such as tulips or daffodils, only grow from bulbs; others, like iris or anemones, may have a mixture of rootstocks depending upon their native habitat and how they have evolved to cope with it. Thus there are bulbous, rhizomatous and herbaceous forms of iris.

Throughout this book the term 'bulb' is used in its loosest sense to mean a swollen underground storage organ – corms, true bulbs, tubers and rhizomes. All are adapted to withstand adverse conditions of heat, drought or cold and all have one thing in common – for part of the year they are completely dormant. In order to withstand this time of inactivity,the bulb must build up its reserves while it is growing, for which the leaves are vital. The importance of this cannot be stressed too much.

Bulbs are essentially ephemeral. Their flowering period can be as long as a few weeks in the early, cooler part of the year, or as short as a few days, but normally they last for about one to two weeks depending upon the weather. However, their leaves, unlike their flowers, persist for many weeks and few are ornamental in their own right. Severe frost, unexpectedly hot conditions, or in particular strong winds can quickly devastate the flowers, leaving an untidy heap of leaves in their place.

Nevertheless it is essential that these are left to die down naturally in order to create a flowering-sized bulb for the following season. It is this mass of slowly fading vegetation littering the border, or having to delay the cutting of the lawn until it looks more like a hay field, that has given bulbs a bad name; and in extreme cases gardeners have been known to banish them altogether. However, if the bulbs are placed with care this need not be an insurmountable problem. Some bulbs such as *Cardiocrinum giganteum*, other lilies and many alliums have attractive, long-lasting seed heads, which are a bonus.

It is impossible to make generalizations about the soil type, conditions, alkalinity and so on preferred by bulbs. They have such disparate requirements that any special needs will be discussed under each specific entry. One point must be stressed, however: that of drainage. Most bulbs have evolved in areas with a Mediterranean type of climate where the summers are warm and dry, unlike those of more northerly areas. Thus the soil must be free draining if the bulbs are not to rot.

The prime consideration when planning a planting scheme must be the compatibility of the bulbs to the situation. The tables in the Appendix at the end of the book suggest appropriate bulbs for different locations in the garden.

Nectarascordum siculum in seed.

Striking seedheads of *Fritillaria imperialis*.

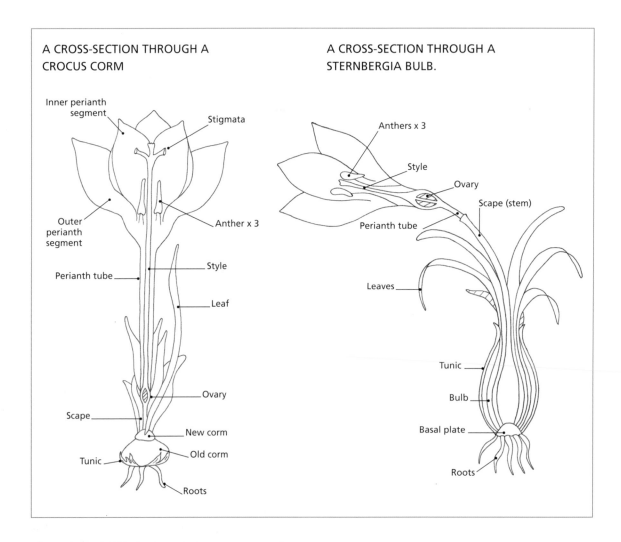

A CROSS-SECTION THROUGH A CROCUS CORM

Inner perianth segment
Stigmata
Outer perianth segment
Anther x 3
Perianth tube
Style
Leaf
Ovary
Scape
New corm
Tunic
Old corm
Roots

A CROSS-SECTION THROUGH A STERNBERGIA BULB.

Anthers x 3
Style
Ovary
Scape (stem)
Perianth tube
Leaves
Tunic
Bulb
Basal plate
Roots

Mixed corms.

What is a bulb?

There are four main types of 'bulbs':

1 Corms are solid structures providing the growing plant with nutrients only. The shoots arise out of the top and the whole corm gradually shrinks as the plant grows. These shrivelled remains can often be seen below the current corm. A new corm is formed on top of the old one within the circle of leaves. As the foliage dies off so the base of the leaves form a tunic, often in concentric circles. This can be papery or netted. In some genera like *Crocosmia* the old corm does not completely disappear but remains below the new one, often in extended chains. Examples of corms include crocus, colchicum, crocosmia, gladiolus and tritonia.

2 Like corms, tubers are solid structures but they are permanent, often living to a great age. They do not have a tunic but most have a hard, corky outer layer. Most tubers do not produce offsets and have only a single growing point – cyclamen, for example – and the only method of propagation is by seed. However, some corms like *Anemone blanda* and eranthis produce multiple growing points and they can be cut up. Examples of tubers include cyclamen, corydalis, eranthis, and *Anemone blanda*.

3 Rhizomes are the default structure for plants growing in cool woodlands. These are modified stems that creep under the ground (or above it in the case of bearded iris). Most are very thin and vulnerable to desiccation if they are left exposed for any time. As with the bearded iris, the rhizomes grow outwards and the end dies off behind. Some, such as wood anemones, form dense mats of twig-like rhizomes which are simply propagated by breaking them up (make sure that there is a growing point, a small white nodule, on each piece). Others, such as trilliums, are much slower and seed is a better method of raising new plants. Examples of rhizomatous bulbs include *Anemone nemorosa*, trillium, and some alliums.

4 The largest and by far the most disparate group are the 'true bulbs'. At first glance there seems to be nothing that links bluebells with daffodils or with lilies and alliums. A closer inspection reveals that they are all made up of one or more scales and a growing point attached to a basal plate. This is the hard bit at the bottom of an onion and it is very vulnerable to physical damage. All the roots arise from it. This basal plate is permanent, continuing from year to year while the scales attached to it turn into flowers and leaves and then die off to form new scales for the following season. In many bulbs the fading leaves turn into a protective tunic. This prevents the bulb from losing moisture while it is dormant; it is hardest in bulbs from hot areas (such as tulips) and non-existent in ones from cooler, damper conditions (such as lilies and bluebells). Those without protective tunics are vulnerable to excessive drying out during the planting season. Most bulbs produce offsets (small bulbs) on the side of the parent bulb, which are removed for propagation. Examples of true bulbs include narcissus, allium, chionodoxa, lilium, fritillaria, erythronium, scilla, hyacinth and tulip.

The amazingly variable true bulb.

Using bulbs in the garden

Bulbs present gardeners, even very experienced ones, with a conundrum: they are among the easiest of subjects to grow but surprisingly difficult to use really effectively. You have only to look around you in the spring to see how badly we often use these simple plants. Whereas considered thought may go into the placing of a shrub or herbaceous perennial, bulbs seem to be randomly shoved into any available space with little consideration other than, hopefully, soil type and aspect.

The fault, if fault it is, lies with the bulbs themselves rather than any design deficiencies of the gardener. Bulbs come as neat packages which are readily planted with little skill, but it is all too easy to forget the time gap between planting and flowering. Autumn is the principal planting time and even if you wait until the correct time of mid-autumn, which can be difficult with garden centres urging us to buy and plant earlier and earlier, the garden is often still bursting with colour from late-summer herbaceous perennials and half-hardy annuals. Just finding a space can be a challenge.

It is difficult to remember that when the bulbs flower, some six months after they were planted, the annuals have long since been consigned to the compost heap and the exuberant perennials have been cut down to size, leaving the bulbs in sole, splendid possession of the border. This six-month time lag often leads to rather random plantings and uncomfortable colour associations

A typical bedding display.

as we try and find a gap in the autumn border to squeeze the bulbs in – forgetting what else will be flowering at the same time in spring. Even a 10cm crocus can dominate a border in winter. It is now that the amount of forethought and planning that may (or may not) have gone into the placing of the bulbs becomes apparent, and our errors glaringly obvious.

The simplest way of avoiding these errors is to make notes, either written or as a photographic record of the border at the time you wish to change it, showing exactly where the gaps are and to make notes about the type, and probably most importantly, the colour of bulbs to be added. Then, when autumn comes round, you are prepared and the purchasing and planting can be done with confidence. If you are uncertain what you want or what will go with what there are a few simple guidelines which will make planting a less hit-and-miss affair.

Bulbs can be used throughout the garden and the next section is divided into the four main areas in the garden where bulbs can be planted – sunny borders, shady borders, grass, and in containers. The aim of this section is to give the principles behind using bulbs to create different effects. The principles will remain the same regardless of the scale of your border or garden. You can then choose the varieties to suit your requirements and taste.

Sunny borders

Sunny borders are a prime garden site and bulbs have to compete with a full range of other garden plants, so they are most likely to take a supporting role rather than centre stage, especially outside spring. Most bulbs, but especially spring-flowering ones, require a relatively dry summer dormancy. They will therefore not be very long-lasting in gardens where there is an irrigation system that waters the borders during the summer, although it is possible to lift the bulbs and store them for the summer. Tulips especially will benefit from this treatment. Alternatively, they can be treated as annuals and new bulbs planted each year. Daffodils are remarkably tolerant and will normally survive, as will small bulbs clustered at the very front edge. Lilies on the other hand will actively revel in the water, as lack of it when they are growing is one of the prime causes of 'blindness' – a failure to flower.

Formal planting

Bedding is the most familiar situation in which bulbs are encountered. Usually mixed with wallflowers or polyanthus, they are to be seen on virtually every roundabout or municipal park. This method is expensive both in bulbs and labour as the display needs to be replaced as soon as it fades, the bulbs being discarded rather than being left to die back naturally. This approach has limited use for the gardener, although it is useful for areas of high visibility such as a small front garden. Here the number of bulbs required is manageable and fun can be had experimenting with different combinations. Local parks departments are often a good source of ideas as it is with these large-scale plantings that the growers often introduce their newest varieties to the public.

However, there are areas in the garden where a certain formality of planting is appropriate. Box parterres, rose beds and narrow borders under pleached trees all lend themselves to this approach.

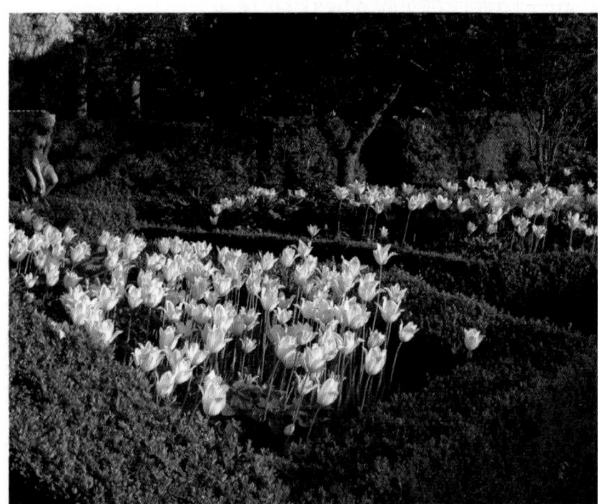

Tulip 'White Triumphator' filling a box parterre.

Tulips are the traditional bulb for these situations. They may need to be lifted after flowering or may be left *in situ*, depending upon the nature of your soil and the variety chosen. On heavy soils they can be left for some years, only topping up the display occasionally, but on lighter soils annual lifting and replanting might be a safer option to maintain the display. The lily-flowered tulips are especially effective massed in parterres where their pointed-tipped blooms seem to hover like butterflies above the low hedges. *T. fosteriana* 'Purissima' is excellent as an earlier-flowering option. Whatever your choice of variety, the density of the bulbs is of the utmost importance. Spread them too thinly and not only will the hoped-for impact be dissipated, the resultant display is liable to be a negative rather than a positive experience. Another simple rule is to plant the earliest-flowering varieties furthest away; thus the display is always freshest nearest the house, hiding the fading flowers of the earlier ones. It is best to keep to the same type of tulip if you wish to mix the colours, whether for complementary tones or contrasts. The purple-edged 'Shirley' and the dark 'Queen of Night' will give a dramatic late display. Drumstick alliums or *Lilium regale* can then follow on.

Short bulbs such as *Anemone blanda* 'White Splendour' or *Scilla sibirica* are perfect for under-planting pleached trees where the soil is too thin for tulips. The anemones do not need to be individually planted but can be scattered on the surface in the late autumn and then covered with compost or bark. Unlike tulips these are left undisturbed, their display improving year on year as the tubers enjoy their dry summers under the trees and increase in size. Grape hyacinths are another suitable subject for these massed plantings. Traditional rose beds lend themselves to similar edgings.

Incorporating bulbs into sunny borders

Location

Bulbs and herbaceous perennials are seen as mutually exclusive by many gardeners. Not only are they difficult to combine successfully with other plants: there is always the ever-present risk of spearing the bulbs when weeding the border in summer. Bulbs planted in the middle of the border, such as tulips, should be planted at least 20cm deep, which will take them well below danger level.

The foliage of many bulbs, but especially that of daffodils, is often perceived as such an insurmountable problem that they are banished from traditional herbaceous borders. The leaves of daffodils elongate considerably after flowering and are vital to maintain the vigour of the bulb for future years. All leaves must therefore be kept for some considerable time after the flowers fade. They then die back, 'flopping in masses of yellow decay', to use Reginald Farrer's evocative description. They can be rather difficult to incorporate successfully, but the problem of fading foliage can be overcome by the simple expedient of disguise. Clumps of early-flowering varieties can be placed along the back of a border where they will bring the border alive early in spring, but then the emerging herbaceous perennials will hide the fading bulb foliage.

A primrose provides the perfect foil for Crocus 'Skyline'.

The bicoloured N. 'Jenny' and 'February Silver' are good varieties for this treatment, being early-flowering and very long lived as well as good looking! The creamy white daffodils from Division 5, such as 'Tresamble' or 'Thalia', are other reliable choices.

The leaves of tulips are much better regulated; even the dying stems stand strongly to attention. The removal of the faded petals is all that is required to disguise them. They should be planted in good-sized clumps through the middle of the border. If these are to be left *in situ* then they repay the excavation of a decent hole – at least 15–20cm deep. They can then be successfully placed between clumps of herbaceous perennials which in turn will flop outwards, giving the tulips the chance of a dry summer dormancy under their protection.

Small, early-flowering bulbs such as crocus, eranthis and scillas, especially *S. bifolia* and *S. mischtschenkoana*, are neat enough in and out of flower to be clustered along the front edge of a border where they will add colour to an often very dreary time of the year. If the border includes shrubs such as roses, small bulbs like snowdrops and particularly chionodoxa can be clustered round their base, where they will be well away from inadvertent damage from the over-enthusiastic gardener. The aim is to add pockets of colour early in the year. The bulbs should therefore be planted in clumps of seven to fifteen rather than scattering them randomly through the border.

Summer bulbs take a much more supporting role in the border than their spring-flowering compatriots. Compared to most perennials they have a relatively short flowering period. However, most have fairly large flowers on tall thin stems so they are ideal as a foil for the more dense herbaceous plants. Alliums and lilies are best rising up through and flowering above the domes of perennials, so they should be planted in the middle of the border rather than at the back as their height might indicate. Bulbs with flowers in a spike, such as gladioli or camassias, should be planted in small groups.

The herbaceous plants will also solve the problem of the unattractive fading foliage of the alliums and camassias, which is so distressing to some gardeners. These bulbs come from areas of limited rainfall so they grow first in the spring then bloom as the leaves fade, rather than flowering first like spring bulbs. If they are planted behind herbaceous perennials their unsightly leaves will be hidden. Mounds of herbaceous geraniums are particularly good or day lilies *(Hemerocallis)*, which have similar linear leaves to the bulbs.

The summer-flowering Allium 'Purple Sensation' follows on from tulips in a border of grasses.

Pink tulip 'Marietta' with *Geranium tuberosum*.

Borders of grasses have become very popular in recent years and these drier conditions suit alliums better than most traditional herbaceous borders, which can be too moist for them in mid-summer. Other small summer-flowering bulbs like triteleias work well here as well.

Whichever bulb you choose, planting small clumps is preferable to dotting the same number of bulbs about. It is also much more practical, as they can be planted deep enough to be well below accidental damage.

Colour

We now come to the vexed question of colour, which is one of the most difficult things for the average gardener to achieve successfully. This is very much a question of personal preference but there are two basic approaches: harmonies, which use colours that are adjacent on the colour spectrum and are the easiest to use; and contrasts, which use colours from the opposite sides of the spectrum.

Harmonies

This is the easiest and simplest method of combining colours, using those that are adjacent on the colour spectrum. Pink with blue and purple or yellow with cream and white provide a safe combination of toning colours, and will always blend and look attractive – although the effect can be rather monotonous if the tones are too similar.

Tulip 'Apricot Jewel' and Aubretia.

Contrasts

Whereas harmonious colours are straightforward, always giving a pleasing result, they can be bland. A contrast, on the other hand, offers the gardener drama as it uses colours from the opposite sides of the spectrum, and although it does not always succeed it is great fun trying different combinations. However, the intensity of the dramatic effect depends upon the saturation and depth of the colour. Pale colours will appear more harmonious.

True scarlet can be a problem but will always go with blue, white or yellow, and of course orange. However, some contrasts are not pleasing, the colours setting up an uncomfortable resonance as they clash. Only experience will tell you what works. One of the safest options isthe purple/gold or the simple yellow/blue combination. The addition of a touch of yellow to blue, perhaps a few primroses or yellow pansies to a mass of rather pedestrian grape hyacinths, is magical.

Although with bulbs there is a tendency to think about spring to the exclusion of the rest of the year, the same principles can be followed in summer through to autumn: white lilies under pink roses, for example, or golden crocosmia with red dahlias.

Shape

Shape may not be the main consideration when choosing bulbs but this is to neglect one of their most useful assets. Some have a very complex shape – crown imperial fritillaries spring to mind – that is not easily associated with other plants. They are best allowed to dominate a border of foliage rather than trying to mix them with other flowering

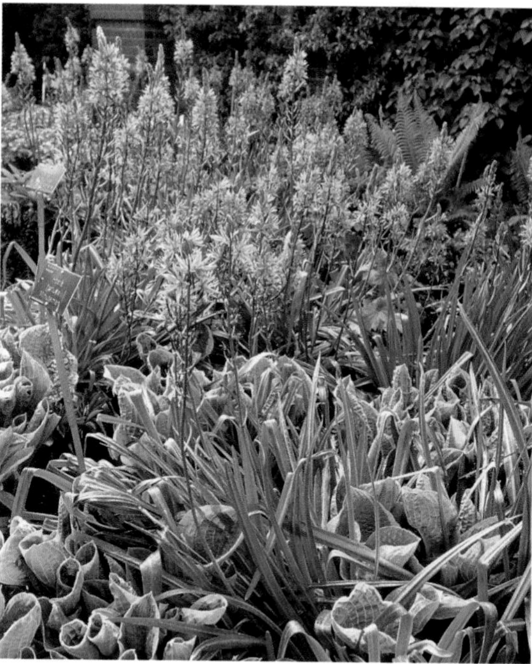

The spikes of Camassia are useful for a semi-shady border.

SPECIAL PLACES

A rock garden provides a natural home for a wide range of shorter flowering bulbs, starting in late winter with crocus pushing up through the low mats of an alpine dianthus, followed by the bright stars of *Anemone blanda* 'White Splendour' or the strident 'Radar', then dwarf daffodils and finishing with a wide range of species tulips, all of which thrive in well-drained, sunny soil.

There are many bulbs which will revel in the warm dry soil under a sunny wall. This is also the province of many South African bulbs; these depend upon a warm, dry summer to trigger their flowering. The season starts with the exotic eucomis followed by the golden cups of sternbergia and the showy heads of nerines and amaryllis.

subjects. Most lilies fall into the same category and are best appreciated standing proud of other plants. In the spring even a dwarf bulb can dominate a border, but come summer the herbaceous perennials swamp all but the boldest and it is now that these taller bulbs are so useful – their spikes (or pompoms in the case of alliums) punctuating the mounds of perennials. Early summer bulbs like camassias and alliums are especially useful to fill that awkward gap between the spring and true summer display.

Shady borders

The circular bed round a tree in a lawn is a natural planting place for massing many of the smaller spring-flowering bulbs such as grape hyacinths in the spring or colchicums in the autumn. They flower when there is plenty of moisture and light available but then are dormant during the summer. But other shady areas of the garden are often considered a problem by gardeners, largely ignored and their potential overlooked. So many gardeners regard a shrub bed as exclusively that – a collection of flowering shrubs, the possibilities offered by the ground beneath or around them forgotten.

Many bulbs, particularly those with rhizomes, are naturally natives of woodland, revelling in the light humus-rich soil found under trees or shrubs. We have only to think of our bluebell woods with their stunning carpets of blue in late spring. There are many other bulbs that are the perfect companions for deciduous trees and shrubs. They make their growth during the winter months when the branches of the trees are bare and moisture is freely available but then go dormant when the umbrella effect of the leaves makes the soil beneath parched. There is a huge choice possible as virtually all spring-flowering bulbs will grow well under shrubs, but there are some for which these cooler conditions in summer are essential: *Anemone nemorosa*, erythronium and trilliums in particular. North-facing walls offer the gardener a perfect alternative site for these bulbs that prefer cool damp conditions as there is no overhead canopy to keep off the rain.

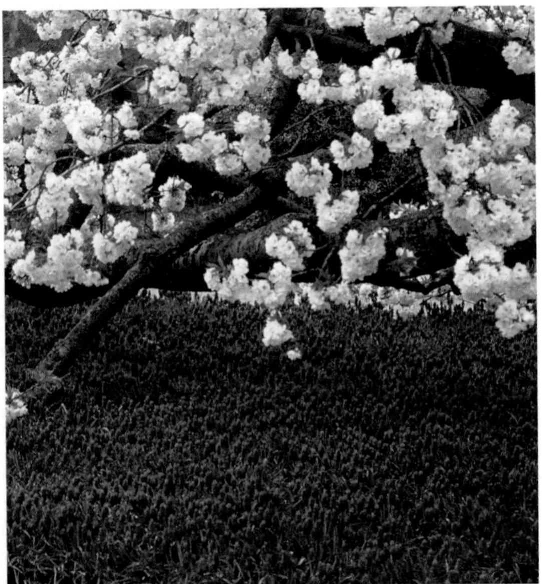

Massed muscari under a cherry tree at Wisley.

Cyclamen repandum, wood anemones and bluebells growing in shade.

The season kicks off in autumn with *Cyclamen hederifolium*, which will freely colonize the dry soils at the base of large trees, and colchicums, which revel in rich deep soils. These are followed in winter by *C. coum*, snowdrops and winter aconites. *Anemone blanda* is normally considered a plant favouring full sun but it will happily spread in light shade to give a glowing blue carpet early in the year, which can then be punctuated by clumps of golden daffodils. Other small blue bulbs such as chionodoxa and scilla like similar conditions. Later in the spring the new foliage of hostas, hellebores and Japanese anemones make the perfect foil for camassia, which could in turn be followed by lilies if it is not too dry.

Summer is more of a problem as the leaves of trees reduce not only light but also moisture. In open glades where the soil is not too dry, or under north walls, lilies,

Narcissus 'February Gold' follow snowdrops and aconites under birches.

especially those with turk's-cap-shaped flowers, are an ideal choice – *L. lancifolium* and *L. martagon*, for example.

The dry bed around the base of a large tree is an often overlooked planting opportunity. These areas are either neglected or restricted to ground cover but as there is no shade early in the year it is possible to construct a raised bed on the sunny side and mass it with small early-flowering bulbs, allowing them to exuberantly seed into each other. Small clumps of new varieties can be added to the mix each year. The season starts with *Eranthis hyemalis* and species crocus, which then segue into *Anemone blanda*, *Muscari latifolium*, and *Iris tuberosa*, followed by daffodils – even small tulips can be added to the equation.

Many gardens have a grassy bank as a boundary. This can be planted with snowdrops to start the season followed by clumps of daffodils mixed with primroses for a perfect spring picture.

Sadly, evergreen trees do not provide a seasonal canopy and there are few bulbs that will survive let alone thrive under them.

Naturalizing bulbs in grass

Whether it is Wordsworth's golden host blowing in the wind or a haze of bluebells staining the woods beneath the fresh young leaves of beech trees, massed bulbs growing in grass provide one of the most evocative sights of spring – although it need not be restricted to that season. It does not matter whether it is crocus studding the lawn or massed daffodils under fruit trees; this is probably the most common and foolproof method of growing bulbs. There is an enormous range of varieties suitable for growing in grass and once planted they can be left undisturbed for many years – the display improving all the time.

However, the inevitable problem with leaves rears its head again. Small, early-flowering bulbs like snowdrops and crocus will be going dormant by the time the grass needs to be cut but the lush leaves of daffodils can be more of a problem. It is recommended that daffodils need a minimum of six weeks' uninterrupted growth once the flowers fade. After that the leaves can be cut at any time without compromising the future performance of the bulbs. Early-flowering varieties are best for those gardeners itching to reinstate their stripes in the lawn, while those who are content to live with or disguise the fading foliage can choose from a much wider range and extend the flowering season into late spring, even incorporating tulips or camassias.

In the strict sense of the word, 'naturalizing' should be applied only to bulbs that will 'grow as in nature' – in other words, species bulbs that will seed around, but most gardeners use it to describe any bulb that is vigorous enough to be grown in grass. There are two distinct approaches to planting bulbs in grass: formal and informal.

Formal planting is where no attempt is made to imitate nature. The bulbs are used to provide blocks of colour and

Narcissus 'Peeping Tom' in grass under birches.

Planting daffodil bulbs.

are particularly useful for the more structured areas of the garden such as along a drive or near the house. The bulbs are planted in controlled groups of one or maybe two varieties. Here the choice of variety is not important; impact is the driving factor. Along a drive edge it is best to leave a 60cm strip unplanted. This not only allows for a straying vehicle, but also means that the edge can be kept neatly mown, which will help lessen the visual impact of the fading foliage later in the season.

With a long drive different blocks of bulbs can be used or later daffodils can take over from early crocus. There are, however, some warnings: circles of bulbs are not only visually uncomfortable – you must also remember that there will be six weeks at least when they must be left uncut. It is tedious to have to drive a mower in a tight circle. Gentle outlines of lozenges make mowing easier, especially around trees. The other warning is to avoid straight lines at all costs. These have a nasty habit of creeping in to the best plantings and once established they can be virtually impossible to eradicate or even disguise. My straight lines of snowdrops planted in error over thirty years ago are still clearly visible.

In informal plantings the gardener is making a conscious effort to mimic nature and free the bulbs from the formal constraints of defined shapes or areas, allowing them to spread around 'naturally'. It might be crocuses or snowdrops by the thousand in the wilder parts of the garden or a mass of daffodils, fritillaries and so on under apple trees. These depend upon sheer quantity for their effect, the bulbs being planted in a random manner. There are many varieties suitable for this treatment and the choice depends upon personal taste.

Another approach is to try to mimic wild plantings more closely. Fine examples of this are the *Narcissus bulbocodium* on the Alpine bank at Wisley, or by the stream in the Savile Gardens, the millions of *Crocus vernus* at Forde Abbey in Dorset or *Fritillaria meleagris* in the meadows at Magdalen College, Oxford. These displays all have one thing in common not shared by most gardeners – time. The bulbs have been seeding for a century or more. However, it is possible to cheat and create a similar natural effect, provided a few rules are followed. The secret lies in the choice of bulbs, or the three 'S's:

1. **Species or near-species bulbs:** these tend to be rather simple flowers that are appropriate for the site. Snowdrops, *Crocus tommasinianus*, small daffodils (such as *N. lobularis*, *N. obvallaris* and *N.* 'Topolino'), *Fritillaria meleagris*, *Ornithogalum nutans* and *Camassia quamash* are all good choices.

2. **Short:** the tall, modern hybrids have no place in this type of planting.

3. **Scattered:** plant the bulbs not in clumps but in a random, scattered manner, as though they had seeded naturally.

For daffodils growing in grass, leaving the surrounding grass unmown as the daffodils fade will aid this disguise – a much easier and less laborious method of hiding the unsightly foliage than attempting to dead head, which only partially tackles the problem as it is the leaves themselves that are so unattractive as they fade. No matter how tempting it might be to 'tidy up' the leaves and tie them in knots, this is not recommended as it is self-defeating, destroying the very cell pathways that enable the goodness to feed the bulb for the next season.

Planting methods

Choosing and ordering the bulbs for a large-scale project is much easier than the actual planting once they have arrived. There are many specialist bulb-planting tools on the market which are designed to create the perfect planting hole for daffodils; alternatively, you can use a trowel for small bulbs like crocus. It is also possible to remove a layer of turf, loosen the exposed soil and then plant directly into it.

Bulbs can also be grown in small pots to be added to an established planting in the spring when the gaps can be seen. This is also a useful method of thwarting mice and squirrels when growing fritillaries or crocus.

Aftercare

The grass must not be cut for at least six weeks after the last bulbs have flowered to give them adequate growing time. If the planting includes bulbs like fritillaries or *N. pseudonarcissus*, which increase by seed, it may need to be left for longer for the seeds to ripen. Once the seeds have been dispersed, strim the area and leave the grass uncollected for a couple of days to allow all the seed to drop. This is not necessary with hybrid daffodils; nor is it necessary to feed bulbs in grass: non-flowering will almost certainly be a result of congestion and overcrowding, which prevents the individual bulbs attaining sufficient size to flower. Physical division of the clumps is the only (rather laborious) way to overcome this, and it can be done at any time you can see them.

Pots of lilies fill this courtyard garden.

Fritillaries with small tulips and daffodils under the canopy of a small tree.

The double tulip 'Monte Carlo' is ideal for pots.

Bulbs in containers

Planting in containers, as with bedding displays, generally involves a single use of the bulbs, but it has the advantage that it is on a much smaller scale than bedding displays and is mobile. Many spring-flowering bulbs, especially tulips, hyacinths and muscari, are suitable for cultivation in containers, as are lilies and eucomis for the summer. Other than the small multi-stemmed varieties, daffodils do not really suit pots as the proportion of foliage to flower is unbalanced.

- Problem areas such as concreted areas can be disguised by the addition of pots. These can either be large mixed planters, to which a few bulbs can be added each autumn, or a collection of smaller seasonal pots.

- Focal points beside a door, gateway or steps benefit from the addition of pots. There is potential for a seasonal change as daffodils are followed by tulips then lilies or eucomis in the summer.

- Mixed plantings of different bulbs in a single container can be very spectacular but difficult to achieve as the foliage of earliest flowering varieties continues to grow after flowering, and can swamp the later varieties as they try to flower. Nearly all tulips

The dwarf Kaufmanniana tulips are perfect for pots.

are ideal for pots and crocus, and *Anemone blanda* and muscari all make excellent subjects for under or inter-planting with them. You can have one dramatic splurge with all the bulbs flowering at the same time or a carefully planned succession. If you wish to use two different tulips in the same container it is important that the later-flowering one is taller than the earlier.

Most daffodils are difficult even on their own as their leaves are sensitive to water, or rather lack of it, and once they have flagged no amount of moisture will revive them. Smaller varieties such as 'Hawera', 'Toto' and 'Tête-à-Tête' are less prone to this and have the added advantage of being multi-stemmed as well as multi-headed. Winter-flowering pansies are the perfect foil for most spring bulbs and extend the display back into winter before the bulbs appear. They will also act as a timely reminder to water the pot!

The scented *Lilium* 'Stargazer' is ideal for pots.

- Although spring is the principal time for bulbs in containers, there are some useful summer-flowering bulbs, especially the shorter lilies and eucomis. Here it is better to have a selection of pots of single varieties to add to a standard display of summer containers as they flower.

- All bulbs need a good depth of compost below them, but it is important that the ultimate size of the flower is also taken into account when choosing a suitable container. Tiny tulips look just as uncomfortable perched in the top of a tall Ali Baba pot as a tall tulip does swamping a pot that is far too small. Bulbs prefer to grow in a loam-based compost. The modern friable all-purpose composts do not give them the stability they need to flower well and are liable to dry out too quickly. Even if it rains, all pots still need regular watering in spring once the bulbs are in active growth. In the summer lilies and eucomis must be watered almost daily and given a regular feed or they may abort their flowers. More information will be found under the relevant sections.

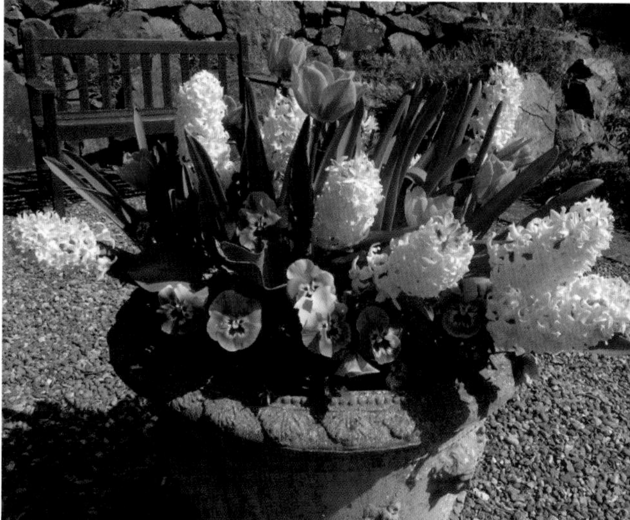

An exuberant mix of tulip 'Prinses Irene' and Hyacinth 'City of Haarlem' with blue pansies.

- There is always some discussion about what to do with the bulbs once they have finished flowering. Most spring bulbs growing in pots are unlikely to have the time or the conditions to make a flowering size bulb for the next season and are probably best discarded. Daffodils and hyacinths can be lifted as they fade and planted out in the garden to recover but tulips are best thrown away. Trying to keep small quantities of different varieties separate in the garage never quite seems to work. It is easier and more reliable to buy some more each autumn. It also allows you to ring the changes. *Muscari armenaicum* 'Blue Spike' is my standard companion for many bulbs in pots and I plant the discarded bulbs along the edge of my rose bed. Here their otherwise annoying habit of producing leaves in the late autumn is a positive bonus, giving a fresh green winter evergreen edge to the bed of stark rose stems. *Anemone blanda* tubers can be rescued and reused for many years – if you can find them.

  Lilies and eucomis on the other hand can be left *in situ* to give many years' service, provided they are well watered and fed. They should be planted into large containers that are not needed for spring bulbs.

CHAPTER 1

BULBS FOR THE AUTUMN

Seed heads of *Eucomis comosa* among grasses.

Say 'bulbs' to any gardener and their mind jumps to drifts of daffodils under cherry trees, but autumn, normally regarded as the season of decay, is the most important time in the life of a bulb. As the first rains fall in the Mediterranean areas or the leaves fall in temperate woodlands allowing more rainfall to reach the soil, so moisture breaks the drought-induced summer dormancy and the bulbs begin to grow. For most it is just the production of the roots that are so essential for future growth but for a few it is their flowering season as well. Surrounded by fallen leaves, they are a sight as welcome as they are unexpected on a sunny autumn day. Most autumn-flowering bulbs are planted in late summer or early autumn, just before they flower.

The showiest of the autumn-flowering bulbs are those from southern Africa such as the autumn lily *Nerine bowdenii* or *Amaryllis belladonna*, which rely on a dry summer to ripen their bulbs. These are planted in early spring as they come into leaf, although pot-grown ones can be planted at any time.

NOTE

Summer-growing bulbs like eucomis, some of which flower in the early autumn, are listed in the summer section.

Acis
(Leucojum)

Long included in Leucojum, these are now a genus in their own right. There are a number of very similar species but only one is really suitable for the open garden. It is often the first sign of autumn, frequently starting to flower in late summer.

A. autumnalis 🏆

As summer draws to a close, these tiny bulbs erupt into flower, almost overnight pushing up their slender stems, each topped with one or two tiny nodding purple-tipped white bells. These are followed by thin, grassy leaves. Northern Spain is their home, so they prefer a dry summer when they are dormant, and grow well on a sunny rock garden or around the base of a small tree. They are clump-forming and give their best display when well established. Height: 20cm.

Amaryllis belladonna.

Amaryllis

This single-species genus from South Africa is often confused with the non-hardy South American relative, the Christmas-flowering *Hippeastrum*. Amaryllis produce a cluster of six or more trumpet flowers on stout stems which are followed much later by the leaves. They can produce flowers at any time from late summer to autumn depending upon the weather in the preceding summer. They are reputed to be hardy to -5°C although we have grown them outside where the

Acis autumnalis.

Amaryllis 'Hathor'.

temperature has dropped much lower. More important is a warm, dry summer to encourage flowering. Bulbs that are overshadowed by neighbouring plants or receive too much water during the summer will fail to ripen and flower. Our bulbs grow freely in an open bed in the nursery but produce only sporadic flowers. Another clump injudiciously planted against a wall became smothered by its neighbours. It grew very well but never flowered until the offending vegetation was removed to allow the sunlight to fall directly upon the bulbs. The ideal position for all these autumn-flowering South African bulbs is against a dry, sunny wall where they can be left undisturbed to form large clumps. Mature, congested clumps flower best. They seem to do best in relatively frost-free locations such as near the sea and especially in the Channel Islands, where virtually every front garden is adorned by dramatic displays in October. The flowers are followed by long strap-shaped basal leaves that grow during the winter, gradually fading as the summer progresses. They make easy and attractive pot subjects for a cold glasshouse or conservatory.

Cultivation

The bulbs are planted in early spring just below the surface of the soil in a very sunny position in well-drained soil. Narcissus fly can be a problem in some gardens and slugs may damage the flowers.

Propagation

Congested clumps can be carefully split in the spring. Small offsets are best grown on under glass for a couple of years. Seed should be sown under glass as soon as it is ripe.

A. belladonna 🏆

This produces an umbel of up to six pale pink, lightly scented flowers in the autumn, followed by long strap-shaped leaves. There are various named colour forms which seem to be less hardy than the type but all make easy pot plants for cold glass. **'Hathor'** has pure white flowers; **'Johannesburg'** is a rich pink. Height: 60cm.

There are various inter-genus hybrids between Amaryllis and other, non-hardy South African bulbs: **× *Amarygia*** (Amaryllis × Brunsvigia, sometimes called Brunsdonna), **× *Amarcrinum*** (Amaryllis × Crinum, sometimes called Crinodonna) and **× *Amarine*** (Amaryllis × nerine). These are not fully hardy and are only suited to mild districts.

Colchicum

Colchicums seem to have more than their fair share of names – most of them wrong. They share the cup-shaped flower form of crocus and are often called Autumn Crocus but are more closely related to lilies. They have six anthers and three separate styles. They have a large, irregular corm, covered in a dark, papery tunic, and handsome and persistent leaves, which can be as large as 13 × 30cm.

Their common name of Meadow Saffron is dangerously misleading. Although they often grow in meadows the whole plant contains the poisonous alkaloid colchicine. Culinary saffron is obtained from the style of a true crocus: *Crocus sativus*. The country name of Naked Ladies describes their habit of flowering long before their leaves appear. In the past they were called 'Filius ante patrem' ('son before the father'). Gardeners had not associated the leaves and its seed pods with the flowers that had appeared the previous autumn and thought the seeds came first, then the flowers! There are some smaller, spring-flowering colchicums but they are not really suitable for the open garden.

Colchicum, especially *Colchicum byzantium*, will flower on a window sill, but must be planted once the flowers fade.

Colchicums have large cup-shaped flowers on tall, slender stalks (more correctly called the perianth tube) that vary in height from 8–30cm. Many of them are more or less chequered ('tessellated' is the correct term for these attractive patterns). The flowers are produced in succession during the autumn. Although they can be top heavy and prone to collapse in bad weather, there are always more to replace them. Planting them beside small herbaceous plants such as pulmonarias or epimediums will help support them. Although small groups are useful to add a touch of colour to an otherwise rather dull shrub bed, they are particularly impressive massed round the base of small trees where their large leaves, which can be an embarrassment in grass, are a positive bonus in the spring. Here they can be left undisturbed to build into impressive patches. One of the joys of colchicums is their attraction for butterflies, and clouds of them can be seen hovering over the flowers on a warm sunny day.

Cultivation

They prefer a deep, fertile soil and most are best grown in light shade among shrubs where their large leaves are a positive feature. Some can be grown in thin grass but their persistent leaves means that mowing must be delayed until July at the earliest. They should be planted with 7cm of soil above the top of the corm.

Problems

On the whole they are trouble-free but they must be protected from slugs, especially those that live underground which can totally devastate the corms. In some seasons digging the corms for sale is more like an archaeological dig than a horticultural exercise, as small black slugs have eaten the entire corm away just leaving the intact tunic to show where it had been.

Colchicum agrippinum.

Colchicum autumnale 'Album'.

C. agrippinum 🏆

This small-flowered colchicum is one of the easiest to grow in a sunny corner and one of the first to flower, often in late summer. Each small, deep purple-pink flower is rather star-like and heavily chequered. The prostrate leaves are slender, with wavy edges and small enough not to be a problem at the front of a border. It is probably a hybrid between *C. autumnale* and *C. variegatum* but has been in cultivation for many centuries. It quickly forms large, long-lived clumps and is excellent on a sunny rock garden. Height: 10cm.

C. autumnale
(Meadow Saffron)

This small-flowered colchicum grows wild throughout Europe, including Britain. The corms are much smaller than most colchicums and produce up to six, but usually fewer, small lilac flowers on slender 12cm stems. Unfortunately bulbs offered for sale as this species are in fact often the larger *C. byzantinum*. The size of the corm is a good guide. Although this plant is not a source of saffron (that comes from *C. sativus*) the chemical colchicine which it contains has various medicinal properties. It has long been used in the treatment of gout and today it is being investigated as a possible treatment for certain cancerous tumours. **'Album'** is a pure white form which tends to be more vigorous than the lilac one; **'Pleniflorum'** is a small double form; 10cm **'Alboplenum'** has large, double white flowers and is late flowering; **'Nancy Lindsay'** *(C. pannonicum)* 🏆 is a vigorous selection from eastern Europe and

Colchicum autumnale.

Colchicum autumnale 'Nancy Lindsay'.

the earliest to flower. Its slender flowers on conspicuous dark stems are rich violet-mauve and have a central white line. It increases freely. Height: 15cm.

'Autumn Queen' 🏆

This is an early autumn-flowering colchicum with rose-pink goblet-shaped flowers that are heavily chequered. Height: 15cm.

Colchicum byzantinum.

C. byzantinum 🏆

Although the name sounds like a species this is a very old hybrid, producing up to twenty small, round, soft lilac flowers in succession in early autumn. It is rather like a more substantial *C. autumnale* and is often erroneously referred to as *C. autumnale* 'Major'. It can be distinguished from the true *C. autumnale* by the dark tips to both its petals and styles and the very large, round corms. These can be placed on a saucer on a windowsill where it will flower without water or soil although it

Colchicum bornmuelleri under trees at Edinburgh Botanic Garden.

must be planted out as soon as it finishes flowering or the corms will shrivel. In the garden it is vigorous in a well-drained position. **'Innocence'** is the new name for the white form. Height: 12cm.

C. cilicicum

This is a small-flowered colchicum with up to twenty rather open, purplish-pink starry flowers on short stems. The flowers often have deeper tips to the petals. It comes from southeast Turkey to Syria and can be rather short-lived in the open garden. Height: 7cm.

C. speciosum 🏆

C. speciosum is one of the best large-flowered colchicums with large, pink, goblet-shaped flowers, each with a white throat. It comes from northeast Turkey and is very

Colchicum speciosum 'Album'.

vigorous, increasing freely, and is ideal for growing among shrubs. It flowers in mid-autumn. Height: 23cm. *C bornmuelleri* is very similar but has purple rather than yellow anthers. **'Album'** 🏆 is a magnificent white form with sturdy goblet-shaped flowers on stiff stems. It is one of the very best whether in small clumps among shrubs or massed around the base of a small tree.

C. tenorei 🏆

This is one of the easiest of the small-flowered species although it is not frequently encountered in commercial lists. The slender, deep lilac flowers with a paler centre have distinct narrow pointed tepals, and are produced in profusion. Height: 15cm.

'Lilac Wonder'

A robust colchicum with large, if rather narrow, clear lilac-pink flowers with little or no chequering. It increases well, each corm producing up to ten flowers. Height: 18cm.

Colchicum 'Rosy Dawn'.

Colchicum tenorei.

'Rosy Dawn' 🏆

This is a very robust, large-flowered colchicum of much substance. The rich purple-pink flowers have a white centre and are lightly chequered. It is better able to withstand the vagaries of the weather than many. Height: 18cm.

'Pink Goblet' 🏆

This excellent hybrid has well-rounded flowers of clear lilac pink without chequering. It is vigorous and strong growing. Height: 18cm.

'The Giant'

Although the large flowers are paler than many they are produced in such profusion that the quantity makes up for any lack in depth of colour. Height: 18cm.

'Waterlily' 🏆

This is reputed to be a hybrid between two white species: *C. speciosum* 'Album' and *C. autumnale* 'Alboplenum'.

Colchicum 'The Giant'.

It really does look like a waterlily in flower and the name causes much confusion at flower shows. It has up to five fully double rosy-lilac flowers with the petals opening out flat, rather than the normal cup shape. The sheer size of the flowers means that they will always tend to droop but this is not unattractive if sufficient are planted in a group. Alternatively the blooms can be supported by neighbouring plants. Primroses and pulmonarias make good companions. Height: 12cm.

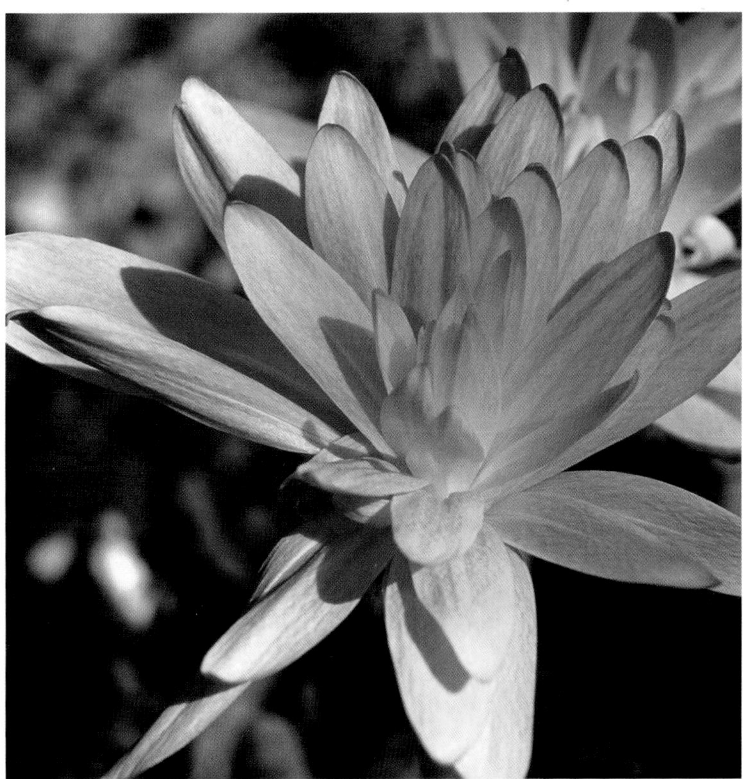

Colchicum 'Waterlily'.

Crocus
(Autumn-flowering)

These are true crocus and are indistinguishable from their spring-flowering relatives other than when they flower. They have similar small corms. In some species the narrow, silver-striped leaves are produced at the same time as the flowers but in others they appear later in the winter. Their cup-shaped flowers, usually supported by long perianth tubes (stems), consist of three outer tepals (petals) that clasp three inner ones. There are three anthers, which are usually white, cream or yellow and a single style which is often much divided and brightly coloured. Many crocus have a honey fragrance which is only really discernible indoors.

Cultivation

In the wild, crocus are found in a variety of habitats, from damp meadows to dry hillsides, so in the garden they have very different requirements. Some will naturalize (too!) freely under small trees whilst others are best given a drier regime on a sunny rock garden. Listed below is only a selection from the wide range of autumn-flowering crocus available. There are many other species more suitable for a bulb frame or a pot in a cold glasshouse, where they can be given the completely dry summer dormancy they require. Most of the ones listed here will grow in the open garden where they like a well-drained soil and a dry summer. The corms should be planted at least 10cm deep.

Pests

Unlike spring-flowering crocus, their autumn-flowering relatives appear to be pretty mouse-proof – possibly because they start growing as soon as they are planted in August, and before the rodents are hungry enough to find these tiny morsels tempting. Even mass mining of colonies in spring by badgers doesn't seem to inflict a great loss on an established colony.

Crocus speciosus naturalized under trees.

Crocus banaticus.

C. banaticus 🏆
(C. iridiflorus)

This is a very distinct crocus with solitary flowers. The stiff inner petals are much smaller and paler than the lilac outer three, which open wide in the sun giving it the appearance of a small iris flower – hence its old name. The strongly divided style is pale lilac. The leaves, which appear after the flowers, do not have a central silver stripe and are wider than most. It comes from damp mountain meadows in eastern Europe and succeeds best in cool, humus-rich soils but can be remarkably persistent, surviving complete neglect here, the flowers suddenly appearing from under a fern or hellebore leaf. It is slow to increase and is best raised from seed. It flowers in early autumn. Height: 10cm.

C. goulimyi 🏆

This is one of the most elegant of the autumn-flowering crocus. The lightly scented, small, round lilac flowers are held on exceptionally long perianth tubes (stems). The inner three petals are slightly smaller and paler than the outer ones. The leaves are just present when the flowers appear in mid-autumn. It comes from dry hillsides in southern Greece where it grows in profusion and therefore needs a dry summer dormancy to thrive outside. It is best grown either in a gritty soil in a raised bed, or in wetter areas it is perfect for an alpine house or bulb frame where it increases freely. It is fully hardy and we find it does well on our raised rock garden in the dry shade of a lime tree. **'Mani White'** 🏆 is a glorious pure white form but sadly not really suitable for the open garden. Height: 10cm.

C. Ligusticus medius 🏆

This late autumn-flowering crocus from southeast France and northwest Italy requires a dry summer to perform well and is ideal for a bed at the base of a small tree, especially one that has good autumn colour such as the clear gold of a ginkgo. The neat flowers are a rich purple with a striking red style. It flowers just as the leaves appear. Height: 7cm.

C. nudiflorus

As its name implies, this crocus produces its flowers before its leaves appear. The solitary slender purple flowers with bold, bright orange

Crocus medius.

stigmas are on rather tall stems which are prone to collapse in bad weather. It is a plant of upland meadows of the Pyrenees and in the garden prefers an open or part-shaded situation where the soil is well-drained, such as on a sloping bank or under shrubs, where they are not going to be disturbed. They will happily co-exist with *Cyclamen hederifolium*. Rather than by seeding they spread by underground stolons which produce a small corm at the end of a horizontal shoot. These new corms are very small and will take some years to reach flowering size but when happy they can form

Crocus goulimyi.

quite impressive patches. It was naturalized in various parts of England where it was originally introduced by the Knights of St John as a source of saffron, which they used for medicinal purposes. *C. nudiflorus* can still be found along the River Mersey in Chorlton Meadows but sadly the Nottingham colonies have largely disappeared under tarmac. Height: 20cm.

C. ochroleucus 🏆

This late autumn-flowering crocus is one of the smallest with one to two tiny creamy-white flowers. A native of Syria, Lebanon and north Israel, it requires a dry, sunny position to do well. It is welcome for its late flowering but it can be rather short lived in wetter areas and is probably best suited to a pot where the flowers are less likely to be damaged by bad weather. Height: 5cm.

C. pulchellus 🏆

This is a vigorous crocus from southeast Europe that produces its flowers over a long period during the autumn. The flowers are soft lilac with faint darker veining. It is very similar to *C. speciosus*, with which it will hybridize, but is easily distinguished by its white anthers. It will naturalize in light grass under small trees or it can be grown on a sunny rock garden. Height: 15cm.

Crocus nudiflorus.

Crocus pulchellus.

C. sativus (saffron)

This very distinct corm with its heavily netted, hairy tunic is a sterile triploid and is one of the oldest plants in cultivation. It has been grown for more than 2,000 years for its striking red styles, the source of culinary saffron. Many hundreds of these are needed to make a few grams of saffron, all laboriously hand picked. The large, deep lilac-purple flowers with darker veins appear at the same time as the leaves. Unlike most other crocus, once opened, the flowers do not close again, making it vulnerable to bad weather. It is sterile, increasing by means of cormlets, and is probably a selection from the Greek *C. cartwrightianus* and requires a very dry summer dormancy to produce its flowers. It is therefore best grown in fertile soil under cover. Huge numbers are grown in Spain and Morocco but especially in Iran and Kashmir, where it is an important commercial crop. Height: 7cm.

The true saffron crocus, *Crocus sativus.*

C. serotinus subsp. clusii 🏆

This is a delightful and easy crocus from northern Spain, flowering in the late autumn. The rounded, deep purple flowers appear at the same time as the leaves. Unlike many autumn-flowering crocus the stems are very short so that the flowers are held within the leaves. **subsp. *salzmanii*** is very similar but

Crocus speciosus.

Crocus 'Zephyr'.

the slender, pointed pale lilac flowers appear earlier in the autumn. This is an easy and long-lived plant for a dry and sunny situation. Height: 10cm.

C. speciosus 🏆

The most vigorous of the autumn-flowering crocus, this Turkish species will spread to form a carpet in grass under small trees. Although it will grow in any dry, sunny border it can be too vigorous, spreading rapidly by offsets and seedlings. Although the flowers make a fine display in the autumn the mass of leaves that follow are just too much of a good thing, swamping out other plants. Flowering begins in early autumn, as soon as the leaves begin to fall from the trees, and continues for two months or more. The large, true blue flowers with darker veins are held on exceptionally tall stems. Although they are prone to collapse in bad weather there is always a succession of replacement flowers to maintain the display, even pushing up through a carpet of fallen leaves late into November. The heavily divided style is bright orange-red and they have the charming habit of showing the tips above the closed petals, rather like cheeky children poking their tongues out. There is just time after they have flowered to cut the grass before the leaves appear in the late winter. Height: 18cm.

There are many named forms that are very similar. The following are distinct: ***f. albus*** 🏆 has large, pure white flowers. It is just as easy as the type but less generous in its offspring so is a good choice for a dry rock garden or perhaps to grow through *Cyclamen coum* leaves under a tree; **'Oxonian'** is the earliest to flower and has very large, violet-mauve flowers on distinctive dark stems.

Crocus speciosus f. albus.

'Zephyr' 🏆

This late autumn-flowering crocus has exceptionally large, pale lilac flowers. It is sterile and gradually forms large clumps. Long lived, it is a hybrid between *C. speciosus* and *C. pulchellus* and will grow in any well-drained soil which is dry in summer, such as that round the base of a tree or at the edge of a woodland path. Height: 18cm.

NOTE

C. laevigatus 'Fontenayi' is often listed as an autumn-flowering crocus, but since it starts to flower in late November and continues through to January, it is included in the next chapter (Winter).

Cyclamen

The small species cyclamen should not be confused with the larger-flowered varieties that have been bred for indoor cultivation. Although some of the smaller-flowered versions of these will survive outdoors in favoured localities most will succumb in a cold winter.

All cyclamen have long-lived tubers with a corky exterior and produce clusters of leaves and small nodding flowers, with reflexed and twisted petals. These usually have a contrasting darker 'nose'. The leaves can be plain green or attractively marbled with silver. In some species there are completely silver-leafed forms. Cyclamen naturally grow in woodland and therefore require a light, humus-rich soil in part shade. Most are summer dormant.

Cultivation

Cyclamen should be planted about 3cm below the surface with at least 15cm between the tubers. An annual top dressing of bark, compost, leaf mould or mushroom compost should be given during summer when they are dormant. Cyclamen do not produce offsets but must be raised from seed. Once pollinated most capsules are pulled down on a coiled stem to nestle safely below the leaves. When the seed is ripe in mid-summer the spring is relaxed and the seeds are dispersed. Each seed has a sugary coating; this attracts ants, which then scatter them away from the parent plant. They can appear in very strange places – we have one in a crevice in the bark part of the way up a tree. Seedlings are easily raised in a shaded seed bed or seed trays and it takes about three or four years for them to start flowering.

Cyclamen associate well with other winter-flowering woodland bulbs such as snowdrops, eranthis, crocus, etc. and in the summer the gaps left by the dormant tubers can be disguised by plants such as deciduous ferns. A decorative bark mulch can be added in the summer where the position is too dry for herbaceous plants to thrive. This not only provides a perfect seed bed: it also protects them from the over-tidy gardener who removes all the leaves that fall in the autumn. In the wild these long-lived tubers (sixty-plus years is normal) have to compete with an ever-increasing layer of leaf mould by slowly pushing themselves upwards. In the garden this means that the tubers regularly become exposed, leaving them prey to the odd nibble or an over-enthusiastic fork. If the tubers do appear above the soil level they should be lifted, the soil deeply dug and humus added before the cyclamen are replanted. This can be done at any time, even when they are in full flower.

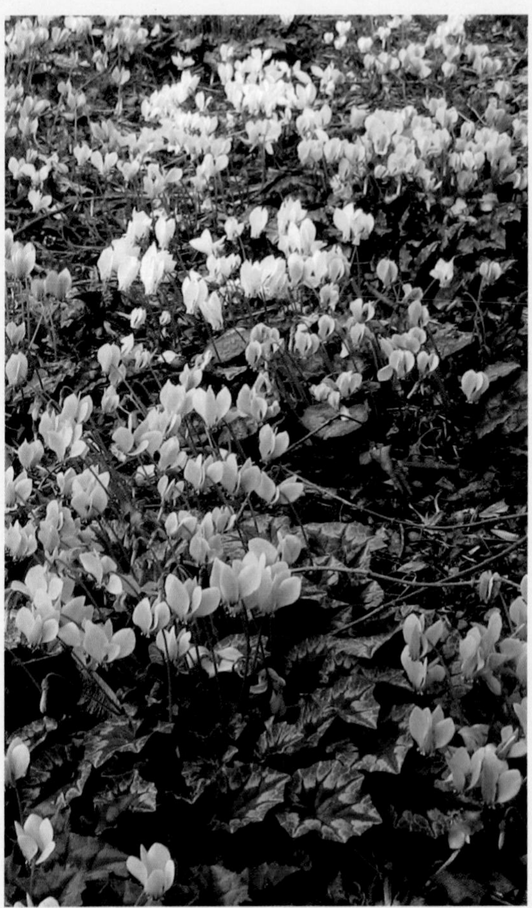

Cyclamen hederifolium in the dry shade of trees.

Pests

They are trouble-free although there may be minor physical damage by slugs, squirrels, etc. Excess wet is more likely to be a problem, which can lead to rotting of the tubers in the summer or botrytis infections of the foliage.

C. cilicium 🏆

The slender, pale pink or white flowers appear at the same time as the round, heavily patterned leaves. This small cyclamen from eastern Turkey has a reputation for not being fully hardy but excess water is the main problem in northern gardens. Provided the situation is dry throughout the year, whether the plant is growing or dormant, it seems to be fine. It thrives here on the sunny side of a mature yew, where it has seeded to form an extensive colony. It flowers in mid-autumn, taking over from *C. hederifolium*. Height: 7cm.

Cyclamen cilicium.

C. hederifolium 🏆

(syn. C. neapolitanum)

The tubers of this hardy species are irregular in shape and very long lived. We have plants that are well over sixty years old and mature tubers can reach the diameter of a dinner plate. We rather irreverently refer to these monsters as 'cowpatiensis'. The flowers are either pink or white with a dark purple mark at the mouth and first appear in late summer before the leaves and then continue to flower sporadically through the autumn with the leaves. Although it is a native of the Mediterranean and prefers a dry summer dormancy under trees it is remarkably tolerant in the garden. It will seed freely, even into thin grass or the desert that is the base of conifers.

The leaves are pointed, toothed and more or less marbled with silver. One of the joys of *C. hederifolium* is the amazingly variable leaf-shape and patterns. As every one is different it is worth choosing plants

White-flowered *Cyclamen hederifolium.*

in leaf rather than flower for although they are principally grown for their flowers they are even more useful in the garden as a winter foliage plant. The flowers may last for six weeks but the clumps of handsome leaves are present for six months. Care must be taken not to allow the large tubers to work their way out of the soil. In the wild they would be covered by an annual layer of leaves but in today's tidy gardens they often push themselves out of the ground where they are vulnerable to physical damage. If this happens they should be replanted with 3cm of soil above them. Mulching them when they are dormant in summer with leaf mould, composted bark or mushroom compost will prevent this and encourage seeding.

The **'Silver Cloud Group'** has similar pink or white flowers but the leaves are completely silver, sometimes with a greenish rim. Height: 12cm.

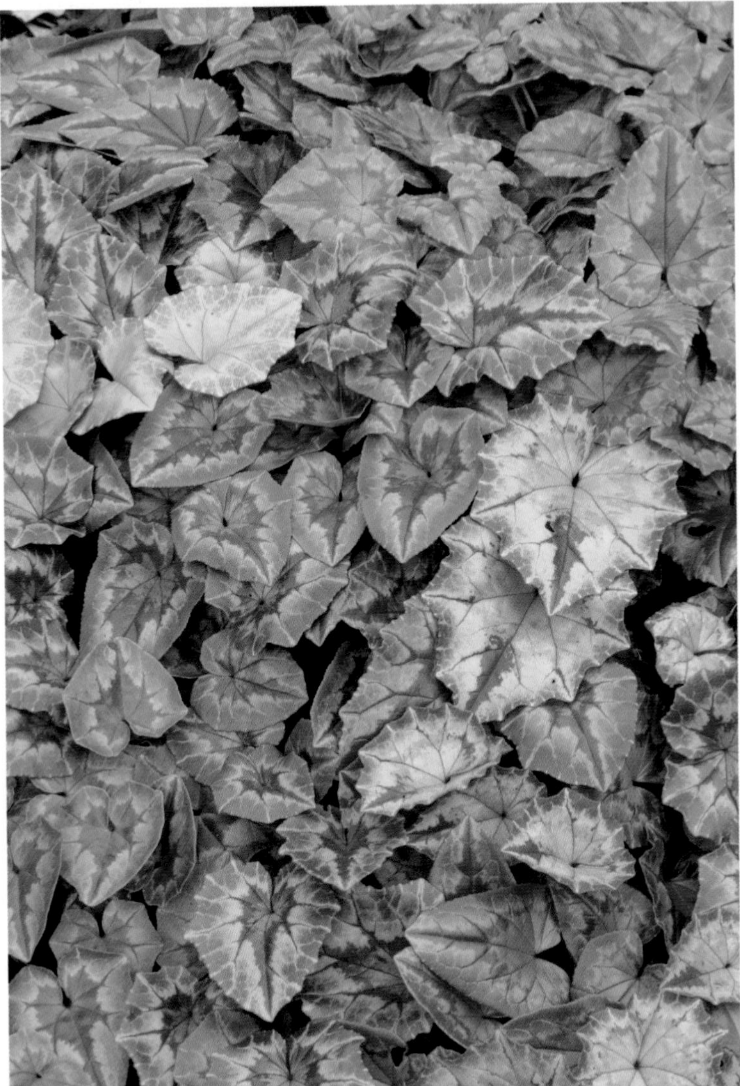

Cyclamen hederifolium

Cyclamen intaminatum.

C. intaminatum

This is one of the smallest of the cyclamen species. It comes from the pine woods of southwest Turkey and will only survive outside in a very dry, sheltered situation though it makes an easy pot plant for cold glass. The tiny grey-veined white flowers appear at the same time as the small, round, dark glossy green leaves. Height: 5cm.

C. mirabile 🏆

This small-flowered cyclamen is very similar to *C. cilicium* but has brighter pink flowers with feathered tops to the petals. The silver patterned leaves are sometimes tinged with pink when they first come through the ground. It seems to be less tolerant of winter wet and requires a very dry, sheltered position in the garden. It makes an easy pot plant for cold glass. Height: 7cm.

Galanthus

Snowdrops are the quintessential winter-flowering bulbs (*see* Chapter 2 for the main entry) but there is one that defies this rule and flowers in the autumn. It comes from southern Greece and flowers in late autumn as the rain breaks the summer drought. In the garden it needs a very dry, well-drained position preferably in full sun, such as a raised bed.

G. reginae-olgae
(G. corcyrensis)

This slender snowdrop, named after a Greek queen, produces its typical snowdrop flowers late in the autumn. Each has a single green mark on the inner tepals. The narrow, grey-green leaves have a distinctive silver central stripe and appear as the flowers fade. Height: 10cm.

Nerine bowdenii.

Galanthus reginae-olgae.

Nerine

(Autumn Lily)

This genus of some thirty South African daffodil relatives produces umbels of showy, lily-like flowers in the autumn as their leaves fade. The leaves may be strap-like, reminiscent of a daffodil, or thin and grass-like. The heads, which vary from 10–20cm across, contain up to twenty-five flowers and vary in height from 15cm to 50cm. Only *N. bowdenii* is truly hardy but the others make attractive and easy pot plants for cold glass or outside in very sheltered gardens.

Cultivation

The bulbs require a sunny situation and should be planted in a well-drained soil/compost. Plant the bulbs with the neck at or just below the surface of the soil. These are amongst those subjects that resent disturbance and newly planted bulbs may take some seasons to flower. Patience is the main requirement. They are easy, trouble-free plants but all flower best when growing in congested clumps. They should be watered well when in active growth. In cold areas they are best tucked in at the base of a sunny wall but in milder districts will grow well in any sunny bed provided the soil is free draining and they are not swamped by neighbouring plants.

Propagation

The bulbs increase by offsets and clumps can be divided in the early spring. Seed should be sown as soon as it is ripe and kept at about 50°C.

Nerine 'Isabel'.

N. bowdenii 🏆

A massed flowering of these showy bulbs against a wall is one of the classic and unforgettable sights of early autumn. Each 20cm-diameter head contains up to ten or more funnel-shaped flowers of clear pink with reflexed tips and undulate (wavy) edges. They flower best in congested clumps where they can be left undisturbed for many years. It is only necessary to remove any loose bulbs or to lift the whole clump and divide it when the display declines. Although the bulbs are hardy, the flowers are frost tender. In mild districts they will grow well in any dry, sunny position but in colder areas they are best planted at the base of a sunny wall, which protects the flowers from damage from early frost. Height: 50cm.

There are many named clones of *N. bowdenii* with very similar flowers but these are some of the most distinctive ones: **'Mark Fenwick'** ('Fenwick's Variety') has flowers of the classic deep pink on dark stalks and is late flowering; **'Molly Cowie'** was discovered in a Scottish garden and has a cream edge to the leaves but otherwise looks exactly the same in flower; **'Quinton Wells'** ('Wellsii') from the north Drakensberg is an exceptionally early-flowering form with large flowers that have a slightly more wavy edge; **'Isabel'** is a new cultivar with intense cerise flowers each with a distinctive pale central stripe, which look as though they are dusted with silver, and the individual flowers are wider and more wavy edged than most; **'Marnie Rogerson'** is a vigorous, pale pink hybrid originally found in Devon, shorter than the type, free flowering and fully hardy; **'Nikita'** is similar; ***f. alba*** has large white flowers and is less hardy than the type, as is the very pale pink **'Stefani'**.

N. flexuosa

This is a small-flowered nerine from eastern South Africa with compact heads of relatively large flowers and neat leaves. The white flowered **'Alba'** is the form usually encountered. Although not fully hardy, only growing well outside in frost-free areas, it makes an attractive pot plant, flowering in late autumn. Height: 45cm.

Nerine flexuosa 'Alba'.

N. sarniensis
(Guernsey Lily)

This late autumn-flowering nerine is the most colourful of the family but sadly it is not at all hardy and must

Nerine 'Marnie Rogerson'.

be kept frost-free. The compact, tennis-ball-sized heads have fully reflexed petals and dramatic stamens. The usual colour is crimson or orange-red, but there are many cultivars available in a huge range of jewel colours from pure white to salmon pinks. All are characterized by an obvious dusting of glistening silvery speckles. **'Corusca Major'** is an old selection with intense scarlet flowers and is grown for cutting. Height: 45cm.

Nerine sarniensis.

N. undulata (N. crispa)

This small late-autumn flowering nerine lives up to its name, producing small heads of delicate pink flowers with very wavy edges. It is hardy in sheltered districts but makes an easy and attractive pot plant for cold glass. Height: 45cm.

'Zeal Giant' 🏆

This Devon-raised hybrid between *N. bowdenii* and *N. sarniensis* produces the largest and most dramatic flowers of all – up to 30cm across with individual flowers to match. They are an intense cerise and despite their parentage are hardy in a sheltered spot, increasing well. They also do not seem to need to be in congested clumps in order to flower. Height: 60cm.

Nerine undulata.

Other species

There are some very attractive dwarf, delicate-flowered nerines with narrow, grass-like foliage which make excellent pot plants for a cold glass house or conservatory, where they can be kept virtually frost-free and dry in summer: ***N. filifolia***, and the similar ***N. masoniorum*** are 15cm tall with tiny 2cm-wide flowers, while the hairy-stemmed ***N. filamentosa*** is 35cm tall with 7cm flowers.

Nerine 'Zeal Giant'.

Schizostylis
(Hesperanthus)
(Kaffir Lily)

Schizostylis coccinea.

This South African plant was always considered as a separate species to the similar *Hesperanthus*, the only difference being that one is bulbous and the other rhizomatous. However, this appears to be purely an evolutionary adaptation to the availability of water: *Hesperanthus* grows in areas of seasonal rainfall whereas *Schizostylis* grows in damp meadows where there is always water available. They have now been combined in the genus *Hesperanthus*.

They are virtually evergreen with narrow pointed leaves, the rhizomes growing into extensive patches in mild districts. In cold winters they will become deciduous and may be killed. The spikes of open, cup-shaped flowers are produced from late summer until the first frost, closing at night but opening wide in daylight. Their appearance in the garden is a clear indication that autumn is approaching. The flowers are frost tender. Although they like a damp position and grow well beside a pond, this is not necessary provided there is ample water early in the summer. In very hot and dry situations the flowering may be sparse and the plants suffer from rust. Some of my best patches are among shrubs where they grow with hostas. Provided they are well watered they even grow and flower well under a north wall. ***S. coccinea*** itself is late-flowering, with rather small flowers that vary from salmon pink to scarlet, but the modern cultivars are more vigorous with bolder spikes of large, showy flowers 5cm in diameter which appear much earlier in the season.

f. alba has small pure white flowers and is not a good plant for the open garden, seeming to be more tender. It grows and flowers well with us under glass.

There are many named cultivars which are very similar but the following are among the best, having large flowers with a silky sheen: **'Major'** (grandiflora) 🏆 in its best forms has very large glistening red flowers on sturdy stems, but there are some indifferent plants masquerading under this name; **'Sunrise'** 🏆 and **'Jennifer'** 🏆 have large pink flowers; the very pale pink **'W.H. Bryant'** has undergone a sex change and is marketed as '**Pink Princess'** – it has very large flowers of the palest pink. It is a sport of 'Jennifer' and was originally named by her after her late husband Wilfred. He had raised the original 'Jennifer', which first flowered on their wedding day. Height: 60cm.

Schizostylis 'Jennifer'.

Sternbergia sicula in a bulb frame.

Sternbergia

These are the final crocus-shaped autumn-flowering bulbs and they are particularly welcome for their bright golden-yellow flowers. They are members of the Amaryllidaceae family so are related to daffodils rather than crocus and are native to the Mediterranean area. Although the ones listed here are hardy they will only flower if given a warm, dry summer dormancy. Congested clumps flower best. If they are too shaded or too wet they will refuse to flower. They are therefore ideal for the base of a sunny wall or around the base of a tree where they quickly form large trouble-free clumps. They associate well with nerines and eucomis, which like a similar situation. The bulbs should be planted about 7cm deep. Newly planted bulbs can be shy to flower and should be left undisturbed.

S. lutea

Traditionally held to be the biblical 'lily of the field', this bulb has narrow, deep green leaves and bright yellow, cup-shaped flowers, which are held at an angle on a long green stalk. The flowers are shorter than the leaves. They flower from mid- to late autumn.

'Angustifolia Group' is similar but has narrower leaves and a more upright flower. In our experience it is also the first to flower. Height: 10cm.

Sternbergia lutea.

S. sicula

This variable bulb is very similar to the above but with smaller, more star-like flowers which come just before or just as the leaves appear, so that they are held above the foliage. The narrow, deep green leaves have a silver central stripe. Although it is hardy it will not tolerate summer rain. Unlike *S. lutea* it seeds freely around our bulb frames. Height: 10cm.

CHAPTER 2

BULBS FOR WINTER DISPLAY

Snowdrops, *Cyclamen coum* and *Eranthis hyemalis* in the snow.

Winter could never be described as the high point of the garden cycle. Rather it is a quiet time where the emphasis is on structural features such as hedges or statues. The silhouette of trees against the sky or the glint of low winter sun on bark dominates the garden, not colourful displays of flowers. A time perhaps to enjoy pots of indoor bulbs like prepared hyacinths and the seed catalogues, but if you are prepared to venture out into the garden there are a number of stalwart bulbs that not only survive but thrive in this often inclement period. Who can forget the uplifting sight of clumps of snowdrops lying like patches of snow under the stark winter outline of trees, or a drift of the delicate *Crocus tommasinianus* studding the grass with the promise that spring is just around the corner. But these are only the most obvious examples of a much larger group of hardy bulbs. Although many are small in stature and rather understated, especially when it comes to colour, they add immeasurably to the gardener's pleasure at this time. As the majority are small and discreet rather than bold and showy they are best given a prominent position, such as the front of a sunny border where they can easily be seen, and where the slightest amount of sun will encourage them to open. Others, such as snowdrops and certain crocus, can spread to form extensive and often dramatic drifts both in borders or in grass.

Crocus

This is a large family of some ninety dwarf autumn- or winter-flowering corms that are found from Europe right through to west China. They grow in a wide range of habitats, from lowland meadows to mountain snowmelt and although most are in cultivation many are not suitable for the open garden, needing the more specialist growing conditions of a bulb frame or alpine house where they will give a beautiful display. Most crocus corms are rather flat in profile with the remains of the previous season's leaves forming a loose tunic on the outside. All produce one flower but most have many more. Each has six petals (or more correctly six tepals) arranged in two rings to form a cup-shaped flower, which opens and closes with warmth and light. In many there is a dramatic contrast in colour between the three outer and three inner petals, the dull outer petals protecting and disguising the flowers until the warmth of the sun opens them to reveal the brighter inner ones that attract the pollinating insects. In the garden some of the mid-winter flowering crocus such as *C. imperatii* seem to appear almost overnight – their presence not having been noticed until the sun opens the flowers wide. All crocus have three stamens and a single style which is subdivided into three. This is often

Crocus imperatii 'De Jaeger'.

Massed *Crocus tommasinianus* with hellebore and aconites.

Crocus tommasinianus.

dramatically frilled or heavily branched. All have upright narrow leaves with a conspicuous silver central stripe; the leaves appear at the same time as the flowers.

Those crocus that are suitable for the garden are easily grown in any well-drained soil in full sun. They have few cultural problems other than the perennial one of predation by mice, squirrels or badgers, which can eat the corms as fast as they are planted. Vigorous species such as *C. tommasinianus* are ideal for naturalizing in grass where they will spread both by seed and offsets to form impressive patches which even the most voracious predator will be unable to deplete. They are ideal mixed with *Galanthus nivalis* (single snowdrops) for a glorious winter spectacle. Their leaves die back in late spring so there is no problem regarding mowing the grass. Others are excellent planted in small clumps along the front edge of an herbaceous border where they add welcome colour and interest early in the year. The spreading herbaceous plants will quickly cover the gaps they leave in the summer and help give the crocus the dry dormancy most of them prefer.

Cultivation

Crocus corms are planted in the autumn at least 10cm deep in small clumps of ten or more. The soil should be well firmed and any loose tunics removed to avoid drawing attention to them. Mice and squirrels seem to have a sixth sense regarding newly planted crocus. A covering of a piece of narrow gauge wire netting may deter them. This is particularly effective for these and other tasty bulbs, like tulips, growing in containers. Alternatively the corms can be grown in small pots and kept mouse-free under netting until they begin to flower when they can be planted out in their final place. At that time the corm will have considerably reduced in size and be less attractive to hungry predators. This is also a useful method of 'topping up' an existing display, as you can see just where the gaps are, rather than rely on the often hit-and-miss affair of adding bulbs in the right place in the autumn.

Those to be grown in grass can be scattered in a random manner with approximately 10cm between them. However, when planting crocus directly into grass, it is best, quicker and probably safer to roll back a whole piece of turf and plant the corms below it, replacing the turf firmly afterwards. The odd corm can then be planted individually around the rectangle of turf to avoid the risk of creating an unattractive regular shape when they flower. In some districts birds seem attracted to the flowers, often shredding them before they have a chance to make any meaningful display. I have no idea why they do this as they just leave the petals scattered. There also doesn't seem to be any pattern regarding which crocus is more attractive. Some gardeners have reported that their birds go for purple crocus whilst in other districts cream is the 'in' colour. A large display can sustain the loss of a few flowers but if the damage is too great the only resort is to crisscross the area with black thread, which is almost invisible to the gardener but not the birds.

Propagation

Most crocus produce a number of small offsets each year and the clumps gradually increase in size. Others, particularly *C. tommasinianus*, spread vigorously by seeding. The seed pods are carried just above the ground, nestling well below the blades of any mower, so the foliage of crocus in grass can be safely cut as soon as it fades in late spring without damaging its seeding potential.

C. angustifolius 🏆

(Cloth of Gold Crocus)

This small, late winter-flowering crocus from south Ukraine produces narrow flowers of deep orange-yellow. The outside of the outer three petals is almost completely brown and they roll back in warm weather rather like a blind to reveal the bright inner petals. It needs a dry sunny spot to do well and is an ideal subject for a trough. Height: 5cm.

C. biflorus

This small winter-flowering crocus is one of the parents of the *C. chrysanthus* group, and is usually found in the form of **subsp. *alexandri*** from the Balkans, which has white flowers. The outer three petals have dramatic deep purple marks on the outside. **subsp. *weldenii* 'Fairy'** has white flowers with a wash of pale grey-lilac on the outer petals. It is a unique and very attractive colour although almost impossible to describe. Height: 5cm.

C. chrysanthus

This is the collective name given to a range of hybrids and selections from two Turkish species – the cream/yellow *C. chrysanthus* and the blue/white *C. biflorus*. These delightful corms produce masses of well rounded flowers in the late winter and quickly increase to give a bold display. They are one of the most versatile groups, being ideal for containers, borders or naturalizing in grass. They are clump forming and do not spread by seed. Height: 7cm.

Among the best cultivars are: **'Advance'** – violet outer tepals which open to reveal a bright gold inside; **'Blue Pearl'** 🏆 – soft, delicate blue with silvery outer tepals and a bronze base; **'Cream Beauty'** 🏆 – pale creamy-yellow flowers with a darker base; **'Gipsy Girl'** – deep gold throughout, and the outer petals are strikingly marked with brown feathering; **'Jeannine'** – larger flowered than most with pale lemon-yellow flowers feathered purple on the outside; **'Ladykiller'** 🏆 – glistening white with a dark purple mark on the outer petals; **'Snowbunting'** 🏆 – creamy-white with light bronze feathering on the outside; **'Zwanenburg Bronze'** 🏆 – an interesting mix of bronzed-violet and yellow; **'E.A. Bowles'** 🏆 – rounded flowers of clear

Crocus angustifolius.

Crocus biflorus weldenii 'Fairy'.

Crocus chrysanthus 'Blue Pearl'.

Crocus chrysanthus 'Advance'.

Crocus chrysanthus 'Ladykiller'.

Crocus etruscus.

lemon-yellow with purple-brown feathering on the outside. Sadly the true plant seems not to be in cultivation at present. **'Romance'** is a similar pale yellow.

C. etruscus 🏆

This compact crocus from north Italy has one or two lilac-purple flowers faintly veined with a deeper shade. The outer petals are slightly paler than the inner ones. It will quickly form good-sized clumps in a sunny spot such as a rock garden or the front of a border, where it is particularly effective pushing through silver foliage such as *Stachys byzantina* or variegated forms of *Lamium maculatum*. Height: 7cm.

C. corsicus 🏆

This large and very showy crocus from Corsica, which flowers from late winter to early spring, needs a dry summer to do well in the open garden but is excellent in a bulb frame where it increases freely. The purple-feathered, pale biscuit-coloured outer petals open in the sun to expose the bright purple inner petals and a conspicuous orange style. Height: 7cm.

C. imperatii 'De Jaeger'

This mid-winter-flowering crocus has relatively large flowers. It is one of the earliest to flower in the New Year. The pale biscuit-coloured outer petals have dark purple stripes and the flowers are easily overlooked until the warmth of a sunny day causes them to open and reveal the bright violet-purple inner petals. As it flowers so early in the year it is best given a choice spot on a sunny, dry rock garden or trough. It is fully hardy and will continue flowering even when surrounded by snow. Height: 12cm.

Crocus corsicus.

C. laevigatus 'Fontenayi' 🏆

Although most books list this crocus as autumn-flowering, it is a true winter bulb, starting to flower in late November and continuing through to January depending upon the temperature at the time, so it is included here.

This crocus has a tiny corm, resembling a shiny hazelnut, producing both leaves and flowers late in the autumn and into the winter. Despite being native to Greece it is remarkably hardy. Even open flowers will stay undamaged in suspended animation through days of unbroken frost, to continue flowering as soon as the temperature

Crocus laevigatus 'Fontenayi'.

Crocus 'Golden Yellow'.

warms slightly. The strongly purple-feathered outer petals are biscuit-coloured and open in the sun to reveal rich purple inner petals. Although it will naturalize easily its short stature means that it never really makes a bold display and it is better suited to a sunny rock garden or trough. It is very long lived – my clumps are now forty years old – although slow to increase; sadly, economies of scale have meant that it is now scarce. Height: 7cm.

C. x luteus 'Golden Yellow' 🏆 ('Dutch Yellow', 'Golden Mammoth')

This is one of the most persistent of all crocus and seems to be remarkably mouse-proof. The flowers are similar in size to the Dutch crocus *(C. vernus)* but it is much earlier flowering, the first flowers often appearing with the snowdrops. The vivid orange-yellow flowers are not to everyone's taste but they are produced in profusion. It will quickly increase at the front of a sunny border to form sizeable patches and it will naturalize in grass, although the colour is somewhat strident. Height: 10cm.

C. minimus

This tiny, late winter-flowering crocus from Corsica and Italy lives up to its name. The small flowers are only 1.5cm long and have a proportionately longer stem than most crocus. However, they are produced in such profusion they make up for their small stature. The inner petals are a dark purple while the outer petals are pale with intense dark violet veins. It needs a dry summer to do well in the open garden but is compact enough to make an excellent subject for a trough. Height: 7cm.

Crocus minimus.

Crocus sieberi.

Crocus sieberi 'Albus'.

C. sieberi 🏆

This vigorous, late winter-flowering crocus from Greece produces its flowers as the snow melts. It is very hardy and is easy to grow in a border or in grass, making long-lived clumps. The dumpy soft pinkish-lilac flowers have a conspicuous white throat. Height: 7cm. **'Albus'** 🏆 flowers in mid-winter before the type and has pure white flowers. It is excellent pushing up through mats of low-growing alpines such as dianthus. (Sadly we can no longer officially call it **'Bowles White'**, a much more evocative and accurate name, which was originally given to the corm to celebrate that great crocus aficionado's thirty-year search for this white seedling.) **'Firefly'** is similar to the type with lilac-pink flowers; **'Hubert Edelsten'** 🏆 is very distinct, as the flowers have whitish inner petals but the outer ones are intense violet and are dramatically lined with white; **subsp. *sublimis* 'Tricolor'** 🏆 is the most striking of the group – the petals are rich purple with a white-edged yellow centre; **'Violet Queen'** has slightly smaller and narrower flowers of deep purple. All of them are excellent and long-lived subjects for a dry, sunny rock garden.

C. tommasinianus 🏆

This well-known and well-loved species is the most vigorous of all the mid-winter-flowering crocus

Crocus sieberi 'Hubert Edelstein'.

Crocus sieberi 'Tricolor'.

Crocus tommasinianus 'Whitewell Purple' and snowdrops.

Crocus 'Vanguard'.

and will spread to form impressive patches. It can be too invasive for a border as the abundant leaves will fill the bed and the millions of minute offsets can be impossible to find and remove. They are ideal naturalized in grass and are a good companion plant for snowdrops and aconites in those problem beds under trees where nothing else will grow later in the year. The pale lilac flowers are very slender and have silvery outer petals. This means that they are often overlooked unless the sun shines when they open to reveal the brighter-hued inner petals. Height: 10cm. **'Whitewell Purple'** is a vigorous form similar to the type but the flowers are in shades of purple both inside and out. They are therefore conspicuous even on an overcast day. They spread freely, both by seed and offsets, and are invaluable for an early display. There are other distinct colour forms that have been named. **'Ruby Giant'** is a sterile hybrid with *C. vernus* and is slightly later flowering. It has more rounded, rich purple flowers and is equally long lived but will only form clumps and not seed about. It is therefore suitable for growing in borders or in more formal plantings in grass. **'Haarlem Gem'** is a similar pale lilac hybrid.

'Vanguard' 🏆

This late winter-flowering crocus is a hybrid between *C. tommasinianus* and *C. vernus*. It has large, pale lilac flowers of much substance and is more like a Dutch hybrid although it flowers a little earlier. The inner petals are slightly darker than the outer ones. It will naturalize well but as it is sterile it will only form clumps, not seed around. Height: 12cm.

C. vernus

The large-flowered Dutch crocus needs little introduction. They are the last to flower in late winter or

Crocus tommasinianus 'Ruby Giant'.

Massed *Crocus vernus* at Sheffield Botanic Garden.

Crocus 'Jeanne d'Arc'.

early spring and have large, rounded flowers. Unlike many crocus there is little difference between the outer and inner petals. Provided the mice can be kept at bay, they are very versatile, suitable for growing in pots, borders or grass where they will clump up well. Height: 12cm. Among the best cultivars are **'Jeanne d'Arc'**, pure white; **'Pickwick'**, pale lilac flowers with conspicuous purple stripes; **'Queen of Blues'**, soft lilac; and **'Purpureus Grandiflorus'**, with intense violet flowers, similar to **'Remembrance'**.

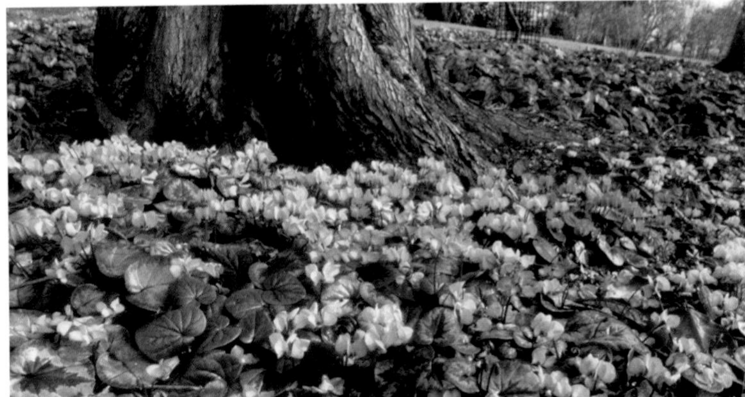

Cyclamen coum round the base of a tree.

Cyclamen

See *Chapter 1* for main description.

Propagation

Cyclamen do not produce offsets and must be raised from seed. They do not breed true: a white cyclamen will produce both pink and white seedlings and the leaf patterns will be similarly variable.

C. coum 🏆

The small-flowered *C. coum* with its tubby flowers in shades of cerise, pink or white, each with a dark maroon blotch at the mouth, is the perfect choice for winter colour, especially planted under deciduous trees where it can be mixed with snowdrops or other mid-winter-flowering bulbs. The small round leaves are a dark green and can be plain or more often attractively marbled with silver. Unlike the autumn-flowering cyclamen these come from the mountains of northern Turkey where they experience a temperate climate not dissimilar to western Europe, with rainfall possible at any time of the year. They therefore do not require a dry summer dormancy and thrive best in light shade and in soils where there is a high humus content. They are fully hardy, the leaves just curling up with frost. Excess wet and strong winds are more likely to cause problems such as botrytis. When happy they can seed to form extensive colonies. Although they are equally long-lived they are a small plant even in maturity and care should be taken that they are not swamped by the more vigorous *C. hederifolium*. Height: 10cm. **'Pewter Group'** 🏆 has pink or white flowers and leaves that are completely or almost completely silver. The name **'Maurice Dryden'** is given to white-flowered selections of this.

Leaves of *Cyclamen coum* 'Pewter Group'.

Eranthis
(Winter Aconite)

A mass of winter aconites carpeting the ground beneath a tree is one of the most memorable sights of winter. These small tuberous plants come from Eurasia, the easiest to grow in the open garden coming from the woodlands of south and east Europe. They have a single, small cup-shaped flower on a short stem above a ruff of much-divided leaves. Their seed pods have five or more follicles. They have small knobbly tubers which gradually increase in size; individually, most are long lived. Eranthis increase by seeding and when happy they can form extensive colonies. Seedlings will take three or four years to reach flowering size.

Cultivation

Eranthis are planted as dormant tubers in the autumn or as growing plants in late winter. They are best grown under deciduous trees or shrubs where they associate well with other winter-flowering bulbs such as snowdrops and cyclamen. Although eranthis will grow in thin grass they prefer to grow without competition in a border. They do not like very acid soils but are quite happy on clay. They are remarkably long lived and persistent. Much to our surprise they appeared as though by magic on our rock garden once we had removed the overgrown shrubs and brambles which had swamped them for decades. They are propagated by seed or by cutting up the tubers.

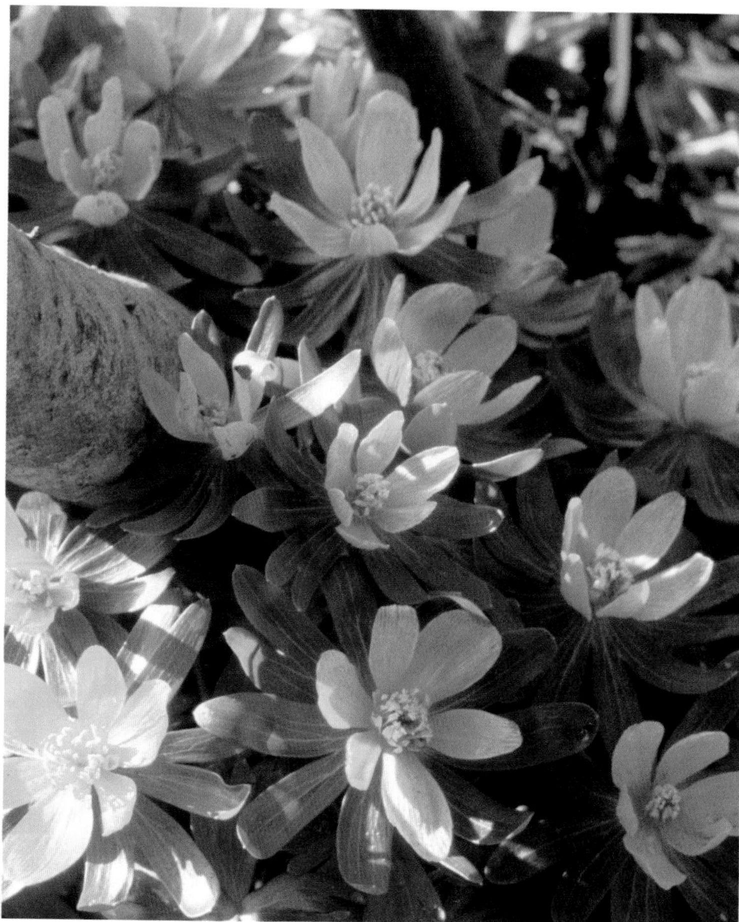

Eranthis hyemalis nestle around the trunk of a tree.

E. hyemalis 🏆

This very hardy tuber is a native of south and east Europe, producing its flowers in the depth of winter. The bright yellow, cup-shaped flowers appear first, followed by a ruff of green leaves below it. It is perfect to mix with other winter-flowering bulbs under trees or it can be tucked in along the edge of a border for an early display. Height: 7cm.

E. Cilicica Group

This group is later flowering. The flowers are similar to *E. hyemalis* but the more finely dissected leaves have a distinct bronze hue when they appear and there are many more seed pods. They are native from Turkey eastwards and in northern Europe need a situation that is very dry in summer or they can quickly fade away. Height: 7cm.

There are a few worthwhile hybrids and selections, all of which must be hand-divided to propagate. **'Guinea Gold'** 🏆 is a late-flowering sterile hybrid with significantly larger flowers, which slowly builds up into large, impressive clumps. The new cultivar **'Schwefelglanz'** has large, pale straw-yellow flowers and is just as hardy, even seeding 90 per cent true if kept in isolation.

Galanthus

(Snowdrop)

Snowdrops are the epitome of the winter-flowering bulb. Superficially they appear to be very fragile but this belies their remarkable resilience. Most of the species naturally occur in mountains, and their spathes, which enclose the bud when it first appears, have specially hardened tips that enable them to push through the snow. Indeed whole clumps will stand proud of blanketing snow. They are also resistant to frost, even in full flower. They are tiny miracles of resilience. Each night they may bow their heads right to the ground but as soon as they thaw in the morning the stems stand erect again. Ones that fail to stand erect are a good indicator that the clump has become droughted, which is a regular if rather unexpected consequence of a long cold period with no rain. Flowering times given in the text are only a guide. In hard winters their flowering will be correspondingly delayed and vice versa in mild winters.

Although the 'common' snowdrop *(G. nivalis)* is much loved in Britain, it is not a native of these islands. Gerard's *Herbal* of 1597 refers to them as occurring in Italy and it was not until some time in the mid-seventeenth century that they finally reached Britain in any quantity. Here they found conditions so favourable that they have spread to form prodigious colonies, especially in churchyards and other places where they would be left undisturbed. Their old country name of 'Fair Maids of February' refers to the Church Feast of Candlemas or Purification, held on 2 February, when a procession of white-robed girls would walk through the churchyard with its white carpet of snowdrops. Other species were introduced during the nineteenth century enabling hybridization to take place between species that normally grew hundreds if not thousands of miles apart, leading to the extensive range available today.

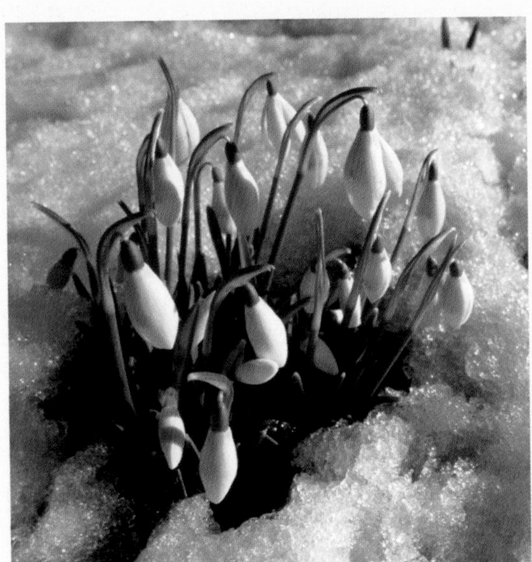

Galanthus 'Atkinsii' pushing through snow.

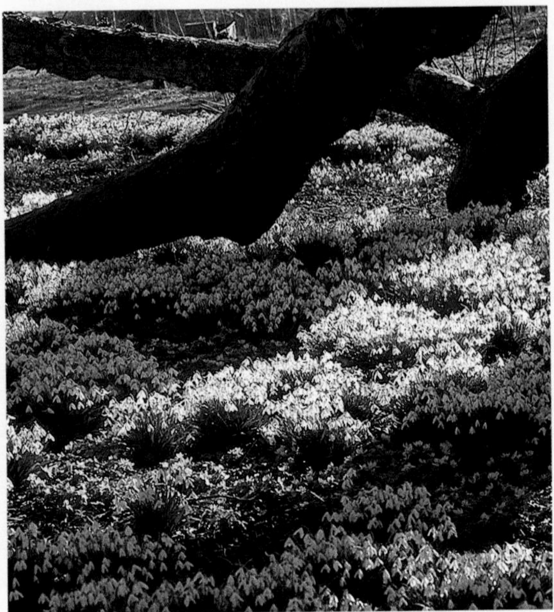

Massed *Galanthus nivalis* and *Galanthus hyemalus*.

Snowdrops are true bulbs with a single pendulous white flower held on a thin arching stalk (the pedicel) at the end of a thicker stem (or scape). Most flower from mid-winter to early spring although there are some autumn-flowering species. In the single-flowered forms there are three large outer petals clasping three considerably smaller inner ones. The double forms have many similar-sized inner petals where the stamens have been replaced by petals. They have two, occasionally three, strap-like leaves which are remarkably variable and one of the easiest means of identification.

What is it about snowdrops that so fascinate otherwise sane gardeners that they will spend inordinate amounts of time, often in the cold and wet, peering at them and even larger amounts of hard-earned money purchasing them?

How can something that is basically small and white with green marks have over 600 different names? There are singles and doubles but the permutations must be restricted, surely? The answer is, not entirely, although I must admit that some of the varietal differences are hard to spot and woe betide you trying to identify a plant once you have lost the label!

In the wild they are found from Europe to West Asia and there are only about nineteen species but in the garden, where different species are grown together, there are many opportunities for hybrids and different forms to occur. The craze known as 'Galanthophilia' has swept through the ranks of gardening enthusiasts in the last few years and many hundreds of these forms have been named. Some of the distinctions are very subtle and certainly not easy to distinguish from the normal observation position standing above the plant! The most obvious difference is the leaves, which vary from small narrow blue-green, to large wide grey or green. Some may be strongly folded (plicate) whilst others have a distinct central silver stripe. Height is another clearly distinguishing feature. Snowdrops vary from 7–25cm in height, with flowers sized to match. However, it is the pattern of the green mark(s) on the inner, and sometimes outer, petals that give rise to most names, although it requires close examination for these patterns to be obvious to the casual observer. Some snowdrops have yellow rather than green marks but, although they make for striking photographs, they tend to be weaker and poorer growers compared to the others.

Snowdrops, with a few exceptions, are bulbs of mountain regions, usually growing in or at the edge of woodland and in the garden they like a well-drained, humus-rich soil in part shade. They do not like very thin, impoverished soil or very wet clay. Nothing is more uplifting than a carpet of white under bare winter trees. They are excellent companion plants for other winter-flowering bulbs such as eranthis and cyclamen, which like similar conditions. Other good companions are hellebores, especially the Lenten Rose, *H.* × *hybridus (H. orientalis)* and deciduous geraniums. The leaves of these will spread in the summer to cover the dormant bulbs and give them a cool dry rest. It also protects them from accidental damage caused by over-enthusiastic weeding and might protect the labels as well! However the old hellebore leaves must be cut back and the dead geranium foliage removed early in the winter before they smother the snowdrops. Named forms are best grown in clumps among shrubs but the more vigorous varieties, especially *G. nivalis*, are excellent for naturalizing in grass where they are the perfect foil for eranthis and *Crocus tommasinianus* in all its forms.

Some of the many markings on snowdrop flowers.

Cultivation

Snowdrops should be planted 10cm deep. They can either be planted as dormant bulbs in the autumn or as growing plants in winter when it is traditional to send them out just after they have flowered. Both methods are equally successful but care must be taken to ensure that they spend the minimum of time out of the ground. Bulbs that are lifted early in the summer then hang around in warm garden centres quickly desiccate and lose their viability. Bulbs posted in growth may well take a couple of seasons to start flowering as transplanting at this time inevitably damages the roots. However, ones moved round the garden in full growth seem to suffer no ill effects at all, presumably because they spend the minimum of time out of the ground. I like to split mine just before they flower or soon afterwards while they are still in active growth. They do not even notice that they have been moved. Later division seems to hasten dormancy (senescence) but does not affect the long-term performance. Bulbs planted in growth must be well watered when replanted, especially if they have come through the post. Few snowdrops will tolerate growing in pots, which is probably the quickest method of killing them.

Ideally, all snowdrops should be planted in small clumps, as those planted singly seem to dwindle rather than increase. It is better to be patient and to buy three of one variety rather than one each of three varieties. Most snowdrops increase by offsets and clumps must be regularly divided after flowering. If left undivided clumps will become congested and their flowering considerably reduced. The display will also remain static whereas regularly divided clumps can quickly be spread to form impressive patches. The easiest method is to lift the whole clump and split it into two by gently pulling it apart. Half can then be planted back in the original hole and the remaining half further split to make two more new groups. In this way large colonies can be established relatively quickly. Research has shown that division every two years gives the optimum increase. This can be done at any time.

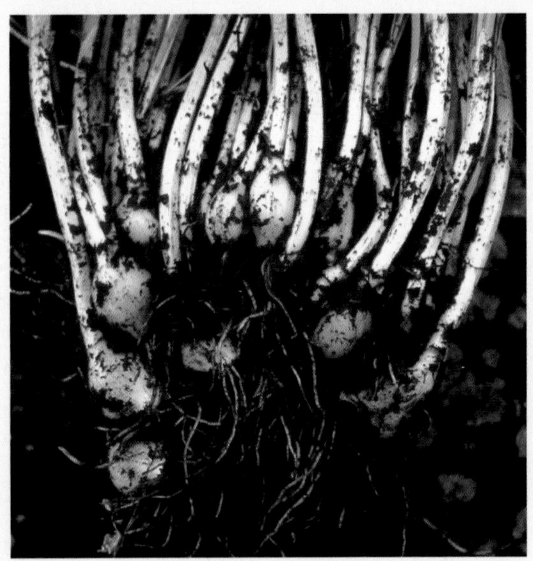

A congested clump of snowdrops ready for division.

Galanthus plicatus with *Cyclamen coum* and primroses.

Contrary to popular opinion not all gardens are suitable for snowdrops. If you do not already grow them it is probably best to try small clumps of the common snowdrop before embarking upon a collection of the more esoteric varieties. They do not appreciate soils that are too fertile so avoid adding any compost or manure to the soil or using fertilizer. Leaf mould, composted bark or chippings are acceptable soil mulches.

Propagation

Most snowdrops, including *G. nivalis*, are largely sterile and are propagated by offsets. Some species are generous with their offspring. Some forms of *G. elwesii* and *G. woronowii* will produce seedlings. *G. plicatus* is a particularly generous seeder.

Pests

Snowdrops are relatively trouble-free although they can suffer from fungal infections that attack the leaves and the neck of the bulb, especially in wet winters. Bulbs with unhealthy-looking leaves should be promptly removed.

Galanthus elwesii.

G. elwesii 🏆
(Giant Turkish Snowdrop)

This very variable snowdrop is readily identified by its broad grey leaves. It occurs from the south Balkans through to eastern Turkey and wild collected bulbs have been imported from Turkey for over a hundred years. Its name honours Henry Elwes, who first introduced it and started a fine snowdrop collection which can still be seen at Colesborne Manor in Gloucestershire. Today the export trade in *G. elwesii* is carefully controlled and most imported bulbs are raised in Turkish nurseries. The traditional form has two marks on the inner petals but these can merge to form a single mark or show any permutation in between. There is a wide range of variation among seedlings and many clones have been named. It is early flowering and prefers a dry position such as the base of a tree. Height: 10–20cm. **var. *monostictus*** 🏆 **(syn. *G. caucasicus*)** has the typical broad grey leaves of *G. elwesii* but only a

Galanthus 'Maidwell L'.

single mark on the flower and also comes from Turkey, not the Caucasus as first thought: the post was rather unreliable 150 years ago when it was introduced. It is very vigorous and can flower at any time from early to late winter. Early-flowering clones are given the name **'Hiemalis'** and are a little shorter than the type, producing their flowers in late November and December. **'Maidwell L'** has exceptionally large flowers with a green mark covering virtually all the inner tepals. **'Green Brush'** has elegant flowers with a bold green mark on the outer tepals.

G. gracilis (syn. *G. graecus*)

This is one of the most dainty and distinct snowdrops. The whole plant seems to 'stand to attention' and the upright, narrow grey leaves have an attractive twist. The delicate flower is slender with twin inner marks and the narrow ovary is a very pale apple green. This snowdrop comes from the pine woods of the eastern Mediterranean and seems to prefer a drier position in the garden than many and does well on my sunny rock garden. Height: 10cm.

G. nivalis 🏆
(Common Snowdrop)

This stalwart of the winter garden needs little introduction. It has slender flowers with a single mark and narrow grey-green leaves. Although it is small in stature, it increases rapidly and is the first

Galanthus gracilis.

Galanthus 'Viridapice'.

Galanthus 'Sandersii Group'.

Common double snowdrop *G. nivalis* 'Flore Pleno'.

choice for naturalizing, whether in grass, under shrubs or even round the base of roses in a mixed border. It is sterile and clumps must be regularly divided if the colony is to increase. Height: 10cm. **'Viridapice'** is taller and later flowering, and very upright with a distinct green tip to the outer petals of the large flower. Height: 18cm. **'Scharlockii'** is like a delicate version of this but the long upright spathe is split like asses' ears. Height: 10cm.

'Sandersii Group' *(G. lutescens)* is one of the yellow, rather than green marked forms, that occur naturally in some naturalized populations of *G. nivalis*. Rather tiny, they are also less vigorous, being extremely slow to increase and often shy to flower. Height: 7cm.

The double **'Flore Pleno'** 🏆 is of a similar stature to *G. nivalis* but the fully double flowers are much longer lasting, giving a bolder display. Unlike some of the named forms, these are rather wayward doubles with a mass of uneven inner petals. Height: 10cm.

'Lady Elphinstone' is one of those frustrating plants that rarely lives up to its description. In good years the inner markings of this double snowdrop are a clear yellow but they can revert to green in some seasons. Direct sunshine seems to have some effect upon the colouring or lack of it. However, unless you actually tip the flower up, the inner yellow markings are only really appreciated by a passing slug – from above they look virtually identical to the standard double! It is, however, very vigorous, increasing freely unlike some of the 'yellow' snowdrops. **'Pusey Green Tips'** is a standard double but with green tips to the outer petals.

G. plicatus 🏆

This snowdrop from the Black Sea area is one of the most easily identified. The relatively wide leaves have a distinct fold (pleat) on either side of the central vein. The leaves vary considerably in colour from grey to green. The flowers, with their single green mark, are often relatively small for the size of the leaves. It has long been in cultivation and will spread vigorously by seed. There are often considerable differences among the seedlings with early- and late-flowering clones and many named selections. Height: 12–20cm.

Galanthus 'Lady Elphinstone'.

Galanthus 'Warham'.

'Warham' is a particularly tall form with a distinct silver centre to the leaves; **'Wendy's Gold'** has bright yellow ovaries and markings and unlike many yellows is relatively vigorous; **subsp. *byzantinus*** 🏆, unlike the normal *G. plicatus*, has twin marks on the inner segments – this is also very variable and there are many named clones available; **'Augustus'** is readily identified by its broad, bright green folded leaves and its well-rounded flowers.

G. rizehensis

This is one of a group of small-flowered and rather insignificant snowdrops from the Middle East with slender flowers and narrow leaves. They are easy to grow in soil that is not too dry where they can form quite large clumps and even seed around. Height: 7cm.

G. woronowii 🏆
(*G. ikariae* subsp. *latifolius*)

This compact, late-flowering snowdrop has distinctive bright green leaves and delicate flowers with a single mark. The flowers are held at an acute angle to the stem and look as though they are facing a strong wind! It comes from the Caucasus and seems to prefer a soil that is not too dry. When happy it can seed quite vigorously. Height: 12cm.

Galanthus 'Wendy's Gold'.

Cultivars

With over 600 named cultivars it is impossible to give more than a small selection, so I have chosen some of the most vigorous, freely available and clearly distinct cultivars. There are many more to choose from, but beware: snowdrops, like stamp collecting, can be addictive!

Atkinsii' 🏆

This is one of the most vigorous of the large-flowered snowdrops. The flowers are large and rather slender, appearing early in the New Year and flowering well before *G. nivalis* even pokes through. It will spread both by division and seeding to form large colonies. It has a single inner mark

Galanthus rizehensis.

Galanthus woronwii.

and narrow grey-green leaves. Stocks of 'Atkinsii' are often mixed with **'James Backhouse'**. This is identical in overall appearance but in some seasons has one deformed inner petal or an extra outer one. Several very similar cultivars have also been named. Height: 20cm.

'Hill Poe'

This distinct double snowdrop was discovered in an Irish garden and has an extra outer petal or two to the large, fully double flowers, which gives it a 'fat' appearance when viewed from above. It is compact and late flowering and seems to prefer a slightly heavier soil than some. Height: 15cm.

'John Gray'

This is one of the earliest, often flowering in December, and has exceptionally large, round flowers on a very long pedicel which are really too large for their stem. They have an unfortunate tendency to bend over, almost touching the ground where they are easily rain splashed or are an instant attraction for slugs. A few well-placed twigs will protect them from this fate. The inner markings are in the form of a bold green cross which pales to the apex as though painted on in watercolour. Height: 18cm.

Galanthus 'Magnet'.

'Ketton'

This is a late-flowering and very reliable snowdrop with relatively large flowers on short stems, forming handsome clumps. The inner marks are very distinct with a dark base and a pair of faint washed lines above. Height: 15cm.

'Magnet' 🏆

The large flowers of this graceful snowdrop are held away from the stems on exceptionally long pedicels which are almost twice the length of the spathe. In warm weather they open wide and seem to dance in the slightest breeze like a ballerina. Overall the clumps are very distinctive in appearance as the stems are also held at a slight angle, making it amongst the few snowdrops that are instantly recognizable at a distance. Height: 18cm. **'Galatea'** is similar but the pedicel has an acute angle in it and the stems are more upright. Height: 20cm. Both are vigorous growers.

Galanthus 'John Gray'.

Greatorex Doubles

This group of tall showy doubles was bred by Heyrick Greatorex in the 1960s and are named after Shakespearean heroines. All are relatively similar but close examination will reveal subtle differences. **'Ophelia'** might not be the most perfect or largest flower but any minor imperfections in the flower structure are far outweighed by its vigour and early flowering. It is among the first to flower, often producing two stems per bulb and forming handsome clumps. Sometimes there is a faint green mark on the outer petals and the inner ones have a narrow deep green mark. **'Hippolyta'** is later with exceptionally well formed and very round large flowers that look as though they have been cut with a knife. **'Desdemona'** and **'Titania'** are similar vigorous hybrids. **'Jaquenetta'** has smaller flowers but is very vigorous, often producing two stems per bulb. It has distinct fat flowers, with an overall greenish cast. The outer petals are short, barely longer than the inner ones which have a long green mark for most of their length. Height: 13cm.

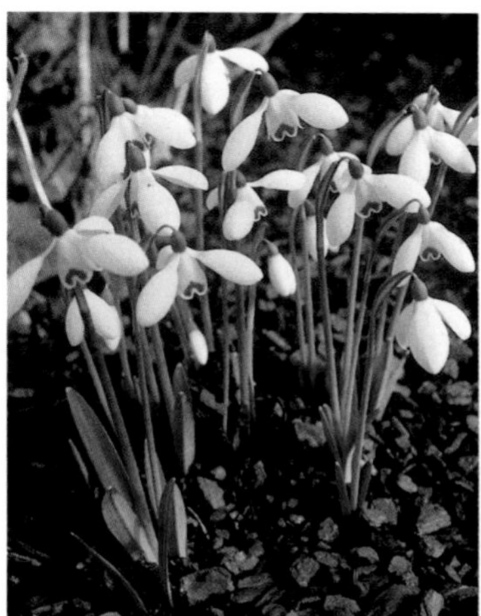

Galanthus 'S. Arnott'.

Galanthus 'Hippolyta'.

'S. Arnott' 🏆

This is one of the best tall cultivars with beautifully rounded, large flowers with a distinct honey (or some say almond) scent which is noticeable even in the open garden on a warm day. When growing well they form very handsome clumps with the flowers held well above the leaves on very upright stems. **'Brenda Troyle'** is similar but earlier flowering. Height: 20cm. Although these two snowdrops are very similar in appearance they seem to have subtly different cultural requirements. 'Brenda Troyle' will cope with dry soils but 'S. Arnott' prefers something slightly more moist conditions.

ODDITIES

Sometimes the usual arrangement of three short inner petals and three long outer petals breaks down.

'Trym' is an idiosyncratic snowdrop with a delightfully undressed look, as though it had forgotten to put on its skirt in its rush to greet spring. In fact it does have a double set of petals but the boldly green marked outer ones are also spade shaped like the inner ones. It is a very attractive plant, if maddeningly slow to increase. It has produced some stunning seedlings. Height: 15cm.

Other cultivars like **'Angelique'** have long thin inner petals echoing the outer ones and look rather like elegant ballerinas waiting to go on stage. **'Blewbury Tart'** on the other hand is just plain bizarre. It is a very readily identifiable and curious double where, instead of nodding, the narrow flower faces outwards to reveal just how awful it is. All the segments are uneven and the whole flower has a green cast. However it is very vigorous and certainly distinct! There are many other curiosities of equally doubtful beauty.

Iris

Reticulata Group

These tiny, winter-flowering iris come from the high mountains of the Middle East where they are buried deep in the snow all winter, flowering as the snow melts and the temperature rises. In our gardens this means late winter to early spring, the first coinciding with the last of the snowdrops. Reticulata iris have a small pointed bulb, with a whitish netted tunic. They produce solitary flowers which have a ridge along the centre of the falls rather than a beard. The long, thin deep green leaves are triangular in cross section. There are various species that make up this section.

It has always been recommended that reticulata iris should be planted on a sunny rock garden. But in this position the bulbs are vulnerable to dry spells and they consequently have an annoying habit of splitting into tiny non-flowering bulblets. These take many years to regain flowering size; thus these iris are often treated as annuals. However, one year I planted a flowering potful of iris in a new shady bed where we grow snowdrops – just to give it some instant colour – and I noticed that the following year they flowered just as well. I now have well-established clumps in cool, humus-rich soil under deciduous shrubs so there is plenty of light/moisture when they are growing but conditions are dry and shady when they are dormant. I have also seen them naturalized in light grass under cherry trees. These were ex-display pots from our flower shows, which normally I would have discarded! The buds will poke through in December and then wait until February to flower.

Iris reticulata growing wild in Iran.

Their early flowering means they also make excellent subjects for pots for the greenhouse, conservatory or house. The pots should be kept outside (protected from severe frost) until the buds appear when they can then be brought into the house to flower.

Cultivation

The bulbs are planted in the autumn in small groups of five to ten bulbs 10–15cm deep. They are traditionally grown as rock garden bulbs in a sunny situation but the dry soil usually causes the bulbs to desiccate and to split into tiny bulblets which will then take some years to regain flowering size. Extra deep planting and feeding with a low-nitrogen fertilizer is often recommended to overcome this. However, bulbs that are planted in a cooler, but equally well-drained, position among shrubs continue growing for longer and do not split up in the same way, continuing to flower for some years. They are excellent subjects for growing in containers and make attractive pot plants to bring indoors once the buds appear.

Pests

These early flowers are like caviar to slugs, which will leave unsightly holes in the petals. The bulbs can suffer from the descriptive 'ink spot' disease. Infected bulbs should be thrown away.

I. danfordiae

This is the first of the group to flower, with very angular yellow flowers with green spots in the throat. It tends to be less reliably perennial than the others and is a rather strident colour. Height: 12cm.

I. histrioides 'Major' 🏆

This old and reliable cultivar has large, deep blue flowers but sadly it is no longer freely available. There are other good, similarly reliable cultivars which have proved to be good garden plants. **'Angel's Eye'** (**'Angels' Tears'**) and **'Lady B. Stanley'** are recommended blue forms. Height: 12cm. **'George'** 🏆 is a hybrid with *I. reticulata* and has exceptionally large flowers of rich purple. Height: 20cm.

I. reticulata

This early-flowering iris grows wild in northern Iran where it flowers as the snow melts. Over the last hundred years many colour forms have been selected. The following are some of the best cultivars: **'Alida'** is a new cultivar with exceptionally large mid-blue flowers and is good in pots; **'Cantab'** is a pale Cambridge blue; **'Edward'** is intense bright blue with a distinct orange ridge; **'Gordon'** has pale blue flowers with a striking deep velvet fall and orange ridge; **'Harmony'** has well-shaped flowers of a good clear blue and is scented (it is recommended for pots as the leaves remain short at flowering); **'Joyce'** is very similar; **'J.S. Dijt'** has rich ruby-red flowers with an orange ridge; **'Pauline'** is deep purple with a distinctive white central stripe; **'Blue Note'** is a new variety with intense blue-purple flowers and a similar white mark. Height: 15cm.

Iris danfordiae.

Iris histrioides 'Lady B. Stanley'.

Iris 'George'.

Iris 'Harmony'.

Iris 'Gordon'.

Iris 'Katharine Hodgkin'.

'Katharine Hodgkin' 🏆

This is an amazing hybrid between *I. winogradowii* and *I. histrioides*. It is much more vigorous than many of the cultivars and has significantly larger bulbs. The flowers are an extraordinary mix of cream and yellow overlaid with blue and green. It sounds dreadful but is very beautiful in the flesh. If planted in shade it will form large, long-lived clumps. **'Sheila Ann Germany'** is another hybrid of similar parentage and vigour with very large flowers of clear sky blue without the yellow background. Height: 10cm.

Leucojum

Although the main entry will be found in *Chapter 3*, some clones of *L. vernum* are early flowering, coinciding with the snowdrops.

Narcissus

Although daffodils are principally spring-flowering bulbs there are some welcome varieties that will flower in the open garden in the winter. See the entry in *Chapter 3* for full details on cultivation, etc.

N. bulbocodium cantabricus etc.

There are various white-flowered bulbocodium species that flower in mid-winter. These come from southern Spain and North Africa and although they are reasonably hardy they will only flower if kept dry in the summer, so they are not really suitable for the open garden, although they do make attractive and easy subjects for cold glass. Height: 15cm.

'Cedric Morris' (Division 1)

This is a rather over-rated daffodil with a reputation for flowering in the early winter, but even this attribute is not consistent: in fact the flowers can appear any time from late November to February. The rather insignificant lemon-yellow flowers are held on relatively tall stems. It is a wild selection of *N. asturiensis* and is in consequence extremely slow to increase. It seems to prefer a cool woodland situation but even here it has a tendency to disappear without trace. Height: 20cm.

'Crewenna' (Division 1)

The bold bicoloured flowers of this variety appear from late January and are ideal to cheer a dark corner. However, it is rather too blousy to take centre stage and its lush leaves can too easily swamp later bulbs. They are best tucked away where their early colour can be appreciated but their later exuberant foliage can be ignored. The large, flared trumpet is deep gold and the petals are white. Height: 35cm.

'Paperwhite' (Division 8)

The name Paperwhite is used to describe a group of many similar Christmas-flowering cultivars, mostly produced in Israel. The most common is 'Ziva', which is almost indistinguishable from the wild plant, with up to five glistening-white, strongly-fragrant flowers per stem. This is the best known of the early indoor daffodils and can flower at any time from November to January, depending upon planting time and temperature.

The pure white, multi-headed *N. papyraceus* grows wild in southern Spain, in the hinterland of the Costas and other areas of the Mediterranean. They appear at any

Narcissus 'Crewenna'.

time from November to January, depending upon the arrival of the winter rain to break their dormancy. They rush into growth almost overnight. A scattering of the ice-white blooms quickly turns into a veritable flood, filling the roadside verges. In the cold north we enjoy their ease of growth in pots for indoors and relish their appearance in mid-winter when the garden can be under snow. However, in their warm Iberian home, they do not have the same resonance and they are given the rather scathing common name of *meao de zorro* (the Spanish name literally means fox piss!), and my interest in them was treated with amazement. If the flowers are cut and brought indoors their strong tazetta fragrance quickly becomes rancid, with a scent allied to that of the fox. Fortunately pots of bulbs retain their sweet perfume.

Paperwhite bulbs are available in the shops from late summer and can be planted in succession, on or under compost, or even on gravel and water. In the house they will spring into flower about six weeks after they are planted. When they are first planted, it is best to put them somewhere cool and light while they root. Although they can be grown entirely indoors, they do tend to become etoliated very quickly in warm conditions. I grow mine in a north-facing porch, and bring the pots indoors in succession when the buds begin to open. Even then, they will need some form of discreet support. I find the silver or white twigs sold at Christmas to be ideal. Bulbs wanted for Christmas or later flowering should be kept in the light in a cool place until mid-November. Any green shoots should be rigorously ignored until you are ready to plant. They quickly straighten up.

N. papyraceus requires a warm dry summer to flower so it is best to buy new bulbs each year, although bulbs planted against a sunny wall in mild districts will survive. Outside it is later flowering.

'Rijnveldt's Early Sensation' (Division 1) 🏆

One of the most surprising sights of mid-winter is to discover a clump of this daffodil in full flower before most daffodils even think of appearing above ground or snowdrops flowering. This is a

Narcissus 'Paperwhite'.

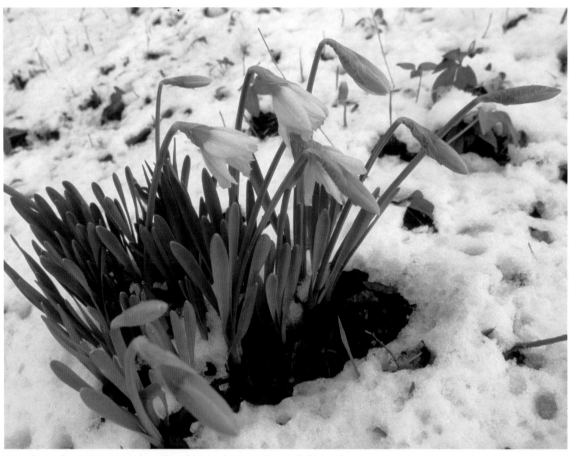

The winter-flowering *Narcissus* 'Rijnveldt's Early Sensation' is fully hardy.

mid-height golden daffodil with an old-fashioned type of flower – the petals are slightly paler than the ruffled trumpet. It is very vigorous, clumping up quickly and requiring regular division, and it is totally hardy, being able to withstand periods of hard frost; the buds may bend over but they will promptly stand up again as soon as it thaws. At a first glance it is a rather poorly shaped flower with little to recommend it but its reliable early flowering means it deserves a place in the garden where it flowers with or even before the snowdrops. It is a plant for the bottom of the garden where it will draw the eye with a promise that spring is on its way. Indeed it regularly fools journalists as this is always the daffodil featured in the regular 'spring is getting earlier' articles. Height: 30cm.

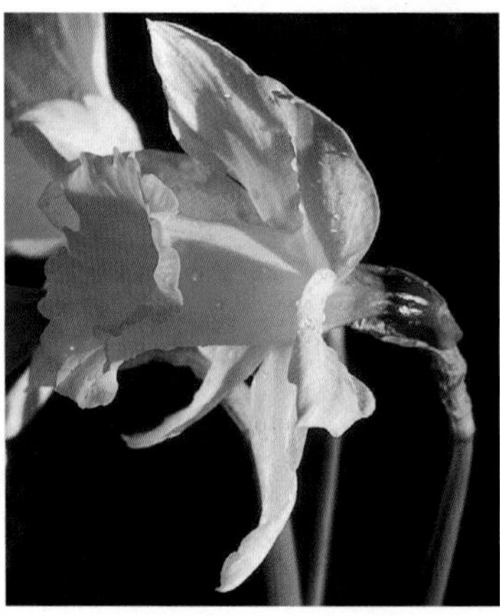

Narcissus 'Spring Dawn'.

'Spring Dawn' (Division 2)

This early-flowering daffodil has creamy-white petals and a lemon-yellow cup and a more delicate, star-like appearance than 'Crewenna'. It can flower at any time from late December to mid-January depending upon the season. Height: 35cm.

Other early-flowering daffodils that are worth considering are: **'Tête-à-Tête'** (Division 12); **'February Gold'** (Division 6), **'Little Gem'** (Division 1), **'Small Talk'** and the Lent lily or ***N. pseudonarcissus (N. lobularis)*** (Division 13). In mild winters these varieties often overlap with the snowdrops. Descriptions will be found in *Chapter 3*.

Scilla

Most of this family are spring-flowering *(see Chapter 3)* but there are two winter-flowering members.

S. bifolia 🏆

This little gem has racemes of intense blue starry flowers. It starts to flower on the cusp of spring as the snowdrops fade. It is too small to make an impact by itself but is delightful dotted in the grass or massed under shrubs where it is a good foil for white snowdrops or cream crocus. Height: 10cm.

S. mischtschenkoana 'Tubergeniana' 🏆

This remarkable bulb from north Iran is one of the very best, if virtually unpronounceable (the fall of the Berlin Wall and the subsequent communication between botanists has a lot to answer for!). This scilla starts to flower with the snowdrops and crocus but the short spikes of small china-blue flowers, each with a darker blue stripe, remain in perfect condition just gradually elongating until the daffodils appear some weeks later. Although it is slow to increase, it is extremely long lived, very versatile and deserves to be much more widely grown. The bulbs look just like miniature hyacinths and can be planted under trees or shrubs, where it is an ideal companion for other early-flowering bulbs such as snowdrops, cyclamen and aconites, or in full sun on a rock garden – or even tucked in along the front of a herbaceous border. Height: 15cm.

Scilla bifolia with an early bee.

Scilla mischtschenkoana.

Tulips

Although these are almost entirely spring-flowering, in mild winters there are some precocious species that will start to flower in late winter: ***T. humilis***, ***T. turkestanica***, and ***T. kaufmanniana*** hybrids are amongst the earliest.

Their descriptions will be found in *Chapter 3.*

Tulipa turkestanica.

CHAPTER 3

BULBS FOR SPRING DISPLAY

Massed tulips edge a driveway.

For all its mid-season fireworks, spring arrives gradually in the garden, seeming to creep in by the back door rather than trumpeting its arrival at the front. One minute it is definitely winter; then, almost overnight, spring is stirring. Many bulbs have already been making their presence felt but for me it is the flowering of hellebores and the strident gold of forsythia that mark the transition: an indication that winter has relaxed its grip and true spring is under way. Then, as every day passes, so more and more bulbs join the display. This starts with early narcissus and the small blue bulbs that are an indispensible foil for the overwhelming yellowness of the daffodils, and continues until the late tulips appear and the whole garden is suffused with colour.

For most people, whether they are gardeners or not, spring and bulbs are synonymous. Bulbs of all kinds feature in everyone's favourite spring picture, whether it is a drift of daffodils gently blowing in the wind or a more formal planting of colourful tulips. This is the season in which the majority of bulbs 'do their stuff', taking advantage of the rising temperatures and bursting into rapid growth before they are swamped by the later perennials. On their own they may be rather small and insignificant, but planted in bold groups they make an impact far exceeding their individual size.

There is a spring bulb for every type of garden and every location, whether it is tulips in a formal border or colourful containers flanking a doorway, massed chionodoxas round the base of a tree, elegant erythroniums in the shade of shrubs, or daffodils growing wild in grass or at the base of a hedge. One of the joys of this season is watching the gradual change in the bulbs as the leaves appear on the trees. Compact varieties start the season but these give way to taller subjects as the herbaceous perennials begin to make their mark or the grass starts to grow. Colours also change, from a predominantly yellow palette of early daffodils to the full rainbow hue of late spring tulips.

Writing a book like this presents the author with the problem of what to include and what to leave out, as an overwhelming number of varieties is available. There is a danger that it becomes just a catalogue of names; this is especially true of daffodils and tulips where there are literally thousands of cultivars. With these I have only chosen a few as a taster of each section to illustrate the enormous range available, concentrating on those that have proved themselves as good garden plants and earned the coveted Royal Horticultural Society Award of Garden Merit 🏆. You will find many more listed in bulb catalogues.

Tulipa saxatalis.

Narcissus 'February Gold' in a shrub bed with scillas and hellebores.

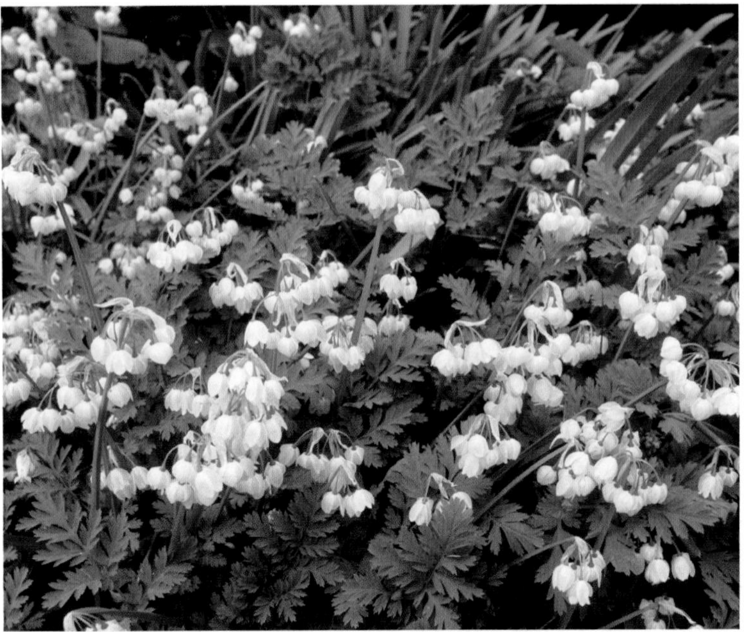

Allium paradoxum v. normale with *Dicentra formosa* leaves.

Allium

Although the majority of these are summer-flowering and will be found in *Chapter 4*, this species flowers in early to mid-spring.

A. paradoxum var. *normale*

Most forms of this Middle Eastern allium should not be allowed anywhere near the garden as they share the unfortunate habit of many other members of this family of producing bulbils rather than flowers in their umbels, which are not only unattractive but also mean they spread almost uncontrollably. This form is well behaved, however, and has attractive, slightly nodding heads of white papery flowers. It is fully hardy and steadily forms small clumps. Although it is not a problem it will gently seed and we recommend removing the seed heads before they are ripe. Like most alliums the leaves are rather fleshy but are neat when the plant is in flower. It is useful as it tolerates dry shade and looks good planted under dwarf pines, or try it mixed with the grey ferny foliage of *Dicentra formosa*. Height: 30cm.

Anemone

The bulbous anemones are one of the stalwarts of any spring display. The smaller varieties such as the blue *A. blanda* or the delicate white *A. nemorosa* will spread to carpet the ground under trees, where they form a delightful background to taller, bolder bulbs such as daffodils. Those from the hotter parts of the Mediterranean have brilliantly coloured flowers and are much showier and taller. Unlike their herbaceous summer-flowering counterparts, the spring-flowering anemones have either small knobbly tubers or slender creeping rhizomes and are summer dormant.

Cultivation

Anemones with rhizomes are naturally plants of cool woodland soils. These slender creeping rootstocks are very vulnerable to drought and should never be allowed to dry out too much, especially when

Anemone blanda naturalized round the base of a tree.

lifted for sale. Twenty-four hours out of the soil and in the open is enough to kill them.

Those with tubers come from hotter, drier areas and prefer a sunny, well-drained position in the garden such as a rock garden. Over-dried tubers will benefit from an overnight soak in cold water prior to planting. Both types may take a couple of seasons to establish themselves but when growing well can spread to form extensive colonies. Propagation is by breaking up the rhizomes of woodland anemones in the autumn or early spring, just as growth begins, or by cutting up the tubers. Some species will seed freely but their offspring will not necessarily have the same colours as the parents. Division is therefore the only method of maintaining particular colour forms like *A. blanda* 'White Splendour'.

A. apennina 🏆

This Greek wood anemone is usually encountered in old gardens where it is naturalized in light grass under trees. Sadly its popularity has

Anemone appenina.

Anemone coronaria.

declined and it is less freely available. In flower it is very similar to *A. blanda* but it is slightly taller with hairy leaves and the rootstock is a fat rhizome rather than a tuber. The easiest way to tell them apart is to look at them in early morning. The flower heads of *A. apennina* bend over through 180° to face downwards, quickly reverting to vertical once the temperature rises. The flowers come in shades of blue or white and there are semi-double forms. If you can track some down they make easy and reliable plants for light shade and will gently seed around. The rhizomes are very vulnerable to drying out and should be transplanted as quickly as possible. Height: 15cm.

A. blanda 🏆

This small, knobbly tuber produces bright blue starry flowers and attractively divided leaves. It flowers for a long time, often starting with the snowdrops and continuing for six weeks. Although they are native to southeastern Europe and Turkey and prefer a well-drained position, they are equally at home carpeting the ground under small trees as on a dry rock garden. Provided the position is sunny when they are in flower and dry in the summer they will seed freely and can spread into impressive colonies. They are usually offered as seed-raised tubers in shades of blue. They are perfect massed around the base of a tree where they can be mixed with primroses and chionodoxas which will seed together. They are also invaluable for underplanting bulbs in containers. Height: 8cm. **'White Spendour'** 🏆 has large, pure white flowers and is probably the best for more formal planting such as in parterres (I grow them round the clumps of bearded iris under my pleached pears). **'Radar'** 🏆 has violent magenta flowers with a bold white centre, but it is unfortunately slow to increase, often gradually dwindling away. **'Pink Star'** and **'Charmer'** are both pink but neither is particularly attractive as their colour is rather pallid. If the various colour forms are planted together their progeny will be a kaleidoscope of shades from pink to purple. Named forms must be propagated by physically cutting up the tubers.

A. coronaria

Careful selection of the poppy anemone of the central and eastern Mediterranean regions has given rise to the well-known florist anemone, which produces long-lasting solitary flowers on tall stems. The showy flowers are in strong tones of red, purple or blue and are ideal for cutting. They are often sold as mixed colours but named single colour forms are available. They are early flowering and are prone to weather damage. Established clumps in sheltered spots flower best or they

Anemone nemorosa with *Scilla bithynica*.

can be grown under glass or cloches. The **'De Caen' Group** have single flowers and the **'St Brigid' Group** have semi-double flowers. Height: 25cm.

A. flaccida

This small anemone comes from the mountains of Japan and neighbouring China and Russia. It has very distinct fat rhizomes, which produce a neat mound of lobed leaves with rounded edges. These are bronze when they first appear but they quickly turn green retaining an attractive silver mark at the base of each lobe. The small, white, typical anemone flowers are produced in mid-spring. They are easily grown in any humus-rich soil, preferably in part shade where they make an attractive foliage plant and are a good foil for other woodland spring bulbs such as erythroniums. However, if it is too hot in the middle of the day they will live up to their name and flop, but they quickly revive in the cooler evening. They are summer dormant. Height: 12cm.

A. × fulgens

This hybrid between two Mediterranean species produces solitary scarlet flowers, each with a dramatic black centre. It is occasionally encountered naturalized in grass where they look rather like out-of-season poppies. They are best grown under small trees such as ornamental cherries, which will provide the dry summer they require. They are propagated by seed and sadly are not often offered for sale. Height: 15cm.

A. nemorosa 🏆

The wood anemone of northern Europe is a vigorous, creeping perennial with dissected leaves and solitary small white flowers, sometimes with a pink flushed back. Although it can be slow to start, once established it can form extensive colonies and should be treated with caution in small gardens. It is happiest in light shade and will compete with thin grass under trees. There are many selected colour forms available. Height: 10cm.

White

'Leeds Variety' has extra large flowers and rather thick rhizomes.

Blue

'Allenii' 🏆 has large pale lilac flowers. **'Robinsoniana'** 🏆 is very similar and has large lavender-blue flowers with cream backs. **'Royal Blue'** is more compact with bright blue flowers.

Double

'Vestal' 🏆 is less vigorous, forming compact clumps which can be smothered by flowers. It has a neat double centre to the small white flowers. There are many other double and semi-double forms. **'Bracteata Pleniflora'** has curious double white

Anemone nemorosa 'Royal Blue'.

Anemone ranunculoides.

and green flowers where the petals and bracts are mixed up to a lesser or greater extent. **'Virescens'** has conical 'flowers' of interleaved green bracts without petals.

A. pavonina

This showy, large-flowered anemone is similar to *A.* × *fulgens* and comes from Greece. The flowers are in hectic shades of pink, red, purple and salmon, which give it its common name of 'peacock anemone'. The selection **'St Bavo Group'** is sometimes offered for sale. In warm counties it will seed around on a sunny rock garden or in light grass under trees. Height: 25cm.

A. ranunculoides 🏆

The variable yellow-flowered wood anemone from European woods is just as easy to grow as *A. nemorosa* although its flowers are rather smaller. It forms neat clumps of divided leaves smothered in flowers. Its cheerful golden yellow is reminiscent of that of celandines but unlike that thug it is non-invasive. It is a good foil for *Epimedium versicolor neosulphureum*. Height: 10–15cm. **'Pleniflora'** has semi-double flowers but annoyingly will produce single-flowered offspring if allowed to set seed.

A. × *lipsiensis*

(A.* × *seemanii; A.* × *intermedia)

This hybrid between *A. ranunculoides* and *A. nemorosa* has creamy-yellow flowers. It is as easy to grow as its parents, spreading to form small patches of attractively divided leaves studded with small starry flowers. It is useful to lighten a dark corner under shrubs. Height: 10cm.

Anemone pavonina naturalized at University of Bristol Botanic Garden (Photo: Nicholas Wray).

The curious 'flowers' of *Arisarum proboscidium*.

Arisarum

These curious arum relatives are grown for their tiny 'flowers', although these are the protecting spathes, not the flowers. The true flower is on an insignificant spadix inside this. They have glossy, dark green leaves and spread to form extensive mats and they are probably more useful as a spring ground cover plant than a flowering plant. They prefer a cool position in the garden.

Cultivation

The small angular rhizomes are planted in the autumn, 5cm deep in a light, humus-rich soil in part shade. Propagate by division at any time. They are reputed to dislike dry soils or to dry out but we have been growing and selling them from an open sunny bed for forty years and never managed to kill them yet. However, they do give their best 'performance' in cool, moist soils.

A. proboscidium
(Mouse Plant)

These have fascinating tiny 'flowers', which look like long-tailed brown mice disappearing down their holes. Unfortunately they are completely hidden below the carpet of glossy leaves and have to be looked for – although growing them on the top of a wall would make this easier. They are easily grown in any humus-rich soil in part shade, where they will quickly spread to form extensive carpets of shiny arrow-shaped leaves. They are summer dormant. Height: 10cm.

Arum
(Lords and Ladies)

These vigorous, tuberous rooted perennials are grown for their clumps of arrow-shaped leaves, which are often attractively marbled. These appear in late autumn and they make a useful winter foliage plant for growing under shrubs. In most cases the flowers, or more correctly, the spathes, are rather dull. The even more insignificant true flowers are inside these. The flowers are followed by spikes of bold red berries. They are summer dormant and all parts are poisonous.
The tubers are usually planted in growth in winter or spring. Plant 10–15cm deep.

A. creticum

As its name implies, this arum is native to Crete and needs a dry sunny place to flourish in the garden, where its glossy, green arrow-shaped leaves appear during the winter. It is grown for its creamy-white or in the best forms striking yellow spathes. It has a foul fragrance but this is not

Arum italicum berries.

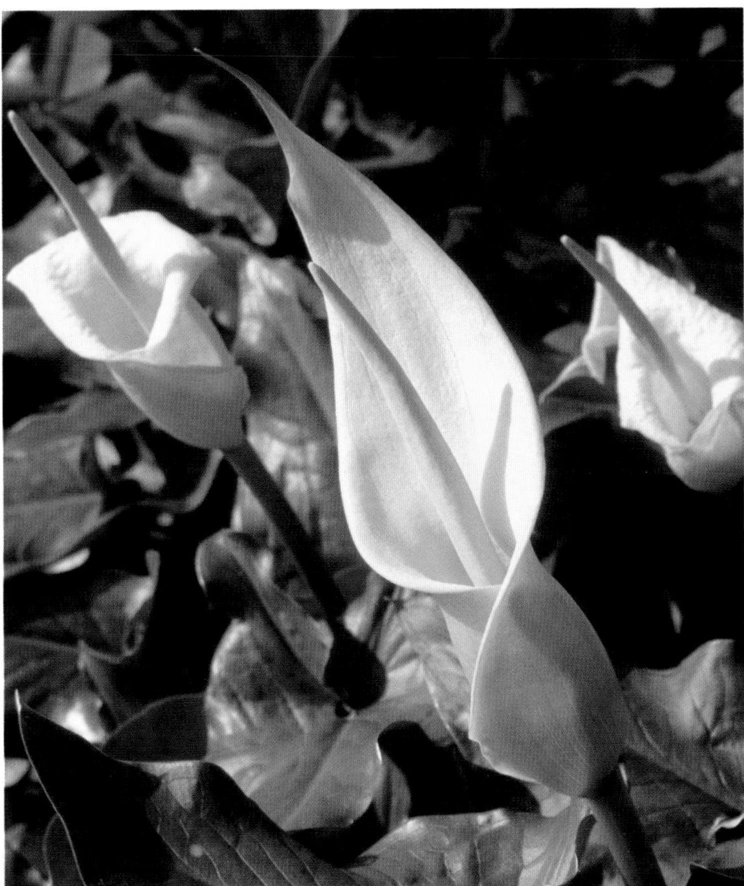

Arum creticum.

noticeable in the open garden. Despite this it makes an easy and attractive pot plant for cold glass, needing little attention. Height: 30cm.

A. italicum

This arum from southern Europe and Turkey is principally grown as a winter foliage plant and is ideal for those awkward areas under large trees where little else seems to grow. It is a vigorous grower, producing many small offsets which are easily and inadvertently spread around borders. These can be difficult to eradicate as they burrow deeply into the soil. There is a wide range of selected cultivars with often dramatically marked or splashed leaves. The most commonly encountered is **'Marmoratum' (syn. 'Pictum')** 🏆, which is grown for its dramatic cream- or white-veined leaves. It should be treated with caution as it can prove invasive. Each tuber produces a mass of offsets, which are easily distributed round the garden but less easily removed. It is also advisable to remove the seed heads, as the leaves of the seedlings are often not as well marked. It appears to be slightly frost tender, preferring the warmer counties, although it has happily survived -15°C here with no damage. Hard frost coupled with wind is more likely to spoil the leaves. Height: 13cm.

Bellevalia

To the casual observer these are grape hyacinths. They produce a similar spike of tubular flowers in the spring, the botanical difference being that the mouth of the individual bells is closed rather than open. They are easily grown in any free-draining soil in full sun, although most are rather insignificant with flowers in shades of brown or off-white. The bulbs are planted in the autumn, 10cm deep and 6cm apart. Propagation is by division of congested clumps.

B. picnantha

This robust bulb comes from the mountains of the Middle East and produces showy spikes of navy blue flowers, each with a yellowish rim to the bells and strap-shaped leaves which appear early in the season. Although it is very attractive in flower, it does need careful consideration before being let loose in the garden as it can be too free with its progeny. Unwanted bulbs are difficult to eradicate as each is topped by a mass of bulblets which quickly replace it, and it seeds freely. The very similar *Muscari paradoxum* may be a synonym but some authorities recognize it as a separate species. Height: 30cm.

Bongardia

This curious tuberous rooted member of the Berberis family comes from the mountains of the Middle East, from Greece to Pakistan. The large tubers should be planted at least 15cm deep in a very well-drained soil or grown in a pot in a loam-based compost. They are

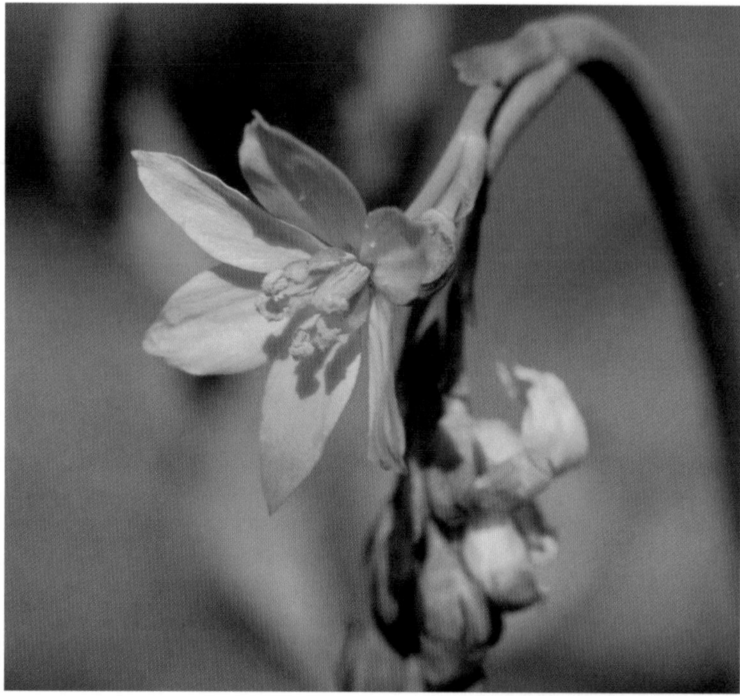

Bongardia chrysogonum.

propagated by careful division of the large tubers when they are dormant in the summer, but as they tend to pull themselves down to remarkable depths, finding them can be difficult.

B. chrysogonum

In late spring the flower heads appear first, curled like a bishop's crosier, gradually elongating to form a well-branched head of tiny starry yellow flowers. The leaves are probably the most attractive part, resembling those of a fern with red marks in the centre of each leaflet, although there are unmarked forms around. It is normally grown under cold glass but it is fully hardy. However, it needs a very dry, warm position such as against a sunny wall, preferably below the canopy of a wall shrub to give it protection from summer rain, as the tubers will rot if it is wet when they are dormant. Height: 40cm.

Brimeura

Although they are hardly in the first rank of spring-flowering bulbs, brimeura have a gentle charm of their own, being rather like a small, delicate bluebell. They like a well-drained soil and will tolerate some shade. Plant the bulbs 10cm deep and 5cm apart in the autumn.

B. amethystina 🏆
(Hyacinthus amethystinus)

These Pyrenean natives have small, open spikes of tubular flowers with attractively rolled rims which will gradually increase to form small clumps. They come in varying shades of blue, the prettiest being a delicate china blue. Height: 15cm. **var. *alba*** has white flowers.

Camassia

Camassias produce their flowers in that dead period between the end of spring and true summer but in an early season they may coincide with the tulips. Full details will be found In *Chapter 4*.

Chionodoxa
(Glory of the Snow)

Their common name may be the Glory of the Snow, but in the garden they are the glory of mid-spring, growing in almost any sunny border where their brilliant true blue flowers are the perfect foil for other spring bulbs, especially early golden daffodils. They are particularly effective under flowering trees such as magnolias or cherries, where they will seed vigorously to form a brilliant blue carpet before the leaves of the trees form an umbrella over the summer-dormant bulbs. They even cope with an annual mulch of rich compost. Chionodoxas are best grown in a border as they prefer not to compete with grass where they gradually dwindle. They have slender, erect basal leaves and a spike of starry flowers. In the past there has been much confusion over their nomenclature and many of the names were misapplied. Today many of the cultivated stocks are still muddled, possibly being of hybrid origin, but they all make excellent and rewarding garden plants. They are native to the mountains of western Turkey, where they flower as the snow melts. The bulbs are planted in the autumn, 10cm deep and 5cm apart. Propagation is by division of clumps or by seed.

Chionodoxa forbesii.

C. forbesii
(*C. luciliae* of gardens)

This vigorous bulb has up to twelve bright blue, white-centred flowers per stem. They are very effective when allowed to carpet the ground around the base of a tree such as a magnolia or cherry, where they will seed to form a sea of intense blue. Height: 10cm.

C. luciliae 🏆
(C. gigantea)

This is similar to the above but the flowers are larger and a softer blue and there are fewer per stem. Height: 10cm. **'Alba'** has large, pure white flowers. **'Pink Giant'** is a very distinct and vigorous variety. It is much taller and larger altogether with a spike of clear bluish-pink flowers with bold white centres. It is quite a difficult colour to use in the garden. Try them massed under early-flowering pale pink cherries such as *Prunus subhirtella* or *Magnolia* 'Leonard Messel' which is the same tone of lilac pink, but avoid pink camellias at all cost as they look awful! Height: 18cm.

C. sardensis 🏆

This small bulb has up to twelve intense bright blue flowers per stem. Unlike the others, these do not have such a conspicuous white centre. It is one of the earliest to flower, preferring a dry, sunny position such as a rock garden or the base of a tree where it will gently seed around. Height: 10cm.

Chionodoxa 'Pink Giant'.

Corydalis

Many corydalis are herbaceous or annual but there are some spring-flowering tuberous rooted perennials that are excellent for the cooler part of the garden. The heavily divided leaves have an attractive ferny appearance. The tubular flowers are carried in a terminal raceme reminiscent of slender snapdragons. They are perfect for underplanting shrubs and make excellent companion plants for other woodland bulbs, such as erythroniums and the smaller daffodils, or to succeed snowdrops. They are summer dormant.

Cultivation

Plant the tubers 10cm deep and 10cm apart in the autumn, or pot-grown plants in the spring. The tubers are vulnerable to drying out when out of the soil, which needs to be humus-rich and in part shade. Propagate by division or seed.

C. bracteata

This attractive yellow-flowered tuber from Russia can be short lived. It needs a moist, humus-rich soil that is free draining. Height: 10cm.

C. cava 🏆
(C. bulbosa)

The curious hollow tuber produces substantial racemes of purple or white flowers and attractively divided leaves. It comes from eastern Europe and can be temperamental in milder climates as the tuber is prone to rot in the winter. Height: 15cm.

C. solida 🏆

The usual form of this vigorous and variable tuber has slender pinkish-purple flowers and quickly forms quite substantial clumps. It will seed around freely and will cross with the other colour forms. They are all excellent companions for other woodland plants such as anemones and erythroniums. They are summer dormant and therefore suitable for dry shade under deciduous trees where they will grow happily for many years. Many colour forms have been named. Height: 12cm.
subsp. *incisa* 🏆 has slender racemes of small pink flowers;
'Beth Evans' is a showy cultivar with large clear pink flowers;
'Dieter Schacht' 🏆 is a compact form with pink flowers;
'George Baker' 🏆 ('G.P. Baker') has intense brick-red flowers.
'White Swallow' has white flowers.

Corydalis 'George Baker'.

Cyclamen repandum at Knightshayes Court, Devon.

Cyclamen

See *Chapter 2* for main description.

C. libanoticum 🏆

This cyclamen has very large, showy flowers of pale pink that fade to white at the mouth which has a bold carmine mark. The flowers are produced at the same time as the large, heart-shaped dull green leaves which have a lighter green pattern on them. As its name implies, it comes from the Lebanon and is not fully hardy but it will survive all but the coldest winters in a sheltered very dry soil such as under large trees or the eaves of a house where it will be dry in summer. Height: 10cm.

C. pseudibericum 🏆

The showy carmine flowers are produced at the same time as the silver-marked leaves. It comes from Turkey and is only hardy in sheltered locations.
Height: 10cm.

C. repandum 🏆

This mid-spring-flowering cyclamen comes from south and east Europe and has heart-shaped leaves that are lightly marbled and slender flowers of rich carmine-red, although there are other paler-flowered forms around. Like so many bulbs, patience is the main requirement as it can be temperamental to establish. It requires a light, well-drained, humus-rich soil in part shade and seems to prefer to choose its own location. The canopy of low spreading shrubs such as *Viburnum* 'Lanarth' is a good protective cover. Once happy it will seed to form extensive patches, especially under large trees, such as at Knightshayes Court in Devon where the colony has spread to spectacular proportions. With us it has spread under box hedges and into thin grass. Unlike other cyclamen it should be planted 10cm deep and firmly left, with the aid of ants, to do its own thing. Height: 14cm.
subsp. *peloponnesiacum* has paler pink flowers and speckled leaves.

Erythronium

(Dog's-Tooth Violet, Trout Lily, Glacier Lily)

These beautiful plants have elongated pointed bulbs and elegant flowers reminiscent of turk's cap lilies. They are found in open woodland or upland meadows in Europe, Asia and North America. The common name depends upon which side of the Atlantic the species originates. The European bulbs are small, like a dog's tooth, whereas those of most American species are very large, their common name of 'trout lily' reflecting the attractive marbling on the rather large leaves. They vary in height from 10cm to 40cm, and there are some fine cultivars. Once established they can form significant clumps and are excellent companions for other spring-flowering plants such as wood anemones and cyclamen, revelling in well-drained, humus-rich soil in part shade. Despite its small stature *E. dens-canis* can be naturalized in thin grass under trees.

Cultivation

The bulbs are planted in the autumn. They are very vulnerable when dormant, and must not be allowed to dry out before planting. Plant the bulbs pointed end upwards with at least 10cm of soil above them and 5cm apart in a humus-rich, well-drained soil in part shade. Some require an acid soil. Patience is the main requirement.

Propagation

Propagation is principally by offsets removed when dormant. We lift them as the leaves are fading and you can still see the plant. The bulbs can reach prodigious depths – 30cm or more – and random digging in the autumn will almost certainly cause damage. If they are not to be immediately replanted they should be put into a deep tray of compost and left in a cool place until the autumn when they can be planted. Some species will seed to form impressive patches.

Erythronium rendutum with *Fritillaria meleagris*.

E. americanum

This small stoloniferous bulb can spread to form extensive patches of attractively marbled leaves, which are rather like a more slender *E. dens-canis*. Sadly it is shy to flower, only producing a scattering of its small, brown-backed yellow flowers. Height: 10cm.

E. californicum 🏆

This beautiful bulb is usually encountered in the form of the vigorous **'White Beauty'** 🏆, which may be a hybrid. It has one to three creamy-white flowers, each with a brown central ring, above attractively mottled leaves. It is one of the most beautiful of all the spring-flowering bulbs and will spread to form large patches. Height: 18cm. **'Harvington Snowgoose'** is an exceptional cultivar, now recognized as a hybrid with *E. oregonum*. It has elegantly twisted and pointed white flowers that do not recurve completely. It is very vigorous, with up to three flowers per stem and dark marbled leaves. It is late-flowering. Height: 25cm.

E. dens-canis 🏆

(European Dog's-Tooth Violet)

The European dog's-tooth violet has small pointed bulbs reminiscent of a canine incisor, which give the genus its common name. It is a plant of open mountain meadows in Europe, flowering as the snow recedes. In the garden it flowers in early spring, sometimes coinciding with the last of the snowdrops. The pointed basal leaves are spectacularly marbled with purple-brown and the solitary flowers can be lilac, pink or white with a darker ring round the prominent anthers. Various clones have been named. It is easy to grow in a humus-rich soil in part shade and can be naturalized in thin grass under trees, often forming substantial clumps, but is one of those frustrating bulbs that requires patience. Fat bulbs regularly fail to live up to their promise, producing little more than a small leaf in the first year, but if left well alone will gradually settle to produce free-flowering clumps. Thin, dry soils and shallow planting are the main problem. Height: 10cm.

Erythronium 'White Beauty'.

Erythronium dens-canis.

E. caucasicum is a large-flowered variant from the southern Caucasus with long, creamy-white flowers with a distinct reddish mark at the base. ***E. sibiricum*** from Russia is the earliest to flower with me and has yellow rather than white anthers and exceptionally large white flowers. It will self-seed. Height: 12cm. ***E. japonicum*** is a Japanese variant of *E. dens-canis* which is regularly offered for sale but seems much more temperamental, the bulbs rarely increasing. The solitary flowers are a deep violet with a yellow throat. Height: 10cm.

E. hendersonii

This is one of the most graceful of a graceful genus. The slender lilac flowers with dramatic brown stamens are held on tall, very upright stems above narrow, lightly marbled leaves. Although it is long lived and easy to grow it increases painfully slowly. Seeding is the recommended method of propagation, but as this variety only rarely sets seed in the UK it is difficult to propagate. Height: 23cm.

Erythronium hendersonii.

'Jeanette Brickell'

This vigorous hybrid has slender, creamy-white flowers on tall stems. There seems to be some confusion regarding this plant and various bulbs masquerade under this name. Height: 23cm.

E. multiscapoideum

This Californian species is very similar to *E. californicum* with similar creamy-white flowers but the flower stems branch below ground so that each flower appears to be solitary. Height: 20cm.

E. oregonum

This is an easily grown species and long lived, although only rarely available commercially. The elegant white flowers only gently reflex from the yellow throat. It hybridizes freely in the garden. The leaves are variably marbled. Height: 23cm.

'Pagoda' 🏆

This is a vigorous hybrid between *E. californicum* and *E. tuolumnense* with large, lightly marbled leaves and four or more large flowers.

Erythronium 'Pagoda'.

These are yellow with greenish backs giving an overall impression of sulphur yellow. It is one of the easiest to grow, producing enormous bulbs which quickly form impressive clumps. Height: 20cm. **'Kondo'** is very similar; **'Citronella'** has flowers that are a clearer yellow and is later flowering.

E. revolutum 🏆

This is arguably the most beautiful of a genus full of beautiful species. It comes from the west coast of America and has up to four slender flowers in varying shades of pink above well-marbled leaves. It can vary in height from 15–30cm and prefers an acid soil that is well-drained but with plenty of rainfall. Individual bulbs are disinclined to form clumps but it can seed to form extensive patches. Some distinct clones have been named.
It associates well with white forms of *Fritillaria meleagris*.

E. tuolumnense 🏆

This is a very distinct erythronium from the woods of California with unmarked green leaves and up to five bright golden yellow flowers.
It is very easy to grow but the leaves can almost swamp the flowers and in some gardens it can be shy to flower. It has been crossed with *E. revolutum* to produce a series of pink flushed yellow flowers which you either love or hate! Height: 30cm.

Erythronium oregonum.

Fritillaria

(Fritillary)

This huge genus of nearly a hundred species is amazingly varied. Some are towering giants whilst others barely hold their flowers above the ground. Only a few can be said to be truly colourful, many having rather subdued flowers in shades of green and brown, but all bear close attention as the patterns on the bells, usually in the form of tessellation or chequering, are often very complex. Whilst most are demanding to grow and are best given individual care and attention in an alpine house, there are some valuable garden-worthy members.

Fritillaries are found in a wide range of habitats throughout the temperate areas of the northern hemisphere, from Eurasia to North America. Most have a solitary nodding bell-shaped flower, although some have a terminal raceme or small spike of flowers. Some are large and showy whilst others are more subdued but all have a conspicuous nectary at the base of the tepals (petals) which sometimes appears as a 'horn' on the outside of the flower, giving them their typical angular appearance. The distinctive bulbs have two or more large, rather open scales without a protective tunic. The leaves are also very variable in colour and shape, and may be slender or wide, alternate, opposite or in whorls. In some species the angular seed pods are almost as attractive as the flowers.

The common snake's head fritillary *(F. meleagris)* is one of the best for naturalizing in grass. Although it is normally associated with damp water meadows, it is much more tolerant of dry conditions once established and will seed freely to form extensive colonies. The process is a slow one at first as the seedlings take five or more years to reach flowering size, but once the first generation starts to flower the increase is exponential.

The stately Crown Imperial fritillaries are among the most handsome of border bulbs and the most contrary. In the wild they inhabit the mountains of the Middle East, growing in deep clay soils that are wet in spring when the snow melts. These then dry out in the summer after the fritillaries have flowered. In the garden they need similar moist, rather heavy soils when they are growing. Any interruption to their water supply before they flower will cause them to abort their buds and go into premature die back with the resultant bulb being too small to flower the subsequent spring. After flowering they need a warm, dry summer dormancy. They seem to grow equally well – or badly – on both acid and alkaline soils but prefer a heavy, water-retentive soil. A timely bucket of water may help alleviate the problem in a dry spring, as will lifting the bulbs and storing them for the summer and planting them again late in the autumn, although this is a rather extreme measure.

Massed *Fritillaria meleagris*.

Cultivation

Many of the hundred or so species come from dry rocky areas with a Mediterranean-type climate and are best suited to a bulb frame or glass house where they can be cherished and given the dry summer dormancy they require. Those from damper areas and woodlands make excellent garden plants. The bulbs should be planted in small groups, 10–15cm deep, in the autumn as soon as you acquire them as they are prone to desiccation if left unplanted for too long. Late planted *F. imperialis* grow and flower surprisingly well. Dry rot may also affect them, and some species, notably those with broad, fleshy leaves, are vulnerable to attack by lily beetle.

Propagation

Seed sown in the autumn will take four to seven years to reach flowering size, but propagation can also be by offsets. Some species produce masses of 'rice-grain' bulbils which can be detached and treated like seedlings.

F. acmopetala 🏆

This fritillary from the eastern Mediterranean is one of the easiest to grow with relatively large, solitary bell-shaped flowers on tall stems of alternate narrow leaves. The flowers are pale green with reddish-brown marks. Although they like a well-drained sunny soil they are equally at home under trees. Height: 40cm.

F. amana

This southern Turkish species has one or two relatively large (7cm) nodding pale green flowers variably marked with brown. It is easily grown in a well-drained soil in full sun or as a pot plant under cold glass. Height: 30cm.

F. camschatcensis

(Black Sarana Lily)

This dramatic fritillary comes from the damp peaty meadows of northwest America, Kamschatka and Japan and is surprisingly difficult to grow well unless the soil is moist throughout spring. It often makes a promising early appearance only for it to abort its flowers as the soil dries out (or it is attacked by the lily beetle which seems to be particularly partial to this species, its suddenly naked stems being one of the first indicators that the pest is around!). In the wild it is variable in colour but the most desired forms have a cluster of up to eight true dark chocolate-coloured flowers at the top of the stem. It has a very distinctive bulb surrounded by masses of 'rice grain' bulblets and it can, if happy, eventually form quite large patches. Height: 10–20cm.

Fritillaria acmopetala.

F. graeca

This small fritillary is easily grown in a well-drained soil in full sun or as a pot plant under cold glass. It comes from Greece and needs a dry summer dormancy. The solitary nodding bell is green but this is almost entirely obscured by heavy chocolate-brown chequering. Height: 15cm.

F. imperialis

(Crown Imperial)

This is the giant of the genus with huge bulbs to match the 1m+ stout stems. The lower part of the stem has whorls of light green, lanceolate leaves. The naked upper stem culminates in a cluster of three to six very large flowers which hang below the top-knot 'crown' of leaf-like bracts which give the plant its common name. The pale cream style and stamen extend well beyond the flowers, protruding even through the closed buds. The flowers are in shades of orange *(**Rubra**)* and orangey-red or yellow *(**Lutea**)*. There are forms with variegated leaves but these tend to look rather diseased to my mind. The whole plant, bulb

Fritillaria imperialis 'Rubra'.

Fritillaria imperialis 'Lutea'.

included, has a strong foxy aroma that some gardeners find unpleasant. They are magnificent bulbs for the centre of a spring border and can be used very effectively in formal plantings, but their complex shape makes them difficult companions for other plants. The bulbs should be planted at least 15cm deep, in a rich soil that does not dry out in the spring. It is often recommended to plant the bulbs on their side to keep water out of the hollow centre of the bulbs, but this is not really necessary. They prefer a dry summer dormancy and seem to grow best on heavy soils in the east of Great Britain. Height: 1–1.5m.

F. meleagris 🏆
(Snake's Head Fritillary)

The snake's head fritillary is a native of eastern Europe through to western Russia. Although it grows wild in huge numbers in some fields, particularly in the Thames valley, it is probably a garden escape and not native. It has narrow alternate grey-green leaves and a large, usually solitary pendent flower. This has conspicuous nectaries, which give it a very angular appearance. The flowers are white or pale purple, more or less tessellated (chequered) with deeper purple. It is an easily grown species in virtually any garden soil, in sun or part shade, grass or border, the main problem in establishing it being depredation by pests. Mice and squirrels, to say nothing of badgers, find newly planted bulbs virtually irresistible. Deep planting may deter them. Pheasants love the flower buds. Alternatively the bulbs can be potted and kept protected until they come into flower when they can be transferred to their final location. This has the added advantage of giving the bulbs a plug of good compost within which to grow in future years. *Narcissus bulbocodium* is a good companion plant in grass. When growing in grass it is important to leave the clumps, and the surrounding area, uncut until the seed heads have ripened fully and the seed dispersed. If the lawn is mown too close to the parent clump the newly emerging seedlings, which look rather like blades of grass, will be mown as well. Although the seedlings will take four to six years to flower this is the best way to establish a large colony. ***f. alba*** 🏆 has pure white flowers. Height: 30cm.

F. messanensis

This easily grown species from the Mediterranean area has a quiet charm. It has narrow leaves and one to three pale green flowers, which are 4cm long with subtle light brown chequering. Although it will grow on a dry, sunny rock garden it is equally suited to light shade. Height: 30cm.

Fritillaria meleagris.

Fritillaria michailovskyi.

F. michailovskyi 🏆

This eastern Turkish species is one of the more showy of the small fritillaries. The small, rich brown flowers have bright golden yellow tips to the recurved petals. Sadly, although it is very easy to grow under cold glass, it tends to be short lived in the open garden. It is small enough to grow in a trough where its beauty can be more easily observed. Height: 12cm.

F. pallidiflora 🏆

This robust central Asian species is easily grown in light shade. It flowers in late spring, producing one to six relatively large, rather square flowers of a creamy-green, sometimes faintly chequered with reddish-brown. It has wide grey-green leaves. It is also prone to attack by slugs, which have an annoying habit of eating through the stem just as they come into flower. Height: 40cm.

Fritillaria persica 'Adiyaman'.

F. persica

In the wild this tall, slender fritillary is very variable. It produces a spike of twenty or more nodding bell-shaped flowers in green or blackish-purple. It has alternate lanceolate grey-green leaves.
The form most commonly encountered in cultivation is **'Adiyaman'** 🏆 from southeast Turkey, which has a tall spike of rich chocolate brownish-purple flowers. Like the Crown Imperial fritillary which comes from a similar area of the Middle East, it tends to be rather temperamental in British gardens, requiring ample water when in active growth but then needing a completely dry dormant period. It seems to thrive best tucked in against a sunny wall or it can be lifted after flowering.
'Ivory Bells' has a stout stem of thirty or more creamy-green flowers and is much more vigorous than the type. Height: 1–1.5m.

Fritillaria persica 'Ivory Bells'.

F. pontica 🏆

Although this fritillary is easily grown under cold glass, it is vigorous enough to grow outside in a sunny well-drained soil or in open woodland. Although it will probably produce fewer flowers there, it is long lived in the garden. It has whorls of grey-green leaves and one to four relatively large pale green flowers, lightly shaded with brown. Height: 20cm.

F. pyrenaica 🏆

This slender fritillary comes from the mountains of southern France and northern Spain. It is very variable in the wild with one, rarely two, nodding brownish-green flowers with recurved tips. The strongly tessellated inside is greenish yellow and it has alternate slender grey-green leaves. It should be easy to grow in light shade but is infrequently encountered. Height: 40cm.

F. thunbergii
(*F. verticillata* misapplied)

This Chinese mountain species is easily grown in any dry sunny position, forming extensive patches, but it can be shy to flower in full sun. It seems to do best when grown under trees where it will quickly form large, free-flowering clumps. It has slender leaves, the upper ones with tendril-like tips and a raceme of six or more angular pale creamy-green flowers faintly tessellated with deeper green. The angular pale green seed pods are an added bonus. Height: 90cm–1.2m.

F. uva-vulpis
(*F. assyraica* of gardens)

Although the yellow-tipped, deep brown flowers are rather too small for the height of the stem, this is an easy fritillary for light shade. It has one, rarely two flowers per stem with narrow alternate leaves. It requires a dry dormant period. Height: 45cm.

Fritillaria thunbergii.

Geranium tuberosum.

Geranium

These two tuberous members of the huge geranium family come from the Mediterranean area through to central Asia and are easily grown in a dry, sunny soil. The ferny leaves appear in mid-winter followed by flowers in late spring. They can be shy to flower unless the soil is dry in the summer and seem to be slightly tender. The showy purplish-pink flowers are carried well above the leaves in a loose head and are more or less veined in deep purple with reddish anthers and style. They make a useful winter ground cover under roses or against a sunny wall. I use them as a ground cover for late-flowering tulips. The strange knobbly tubers are linked by short rhizomes and will spread to form extensive colonies, although flowering may be sparse unless there is sufficient sun to ripen the tubers in summer when they are dormant. *G. tuberosum* and *G. malviflorum* are very similar with superficial botanical differences. Height: 40cm.

Hyacinthoides

This is the name currently applied to the bluebell family, although whether they will keep this name for long is a moot point. They have waxy white bulbs which are remarkably variable in shape. Some are the traditional round shape with a pointed top but many are more or less elongated, with the most extreme looking more like a rhizome than a true bulb. This reflects their woodland habitat where they grow in light leaf mould. They do not have a tunic and are vulnerable to physical damage caused by mechanical handling and are prone to rot. They should be planted 10cm deep and 10cm apart as soon as they are received in the autumn. They are propagated by offsets or by seed sown as soon as it is ripe.

H. hispanica
(Endymium hispanica, Scilla campanulata, S. hispanica)
(Spanish bluebell)

In the wild the Spanish bluebell is a very shy and retiring small bulb, nestling among the rocks of its mountain home in southern Spain. However, it has gained a fearsome reputation as a garden thug. The bulb that is cultivated under this name is almost certainly a vigorous hybrid and not the gentle Spanish species. It has long, strap-like green basal leaves and a tall multi-sided spike of blue, white or pink tubular flowers. In the garden it is extremely vigorous, producing masses of large white tunic-less bulbs which delve deeply in the soil and are almost impossible to eradicate. Constant pulling of the leaves, it being almost impossible to reach and remove all the bulbs without the stems

Hyacinthoides hispanica massed under trees.

breaking off first, seems to have no effect upon subsequent performance whatsoever! However, this iron constitution and rapid rate of increase can be utilized in the garden by using them to colonize those difficult dry-as-dust areas under large trees. Seen en masse they are an unforgettable sight. Established colonies can be controlled by removing the flower spikes as soon as they fade. I strim them off, leaves and all, and still they grow happily. Height: 45cm. **'Excelsior'** is deep blue; **'La Grandesse'** is white and **'Rosabella'** is pink.

H. non-scripta
(Endymion non-scriptus, Scilla non-scriptus, S. nutans)
(English Bluebell)

Massed bluebells under the fresh green leaves of mature beech trees is one of the unforgettable sights of the English countryside in spring. Given that it is a native to Western Europe including Great Britain it can be surprisingly difficult to establish in gardens and, once successfully established, equally difficult to control! It is smaller in all its parts than the hybrid Spanish bluebell, having a nodding one-sided raceme of slender scented tubular flowers of deep blue, occasionally white. Its white pointed bulb is also much smaller. It prefers a light humus-rich soil in shade and will not grow in heavy clay. Established colonies can spread rapidly by seeding as well as bulb increase. This can be controlled if necessary by removing the seed pods as soon as the flowers fade. New colonies can be established by broadcasting ripe seed or simply laying the seed pods down. They should be treated with caution in small gardens. Height: 40cm.

The common bluebell *Hyacinthoides non-scripta*.

Hyacinthus
(Hyacinth)

A typical bedding scheme of hyacinths and polyanthus.

There is only one garden-worthy member of this Middle Eastern family.

H. orientalis
(bedding hyacinths)

The bold, heavily scented hyacinth is usually grown as an indoor bulb but those that have not been treated for early flowering make excellent garden plants, flowering in mid-spring. They originally come from southern Turkey and neighbouring areas but the plants in cultivation are all showy cultivars. The very large bulbs have erect channelled leaves and a single raceme of up to forty tubular flowers in a compact spike. Most are single but there are some with double flowers which are rather overwhelming. Festival hyacinths (see below) are more closely allied to their wild antecedents and have multiple stems and a more open and delicate flower spike. There are some multi-flowered forms where the bulb of a standard variety has been partially cut so that it produces more than one small flower spike. These will gradually return to the normal single-flowered form.

Hyacinths are principally associated with bedding schemes and container culture, but they are useful trouble-free subjects for the front of a border where their scent will fill the garden. Although the flower size may diminish in the initial years after planting they are very long-lived, only slowly increasing so they can be planted close together in a compact clump. They can also be planted above early-flowering tulips in the same planting hole. *Tulipa* 'Purissima' associates well with white or cream hyacinths. Bulbs that were prepared for Christmas flowering can be planted out in the garden when they fade for future years. Hyacinths have been rather neglected but in recent years there has been a surge of interest and a consequent increase in the range of colours available. All have the same overwhelming scent.

The bulbs should be planted 5–10cm apart in the autumn with 5cm of soil covering them. In shallow containers such as garden urns they may prove to be susceptible to frost damage, turning into a soggy mess. Rather than planting them directly into such containers they can be first lined out in the garden and only lifted and put in their container once the buds are visible and the danger of severe frost is over. I have done this for many years and the bulbs continue to grow and flower as though they had been left undisturbed. Height: 15cm.

Pink shades

'Anne Marie' 🏆 is pale pink; **'Gipsy Queen'** 🏆 is salmon-orange; **'Jan Bos'** 🏆 has relatively small spikes of an intense reddish pink, and is good in pots but difficult to blend into the garden; **'Paul Herman'** has large spikes of delicate lilac-pink; **'Pink Pearl'** 🏆 has neat mid-pink flowers that pale towards the edge.

Blue shades

'Blue Jacket' 🏆 has a large spike of mid-blue flowers; **'Delft Blue'** 🏆 is mid-blue; **'Ostara'** 🏆 is violet-blue; **'Woodstock'** 🏆 has deep purple flowers and is a good foil for short yellow tulips such as 'Sunny Prince'.

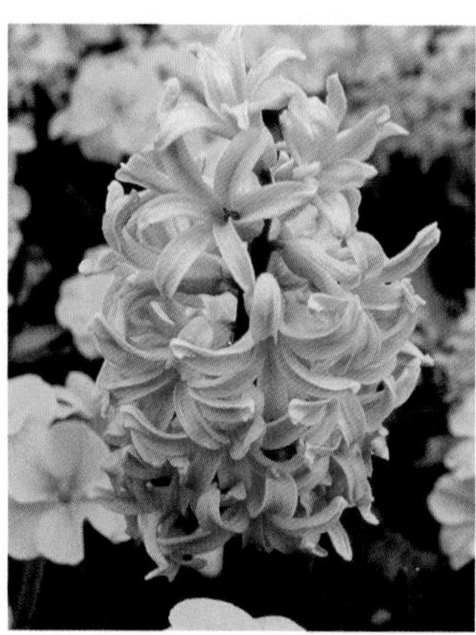

Hyacinthus 'Gypsy Queen'.

Hyacinthus 'Pink Peril'.

Hyacinthus 'Blue Jacket'.

Hyacinthus 'Woodstock'.

Yellow shades

'City of Haarlem' 🏆 is late flowering with creamy yellow flowers; **'Yellow Queen'** 🏆 is a rich egg-yolk yellow.

White shades

'L'Innocence' 🏆 and **'Carnegie'** are pure white and associate well with short red tulips.

Hyacinthus 'Carnegie'.

FESTIVAL HYACINTHS 🏆

Unlike the multiflora hyacinths these are naturally multi-stemmed, each bulb producing up to four slender, open spikes of flowers. They are available in pink, blue or white and have the same strong scent of the larger forms but are less inclined to collapse in bad weather.

Hyacinthus 'Blue Festival'.

MULTIFLORA HYACINTHS

These are top sized bulbs that have been hand cut so that they produce a mass of smaller bulbs, which contrary to normal behaviour will each produce an equally small flower. These clusters of bulbs tend to fall to pieces but it doesn't matter. They are best grown in pots for the house but they can be used for bedding. In subsequent years each part gradually reverts to full size.

Ipheion

These small, clump-forming South American bulbs are very vigorous, often producing their leaves early in the autumn. Their solitary showy star-shaped flowers are carried on slender stems and are produced virtually all spring, even starting in the autumn if the weather is suitable. The leaves smell of garlic if crushed but the flowers have a warm honey scent and make excellent cut flowers. Although they can be rather too vigorous for a small garden, spreading to form large, almost ineradicable patches and seeding freely, in the right place such as the top of a dry wall or under roses they are very useful carpeters. They are particularly attractive when mixed with the deeper blue of equally vigorous grape hyacinths. There are some new varieties with much brighter colours than the standard wishy-washy blue. However, one of the main problems is that they all seed vigorously; unfortunately the seedlings will not be true to name so that in time they become very mixed, tending to revert to a uniform pale blue. Scrupulous dead-heading will stop this but it is time consuming and it may be easier to dig out contaminated patches and start again.

Ipheion 'Rolf Fiedler'.

Cultivation

The bulbs are planted 10cm deep, 10cm apart in the autumn or as potted plants in the spring. The clumps are easily split at any time.

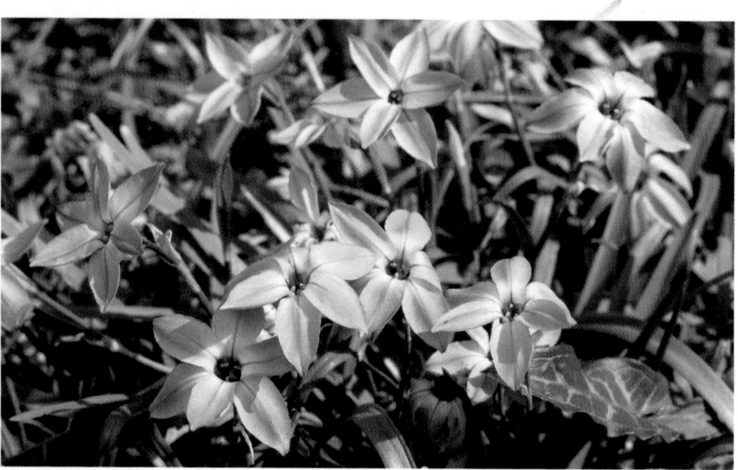
Ipheion 'Wisley Blue'.

Ipheion 'Charlotte Bishop'.

'Rolf Fiedler' 🏆

The leaves of this ipheion appear in spring rather than autumn and are much shorter than *I. uniflorum*. The rounded flowers are an amazing electric blue and have the charming habit of all facing the same way. It seems to be more tender than the others.
Height: 12cm.

I. uniflorum

This very vigorous clump-forming bulb has narrow grey leaves which appear in late summer followed by solitary star-shaped flowers that are produced in profusion all spring. It revels in thin, dry soils. Mixed with grape hyacinths it makes an easy and trouble-free edging for a sunny border or path. Height: 15cm. **'Alberto Castillo'** has extra large white flowers; **'Charlotte Bishop'** is deep pink; **'Froyle Mill'** 🏆 has purple flowers; **'Jessie'** has similar electric blue flowers to 'Rolf Fiedler' but with pointed tips; **'Wisley Blue'** 🏆 has clear blue flowers.

Iris

There are a small number of bulbous iris that flower in the spring. The bulbs of Juno iris are very distinctive, comprising a cluster of relatively large, shiny pointed bulbs attached to persistent long fleshy roots. These help them survive the severe heat and drought of their native habitats which are the inhospitable mountains of the Middle East and Central Asia where they grow in dry, sandy soil. Most are suited only to the carefully controlled environment of the alpine house, but the ones listed below will grow in a sunny, well-drained spot.

I. bucharica 🏆

This vigorous Juno iris comes from Central Asia and is the easiest of the group to grow outdoors. It has shiny green folded leaves arranged rather like a leek and a succession of small flowers in the upper axils. In the wild the flower colour is variable but the form common in commerce has white flowers with yellow falls. When happy they can form good sized clumps. Height: 30cm.

I. magnifica 🏆

When growing well this robust Juno iris certainly lives up to its name, the stems reaching 60cm. However, the soft lilac flowers are rather insignificant and are somewhat lost in the lush foliage.

I. tuberosa
(Hermodactylus tuberosus)
(Black widow iris)

One of the most unusual sights of spring is this solitary greenish-yellow flower with its short velvet brown falls that look as though they are made of moleskin. The slender

Iris bucharica.

leaves appear in the winter, followed by flowers in early spring which can be easily overlooked amongst the mass of foliage. It has curious rhizomes that look like bent arthritic fingers. It comes from southern Europe and when happy can form extensive colonies, but flowering can be variable. It requires a really warm, dry summer to flower well. It will naturalize in light grass under trees or on a dry sunny bank. In cold districts it is best grown under glass. It is scented and makes an excellent cut flower. For some years it was classified in the separate genus *Hermodactylus* but it has now returned to *Iris*. Height: 23cm.

Iris tuberosa.

Dutch iris 'Silver Beauty'.

Dutch iris

The florist iris needs little introduction and flowers in late spring or early summer depending upon the season and when the bulbs were planted. It is derived from the wild bulbous iris of Spain, *I. xiphium* and *I. tingitanum,* which are not in cultivation. For historic reasons their hybrids are referred to as 'Dutch iris'. Each bulb produces an upright stiff stem with one or usually two showy flowers and narrow stem-clasping leaves. The old varieties were in single colours but they are now available in a huge range, from pure white through gold to brown and blue, often in attractive combinations. Individually they are rather stiff and can look somewhat artificial in a border but the more delicate colours are effective when planted as dense clumps. They associate well with dainty flowers like aquilegias. They need a well-drained soil in full sun. Tucked in against a sunny wall they will soon lose their stiffness as they clump up. Height: 60cm.

The other Spanish iris, *I. latifolia*, is hardier and later flowering, with much wider falls to the flowers. This is commonly called the **English iris** and requires a moist, acid soil. Height: 60cm.

Leucojum
(Snowflake)

This relative of the snowdrop has nodding white flowers with six petals, all the same size. Each petal has a bold green tip. The flowers can be solitary or in a cluster. The basal leaves are long and strap-like. They are easy to grow in soil that is not too dry in the spring and are perfect for growing in light shade. They increase by producing offsets, although *L. aestivum* will seed. Bulbs are planted in the autumn 15cm apart and 10cm deep. They may be planted in growth in the spring.

Leucojum vernum.

L. aestivum
(Summer Snowflake)

This bulb is native to much of northern Europe including the British Isles. It has a cluster of six to eight nodding white flowers with green tips on a leafless stem. The individual flowers are rather sparse and often swamped by the large strap-shaped leaves. It is good for naturalizing in rough grass under trees or in light woodland where it will gently seed around. The leaves first appear in mid-winter and it can flower at any time from late winter to mid-spring. Height: 60cm. **'Gravetye Giant'** 🏆 is a robust, sterile cultivar with up to eight relatively large flowers per stem. The flowers are carried well above the leaves although these elongate considerably after flowering and are very persistent. It quickly forms very large clumps and is almost too vigorous for all but the largest borders. It is excellent growing with shrubs, where the white flowers will lighten a dark corner, or beside a pond or stream. The clumps may well need staking if they are in part shade. Height: 1m.

Leucojum aestivum 'Gravetye Giant'.

L. vernum 🏆
(Spring Snowflake)

This is a very variable bulb from the damp meadows and woodlands of southern and eastern Europe. It has daffodil-like leaves and a robust stem with one or two nodding white flowers. Unlike the snowdrop, the six segments are all the same length, each having a small green mark on the tip. Some clones will flower at the same time as the snowdrops whereas others flower with the daffodils. Some are twin-headed but this characteristic seems to be rather dependent upon the amount of moisture available. I have seen them growing prolifically in the wet bottom of a Devon valley virtually in a stream. These were all twin-headed but in my dry sandy soil the same clone only produces a single flower. The green marks can also be more or less yellow but again this seems not to be consistent. Clones with two heads are sometimes called var. *wagneri* and those with yellow markings var. *carpathicum*. Height: 30–45cm.

Muscari

(Grape Hyacinth)

There are around thirty species of grape hyacinths. They are found in a wide range of habitats from dry hillsides at sea level to moist mountain pastures and many make excellent garden plants. The small bulb produces a cluster of slender fleshy basal leaves which tend to flop, although some species only have a single broad upright leaf. The flowers are carried in a stiff, upright raceme on the top of a tall stem, with the buds nestling together rather like egg boxes. They are often crowned with a cluster of sterile florets. In many species there is a distinct contrast in colour between the upper and lower flowers.

The humble grape hyacinth is much maligned by many gardeners for an over-enthusiastic increase by some species and the emergence of the leaves of some in mid-autumn. This vilification should only apply to one or two species. Many are well-behaved, virtually indestructible and extremely useful, not to say attractive, garden plants. Blue is a curious colour that fades into the background rather than taking centre stage but it is the perfect foil for virtually any other colour, especially the predominantly primary colours of early spring. Not all grape hyacinths are blue flowered; there are white and creamy-yellow flowered varieties and recent breeding has resulted in an increasing range of these excellent garden plants. Pink tones are creeping in but as yet they are rather poor.

Their resilience, which is so often bemoaned, can be turned to advantage. Unwanted *M. armeniacum* will happily naturalize in grass with daffodils under flowering trees where they can be planted to follow on from snowdrops. Alternatively they will thrive clustered against the trunk of a tree in a border where nothing else will survive the excessively dry conditions, or they can make the perfect edging to a sunny border. The double-flowered *M. armeniacum* 'Blue Spike' can be used to make a bold edge to a rose bed. Shrub or rose beds can be enhanced by massing grape hyacinths with other blue bulbs such as chionodoxa and especially ipheion 'Wisley Blue' for an early display before the roses start into growth. They are of course dormant in the summer so do not detract from the roses. Others are more delicate and can find a place on a rock garden. They are also the perfect companion plant for bulbs in pots: their slender leaves hang down, softening the edge of the pot and they flower below the taller daffodils or tulips.

Cultivation

Plant the bulbs 10cm deep and 2–5cm apart in the autumn in virtually any reasonable garden soil in sun or part shade. It does not matter if the situation becomes fully shaded and dry in the summer when the bulbs are dormant. They are trouble-free.

Massed *Muscari armenaicum* carpet the ground beneath a cherry at Wisley Gardens.

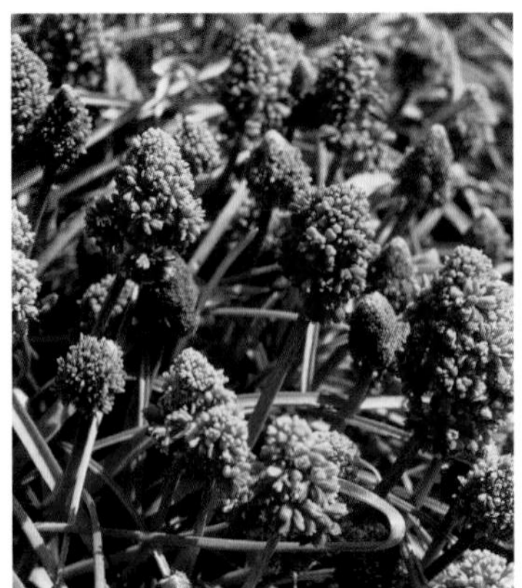

Muscari armenaicum 'Blue Spike'.

Muscari 'White Magic'.

M. armeniacum 🏆

This grape hyacinth is one of the most vigorous and indestructible of all spring bulbs and has a bad reputation among some gardeners. However, for massed planting, such as along the edge of a rose bed, or to enliven the base of a dull hedge, they really come into their own. The main complaint levelled against them is their leaves. Individually these are slender but they appear in great profusion in late autumn; however, their vivid blue flowers are also produced in equal profusion. The individual flowers, each with a distinct white rim, are tiny, and carried in a tightly packed, pointed raceme. Yellow pansies and primroses make a good foil for their overwhelming blueness. They make excellent cut flowers or can be forced for indoor display. Height: 20cm. **'Saffier'** 🏆 is very similar to the type but with well-shaped flowers. **'Blue Spike'** has curiously 'fat' heads of double flowers and is an excellent subject for adding to pots of tulips or for use as an edging plant. **'Fantasy Creation'** is very similar. **'Valerie Finnis'** has beautiful pale powder-blue flowers and is slightly shorter and possibly a little tender. It is perfect to tuck around the base of potted tulips. Height: 15cm. **'Jenny Robinson' ('Baby's Breath')** 🏆 is very similar with neat powder-blue flowers and seems to be less tender. Both will seed gently.

M. aucheri 🏆

This neat Turkish grape hyacinth has rather stocky blue flowers crowned with a cluster of paler, sterile flowers at the top of the spike. The leaves appear at the same time as the flowers in mid-spring. These are all very long lasting and excellent in pots. Height: 15cm. **'Ocean Magic'** is very free flowering with relatively large flowers that darken with age from pale to very dark blue but retain their paler top. **'White Magic'** has bold white flowers opening from green buds in a showy spike. **'Blue Magic'** has clear blue flowers.

Muscari azureum.

M. azureum 🏆
(Hyacinthus azureus)

As its change of name suggests, this is a very distinct grape hyacinth. The flower heads are densely packed and the individual flowers flare out rather than turn in, which gives an overall shaggy impression to the spike. It is very compact, with neat, short leaves that do not swamp the flowers. The colour is as it says – a beautiful azure-blue. It is one of the neatest and prettiest of all grape hyacinths and is perfect for the front of a sunny border or a rock garden where it will gently seed around but never become an embarrassment. Height: 10cm. **'Album'** is a similar shape but with pure white flowers.

M. botryoides

This non-invasive species from south east Europe has two or three upright leaves and narrow cylindrical heads of small blue flowers. It is usually grown in the form **'Album'** (Pearls of Spain) which is scented. Sadly, it can be rather disappointing in the garden, possibly needing a more continental climate with cold winters and hot summers. Height: 15cm.

M. comosum
(Leopoldia comosa)
(Tassel Hyacinth)

This hardly looks like a grape hyacinth at all with its wild top-knot of sterile purple flowers crowning a spike of brownish flowers. The leaves are long and spreading and can swamp neighbouring plants. It has a huge distribution throughout southern Europe right through to Iran and is an unexpected inhabitant of the hay meadows of northern Spain and as such it might naturalize in similar conditions in Britain. It is certainly very generous with its progeny, producing both masses of tiny bulblets and being very free with its seed. It is easily grown in any dry, sunny soil, flowering in late spring. Height: 30cm. **'Plumosum'** ('Monstrosum', 'Feather Hyacinth') really is a monstrous bulb with huge heads made up entirely of sterile flowers on long threads that twist and turn in a most alarming manner. The top-knot is equally enlarged. This feathery curiosity can hardly be described as beautiful but it has the advantage of being the last grape hyacinth to flower in early summer. Height: 20cm.

M. latifolium 🏆

This instantly recognizable, rather tall and elegant grape hyacinth from west Turkey has slender heads of darkest blue flowers crowned by a top-knot of pale, sterile ones. It is accompanied by a single, relatively wide upright leaf. Although it will seed freely it is not an embarrassment and is an excellent companion for other spring bulbs or pushing through the lime green heads of

Muscari latifolium.

Muscari macrocarpum.

Euphorbia myrsinites. At Wisley it was mixed with alliums and used to underplant shrub roses. Height: 25cm.

M. macrocarpum (syn. *M. moschatum*)

This is a most unlikely grape hyacinth from Greece. It is immediately recognizable from its bulb, which has thick fleshy roots that remain attached when it is dormant. The basal leaves are rather long and untidy and the flower stems have an annoying habit of flopping but it is worth growing for its strong perfume. It has rather lax spikes of long, yellow tubular flowers, each with a dark rim, which

Muscari 'Mount Hood'.

open from purple buds; the top few flowers often retain the purple colour. It is hardy only in sheltered districts, requiring a dry summer to flower well, but is easily grown under cold glass where the fragrance will fill the air. **'Golden Fragrance'** 🏆 is virtually indistinguishable from the species but is a more easily marketable name! Height: 15cm.

'Mount Hood'

This is a new clump-forming cultivar with intense blue flowers, each with a distinct white top to the raceme. Height: 15cm.

M. muscarimi (*M. moschatum*)

This is a bulb that has regularly changed its name and even its family and is another of the slightly tender grape hyacinths. The relatively large, whitish flowers, each with a brownish rim, are in a long, rather open spike and have a musky scent. The top florets are shaded more or less with purple. It requires a sheltered spot in full sun to do well. There seems to be some confusion regarding the plant in cultivation known as *M. ambrosiacum*, which is probably a selection. Height: 15cm.

M. neglectum (*M. racemosum*)

At first glance this strongly coloured grape hyacinth seems highly desirable and easily seduces the unwary gardener with its bold heads of white-rimmed, almost black-blue flowers, each with a paler top-knot. However, it is far too vigorous and almost impossible to eradicate once it has established itself – producing vast numbers of bulblets and seeding madly. It is found widely throughout Europe to Asia. Height: 20cm.

Narcissus
(Daffodil)

There can be no bulb more strongly associated with spring than the daffodil. It is the quintessential spring bulb, whether it is Wordsworth's 'hosts of golden daffodils', the delicate white of the scented poet's daffodil or a clump of the blousy yellow stalwart, 'King Alfred'. It is this large golden trumpet that tends to spring to mind when the word 'daffodil' is mentioned. However, 'King Alfred' is susceptible to fungal infections and is no longer cultivated. Although the name may appear in nursery lists etc., the plant supplied will almost certainly be a more modern hybrid.

There is much confusion among gardeners about the distinction between daffodil and narcissus. Traditionally the yellow-flowered narcissus is referred to as daffodils and the white ones as narcissus. However, *Narcissus* is the correct botanical name for all daffodils, regardless of what they look like, while 'daffodil' is the common English name for all members of the genus *Narcissus*.

There are about fifty wild species of narcissus which occur throughout Europe and North Africa, where they are found in a wide variety of habitats, from damp water meadow, to snow melt, to hot dry mountainsides. This disparate habitat affects the cultural requirements of the species, a characteristic that has been inherited by some of their progeny, especially the smaller, more closely related, hybrids. It is a common assumption that small daffodils should be grown on a sunny rock garden when in fact many are happier in a cooler, more shaded part of the garden.

Daffodils are a true bulb with a basal group of strap-shaped leaves which vary in width from a few millimetres to a centimetre or more. Most have solitary flowers but others are multi-flowered. Most only produce one stem per bulb but there are varieties that produce more than one stem. They vary in height from 5–60cm. Their shape is similarly very variable. All have a central trumpet or cup (corona) with six outer petals (the perianth). There is often a striking contrast in colour between the corona

The bulb field of daffodil groves, R.A. Scamp in Cornwall.

and the perianth. Yellow tends to dominate the early-flowering varieties, then gradually white becomes more common as the light levels change. Jonquils, tazettas and poeticus (see below) all have a strong, and noticeably different, fragrance which has been inherited by some of their hybrids.

Over the years the all-yellow trumpet has retained its place in the popularity stakes but the form of the modern hybrid is far removed from its antecedents. Gone are the slightly ragged cup and the uneven, thin petals, to be replaced by the almost perfect flower of the exhibition daffodil. Despite their perfection many make equally excellent and vigorous garden plants. The overriding yellow and white of daffodils is also giving way to a much wider palette. Although daffodils are still mainly yellow or white, recent breeding has introduced red, orange and pink shades, at first into the cup but now it is spreading to the petals as well. In some the normal balance, where the cup is the same or a darker hue than the petals, has also been reversed and varieties have been bred where the cup fades while the petals darken with age. These are known as reversed bicolors.

Most modern hybrids were bred originally for the show bench, where smooth round petals that overlap and well-formed cups win prizes. The best look as though they are made of wax. Thus the modern daffodil is far removed from its early antecedents. However, the older varieties have a charm and grace lacking in many of the bold modern hybrids and still have a place in the garden. Breeders have been hybridizing daffodils for 150 years and as a result there are many thousands of registered hybrids. For ease these are classified according to their shape and allocated to one of thirteen Divisions.

Those awarded the coveted RHS Award of Garden Merit (🏆) only achieve this after three years' rigorous trials in the open ground, where they are tested for vigour and resistance to sun damage. This award is then reviewed regularly.

Using daffodils in the garden

A surfeit of daffodils can be overwhelming in a small garden; it is definitely a case of 'less is more'. Repeated clumps of the same variety planted along the back or a good-sized clump strategically placed can be far more effective than a mass of mixed varieties scattered through a border. An early-flowering variety such as 'Crewenna' or 'February Gold' glimpsed beyond the bare branches of a shrub is much more dramatic than an overwhelming close-up display. Their fading foliage, which is not the strong point of daffodils, will also be less obvious.

Narcissus 'Tete-a-Tete' with *Chionodoxa* and *Pulmonaria*.

They make excellent subjects for planting under deciduous trees and shrubs where they flower before the leaf canopy significantly cuts the light and moisture levels. They also enjoy the dry summer dormancy afforded by such situations. The early-flowering varieties are especially useful as they take over from the snowdrops.

Some of the short flowered varieties are suitable for the drier conditions of rock gardens and raised beds and many are excellent subjects for pot cultivation. The tiny species such as *N. rupicola* and other small jonquils are perfect for growing with other alpine plants in a trough.

Daffodils are the ideal bulb for growing in grass. Only some species can be truly said to naturalize and increase by seeding. *N. pseudonarcissus* (Lent lily) is probably the best but many others, especially those of Divisions 6 (cyclamineus), 5 (triandrus) and the shorter trumpets such as 'Topolino' or 'W.P. Milner' are equally at home in these conditions, quickly clumping up. If the area to be planted is formal, such as around a tree on a lawn or along a drive, then it is best to keep to a few varieties planted in bold blocks. However, if the area is more informal then they can be scattered to give a less structured effect. But at all costs they should never be planted in a straight line as this will persist indefinitely. The fading foliage of daffodils growing in grass can most easily be disguised by leaving an unmown strip around the area containing the bulbs. This fresh green grass will distract the eye from the dying daffodil leaves.

Cultivation

Most hybrid daffodils are easy to grow, having no specific needs beyond a reasonable soil with good drainage and high levels of light and moisture when they are growing.

Daffodil bulbs are planted in the autumn. In borders they are best planted 10–15cm deep in clumps of five or more. As they flower before the herbaceous plants appear they can be planted at the back of a border so that the extending stems of the emerging plants will hide the daffodils' unattractively fading foliage. In grass they should be planted 15cm apart and 15cm deep. In time congested clumps will cease to flower. They must then be lifted and divided. This can be done in late spring as the leaves fade or if they are growing in grass you can split them as soon as the leaves appear through the ground in late winter. In this way there is minimal disruption and both grass and daffodil quickly recover.

The continued growth of the leaves after flowering is essential to maintain the future vigour of the bulb. It is recommended that at least six weeks is allowed after the flowers fade before the leaves are removed. Tying the leaves may be tidy but it will reduce the future performance of the bulbs as it destroys the cell pathways within the leaves. It is better to plant the bulbs so that the fading foliage can be hidden or disguised.

Deadheading is often recommended but it need only be done for aesthetic purposes to disguise the fading flowers. Contrary to popular myth, leaving the heads on does not reduce the size of the bulb in any significant way and as most hybrids are sterile there is little danger of self-sown seedlings appearing. With many species, where seed is the only method of propagation, the seed heads must be allowed to ripen fully and the seed dispersed.

Species daffodils have very specific cultural requirements – see the individual entries for details.

Pests

On the whole daffodils are easy, undemanding bulbs but waterlogged soil can cause basal rot, a fungal infection which destroys the bulb. Some varieties seem more susceptible to this. Daffodils can also be affected by viruses and attacked by slugs and narcissus fly.

Propagation

Daffodils are propagated by offsets which are removed when the bulbs are dormant. Species are principally raised from seed, which can take up to seven years to flower.

Naturalized *Narcissus bulbocodium* at the RHS garden at Wisley.

The Divisions

The species or wild daffodils of Division 13 are described first in this book, as they form the basis for the other divisions, which are listed in numerical order.

Species or wild daffodils (Division 13)

Of the fifty or so wild daffodil species only a few are suitable for cultivation in the open garden. Most do not form offsets like the hybrids and must be raised from seed. These were the building blocks from which our many thousands of hybrids have been bred and they have given their name to some of the classification divisions where their characteristics of shape or poise are still clearly evident.

N. asturiensis (N. minimus)

As its old name implies, this is one of the smallest trumpet daffodils, with tiny, rather pinched flowers held on slender stems and with narrow leaves. This tiny species comes from the mountains of Asturias in northern Spain where it flowers as the snow melts. It was introduced to the gardening public in the early 1970s when it was imported by the thousand. This plundering of the wild has now ceased and only seed-raised bulbs are occasionally available. Sadly it is not at all easy to satisfy in our damp northern climes, preferring the hot, dry summers of Spain. Surprisingly it will survive in part shade in a humus-rich soil tucked under the base of a shrub, but the individual bulbs do not produce many offsets and my small clump has never set seed in thirty years. Height: 10cm.

Narcissus asturiensis.

N. bulbocodium
(Hoop Petticoat Daffodil)

The hoop petticoat is a curious daffodil with its expanded trumpet and an apology for petals stuck onto its side. This group, from southwest Europe and North Africa, is extremely variable with a host of botanical names. They have solitary white or yellow flowers held at an angle to the stem. Most of them are not suitable for the open garden. The white-flowered bulbocodiums, based on *N. cantabricus*, are hardy but require a hot, dry summer to initiate flowers. An extremely dry position such as under a dwarf pine might suit them. They make easy and free-flowering subjects for cold glass where they flower in the early winter, shortly after they are first watered.

The later-flowering golden yellow forms are more easily grown. Botanically they are described correctly (if somewhat long-windedly) as *N. bulbocodium* subsp. *bulbocodium* var. *conspicuus*. In the trade this unwieldy name is usually abbreviated to *N. bulbocodium* or *N. conspicuus*. When conditions really suit them they can seed, as at the RHS garden at Wisley or Savile Gardens, Windsor, to cover prodigious areas. Their grass-like leaves appear in the winter and they flower in mid-spring. They need a moist soil, preferably neutral or acid, that dries out in the summer. In the wild, in the mountains of central Spain, they flower as the snow melts and where they are often completely inundated. They can be grown in light grass or part-shaded borders. They are very variable in colour, height and shape but most of those in commerce have deep yellow flowers, although the attractive pale-lemon-flowered form *N. b.* var. *citrinus* is sometimes available. Height: 10–20cm.

Narcissus cyclamineus.

N. cyclamineus 🏆

This is one of the most distinct of all narcissus, looking more like a sea-horse than a daffodil. The completely reflexed (swept back) petals are as long as the slender nodding trumpet, which can be straight or flared. It has been known about for centuries (although it was not connected to the *Narcissus* genus at that time) but it was lost to cultivation and was thought to be a figment of the herbalist's imagination. At the beginning of the twentieth century it was 'rediscovered' still growing in northern Spain where it flowers in winter when it is very cold and wet and few botanists visit. It has subsequently been used to produce some of the most vigorous and useful garden hybrids (Division 6). The species has a solitary golden yellow flower and deep green, upright leaves. It requires an acid soil and does best in moist conditions, preferring a border in part shade to grass. Like most species it increases principally by seed although some clones do produce offsets. The seeds seem to have an affinity with moss and scattering then directly into a patch of moss is the quickest way to germinate them! Natural hybrids between *N. cyclamineus*, *N. asturiensis* and *N. pseudonarcissus* can occur spontaneously in the garden. Height: 20cm.

N. jonquilla

This is one of the last daffodils to flower, with narrow, cylindrical leaves and up to eight strongly scented deep golden flowers per stem. It comes from the river valleys of Spain and Portugal and requires a sunny position that is wet when flowering but dry in summer. It actively likes limey soils. Most of its larger cultivars (Division 7) have the same round stems and delicious scent. Height: 30cm. Var. *henriquesii* is a shorter version which may be a separate species and not related. It is easy under glass but can be short-lived in the open garden. Height: 25cm.

N. minor

This is one of those mystery plants that has been in cultivation for many centuries but is unknown in the wild. It is a very short, early-flowering trumpet daffodil with neat yellow flowers. It is excellent for naturalizing in light grass. Height: 15cm. ***N. nanus*** is a similar small yellow daffodil but with a frilled end to its long trumpet.

Narcissus moschatus.

Narcissus jonquilla.

N. moschatus 🏆

This beautiful creamy pseudonarcissus species probably originated in the Pyrenees although it has not been recorded in the wild and may be of hybrid origin. It has graceful nodding heads and is easy to grow. Like all the Lent lily group it is early flowering and prefers the cooler part of the garden and is therefore perfect for growing among shrubs. *N. alpestris* from the Pyrenees is similar and smaller although less easy to grow in the garden. Height: 30cm.

N. obvallaris 🏆
(Tenby Daffodil)

This is one of the many conundrums in the daffodil world. The cultivated clone of this well-known plant may or may not be a true species. It is sterile which suggests it is not, but whatever it may be it is an excellent garden plant. It is early flowering

Narcissus obvallaris.

Narcissus pseudonarcissus.

with perfect golden trumpet flowers on sturdy stems with neat leaves. It is reliable for naturalizing in grass where it grows into sizeable clumps provided it is not too dry, when it will cease to flower. Height: 20cm.

N. poeticus var. *recurvus* 🏆
(Pheasant's Eye)

The late-flowering poet's daffodil from the mountains of Europe is one of the most instantly recognizable daffodils with its glistening white petals and the tiny red-rimmed eye of a cup. It is sweetly scented.

There are many regional variants of *N. poeticus*, but the plant most commonly encountered is the variety recurvus from Switzerland, which has slightly reflexed petals and a very distinctive long bulb. It is the perfect choice for planting as small clumps among shrubs where it is a good foil for their new foliage. Although it will easily naturalize in grass it can be temperamental and may take some time to settle. It is the last to flower and care must be taken as the buds may abort if the weather is too warm and dry. Height: 40cm.

Narcissus poeticus var. *recurvus.*

N. pseudonarcissus
(Lent Lily)

This is the native daffodil of northern Europe and has narrow, twisted straw yellow petals that clasp the darker-hued trumpet. It is one of the first to flower and in the wild it is remarkably variable. Some clones are very dwarf whilst others are taller. The colour of the trumpet varies from deep egg yolk to lemon yellow and the shape of the trumpet is straight or frilled. It can be slow to establish but if grown in a soil with plenty of moisture in the spring it will happily seed about in light grass where it associates well with wood anemones. The variety usually encountered in commerce is the seed-raised clone *N. lobularis* which is indistinguishable from *N. pseudonarcissus*. Height: 15–25cm. ***N. nobilis*** is a particularly large-flowered form from the Pyrenees and Picos de Europa where it grows in abundance. It is very similar to **'Gayi'**, an old cultivar which is frequently encountered in old gardens or orchards. Height: 35cm.

N. rupicola

This tiny gem from the mountains of central Spain flowers in mid-spring and requires a moist acid soil that is free draining and dry in summer. It is small enough for a trough and makes an easy pot subject for an unheated greenhouse. Height: 10cm.

N. triandrus

The delicate Angel's Tears from central Spain is one of the most distinctive daffodils. It was named after young Angelo, who was helping the botanists and not a celestial being. The slender stems bear two or more creamy-white nodding flowers with fully reflexed petals and a short, rounded cup. Sadly it is not easy to satisfy in the open garden, needing a dry acid soil. It is not clump forming and grows best when allowed to seed into light grass under the canopy of trees, but even when growing well it is too delicate to make a real show. Its progeny (Division 5), however, are some of the most versatile daffodils ever bred. Height: 23cm.

Narcissus triandrus.

Hybrid Daffodils

Most daffodils are hybrids and this list is arranged according to the Division to which they are allocated. The official Royal Horticultural Society description of each Division is given in italics at the start of each section.

Division 1
TRUMPET
DAFFODIL
CULTIVARS

Division 2
LARGE-CUPPED
DAFFODIL
CULTIVARS

Division 3
SMALL-CUPPED
DAFFODIL
CULTIVARS

Division 4
DOUBLE
DAFFODIL
CULTIVARS

Division 5
TRIANDRUS
DAFFODIL
CULTIVARS

Division 6
CYCLAMINEUS
DAFFODIL
CULTIVARS

Division 7
JONQUILLA &
APONDANTHUS
DAFFODIL
CULTIVARS

Division 8
TAZETTA
DAFFODIL
CULTIVARS

Division 9
POETICUS
DAFFODIL
CULTIVARS

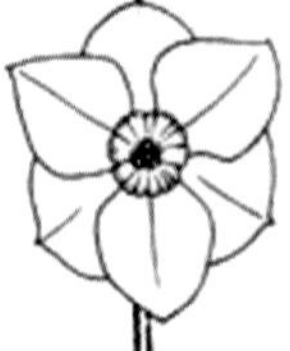

Division 10
BULBOCODIUM
DAFFODIL
CULTIVARS

Division 11
SPLIT-CORANA
DAFFODIL
CULTIVARS
a) Collar Daffodils

b) Papillon
Daffodils

Division 12
OTHER DAFFODIL CULTIVARS
Daffodil cultivars which do not fit the definition of any other division

Division 1

Trumpet Daffodils

This group has solitary flowers with the trumpet as long or longer than the petals.

The bold golden-yellow trumpet daffodil is the quintessential spring bulb and is probably the most popular of this popular genus, having long been grown in our gardens. Thousands of them billow along verges outside many villages. The variety 'King Alfred' was the first of the then modern daffodils to be mass marketed in the late 1800s. It is a hybrid of the Spanish species *N. hispanicus* and was valued for its large, golden yellow flowers on sturdy stems, so different from the dainty native Lent lily. The name 'King Alfred' is still familiar to gardeners today but this rather weak variety with its thin, twisted petals is no longer grown and has long been superseded by more vigorous modern cultivars which have the added bonus of better-shaped flowers. The ideal flower has smooth overlapping petals and a trumpet that is round in cross section. Trumpet daffodils can be grown in virtually any garden setting, sun or shade, or in grass. Modern breeding has also seen a move away from the traditional white or yellow into ever more dramatic colours and colour combinations. Reversed bicolor is the term used when the normal dark cup and pale petal arrangement is reversed so that the cup or trumpet fades to almost white leaving a rim of darker petals around it.

Trumpet daffodils.

Narcissus 'Dutch Master'.

However, not all of the trumpet daffodils are the tall stately flower we immediately think of. They vary in height from 7–50cm. Although many are strong enough to grow in grass the short varieties are also ideal for a rock garden or the edge of a shrub bed.

Yellow

N.'Dutch Master' 🏆 is one of the best modern trumpet daffodils. It is very vigorous and free flowering with large, golden yellow trumpet flowers. However, it is prone to basal rot.

'Arctic Gold' 🏆 and **'Gold Finger'** 🏆 are more vigorous, with similar perfect yellow trumpets. **'Spellbinder'** and **'Gin and Lime'** have attractive, soft lemon yellow flowers.

Narcissus 'Gold Finger'.

Narcissus 'Mount Hood'.

Reversed bicolor

'Trumpet Warrior' 🏆 has clear yellow petals while the trumpets fade to white, leaving a neat yellow rim. **'Glover's Reef'** and **'Sargeants Caye'** are similar. **'Pay Day'** opens a rich lemon yellow but the cup fades to white with age.

All white

'Mount Hood' 🏆 is the classic white trumpet with an iron constitution and well-formed, very large flowers. These open creamy but quickly fade to white. **'Silent Valley'**, **'Empress of Ireland'** and **'Vigil'** are similar large white trumpets but tend to be prone to basal rot.

Bicolor

'Bravoure' 🏆 is one of those daffodils that elicits strong feelings. Love it or hate it, it certainly cannot be overlooked. It has large white flowers which are dominated by its exceptionally long, rather narrow

Narcissus 'Bravoure'.

Narcissus 'Elka'.

lemon yellow trumpet. **'Foresight'** has large flowers with pure white petals and a mid-yellow trumpet. **'Pink Silk'** and **'Chanson'** have dramatic white flowers with a pink trumpet. **'Glenfarclas'** 🏆 and **'Uncle Duncan'** have yellow petals and a bold orange trumpet. The similar **'York Minster'** has a darker red trumpet. **'Lorikeet'** is one of a new group of daffodils with yellow petals and a pink trumpet.

Early flowering

Details of the January-flowering **'Rijnveld's Early Sensation'** 🏆, **'Crewenna'** and **'Cedric Morris'** may be found in *Chapter 2*.

Dwarf

'Elka' 🏆 is a tiny, early-flowering hybrid with white petals and a slender lemon-yellow trumpet. It is perfect for part shade where it associates well with *Corydalis solida,* although it can split into masses of

Narcissus 'Lorikeet'.

Narcissus 'Midget'.

non-flowering bulbs if the soil is too dry. Height: 12cm.

'Little Gem' 🏆 is a dwarf trumpet daffodil with a neat yellow flower and grey-green leaves. This vigorous cultivar is probably a selection from *N. minor* and is easy and long lived, being one of the earliest to flower. Although it is not one of the most beautiful, its 'unimproved' appearance makes it excellent for naturalizing in grass. Height: 18cm.

Narcissus 'Topolino'.

Narcissus 'Small Talk'.

***N. nanus* 'Midget'** is a tiny daffodil with narrow grey leaves and a slender golden-yellow flower with a long trumpet and rather twisted petals. The flower barely clears the ground when it first opens but gradually the stems elongate to 12cm. Although it is small enough for a rock garden or trough it is shy to flower if the soil is too dry. It is probably an historic selection from *N. minor*. Height: 10cm.

'Small Talk' 🏆 is a tiny gem for a rock garden or trough where it flowers as the snowdrops fade. The little golden flowers are well formed and held on stiff stems. It is a strong grower, free flowering and increasing well. Height: 10cm but gradually elongating to 20cm.

'Topolino' 🏆 is very similar in flower to the wild Lent lily *(N. pseudonarcissus)*, with pale creamy petals and a slender yellow trumpet, but is easier and less fussy regarding growing conditions. It is neat enough to plant on a rock garden or even in large tubs but it is free flowering and vigorous enough to grow in grass. It does not set seed. Height: 20cm.

'W.P. Milner' is an old Victorian variety which still has a place in the wild garden. It has nodding flowers of pale cream with a slightly darker cup. It looks like an improved pale Lent lily but flowers a little later. Height: 20cm.

Narcissus 'W.P. Milner'.

Division 2

Large-cupped Daffodils

These have solitary flowers where the cup is more than 1/3 of the length of the petals.

This is a very mixed bunch of daffodils with no really obvious unifying characteristic. It is a sort of catch-all division for misfits! The coronas are either just too short for a trumpet daffodil (Division 1) or just too large for a short-cupped daffodil (Division 3). Most are very vigorous and easy to grow with no special requirements. The early red-cupped **'Fortune'**, bred at the beginning of the twentieth century, is a classic example of this group. Height: most are 60cm.

All yellow

'St. Keverne' 🏆 is a very vigorous and beautifully shaped daffodil which could, at first glance, pass for a trumpet (Division 1). Other good, bold all-yellow members of Division 2 are: **'Bryanston'** 🏆; **'Camelot'** 🏆; **'Gold Convention'** 🏆; **'Golden Aura'** 🏆; and **'Golden Jewel'** 🏆. **'Whisky Mac'** is a lemon yellow. **'Skilliwidden'** is a useful early-flowering variety that is not too tall.

Reversed bicolor

'Pineapple Prince' 🏆 opens a uniform pale yellow before the cup fades to white and the petals darken. **'Carib Gipsy'** 🏆 is similar but the cup retains a yellow rim. **'Cloud Nine'** is a late-flowering, intermediate-sized daffodil with similar colouring. Height: 45cm.

Narcissus 'St Keverne'.

Narcissus 'Ice Follies'.

All white

'Ice Follies' 🏆 is a classic daffodil with large, creamy-white flowers and a widely flaring cup which opens lemon and gradually fades to white. It is very prolific and excellent for bold plantings in grass. **'Broomhill'** 🏆, **'Desdemona'** 🏆, **'Misty Glen'** 🏆 and **'Torianne'** 🏆 are similar white-flowered daffodils.

White with coloured cup

'High Society' 🏆 has large white flowers and a pink-rimmed white cup. **'Notre Dame'** and **'Rainbow'** 🏆 are similar. **'Salome'** 🏆 has large white flowers with a long salmon-pink cup. **'Precocious'** 🏆 has round, white petals and a flattened and ruffled deep pink cup that seems to be reasonably weather resistant, keeping its colour well. **'Chromacolour'** 🏆 has white petals and a

Narcissus 'Pineapple Prince'.

Narcissus 'Broomhill'.

deep reddish-pink flared cup. **'Brooke Ager'** is an attractive, intermediate-sized daffodil with white flowers and a neat pink cup.

Yellow with coloured cup

'Boulder Bay' 🏆 is yellow with a bold red cup. **'Freedom Rings'** is a new daffodil with yellow petals and a pink cup. **'Bantam'** 🏆 is a sturdy daffodil of intermediate size. The slightly nodding flowers have bright yellow petals and a flaming orange-red cup. It is useful to cheer up a dark corner under shrubs but neat enough for a more prominent situation at the front of the border. Height: 25cm.

Narcissus 'Chromacolour'.

Narcissus 'White Lady' naturalized with camassias.

Division 3

Small-cupped Daffodils

These have solitary flowers where the cup is less than 1/3 of the length of the petals.

This is the flower that many gardeners associate with the name 'narcissus'. The typical variety has a flat white flower with a small coloured cup but this colour combination no longer dominates: pink, red and orange are now present in the cup or the petals.

The old Victorian hybrid **'White Lady'** is probably the quintessential Division 2. Although it was bred 200 years ago, the gentle unassuming charm of its twisted white petals and tiny lemon cup is still popular. Large clumps of it are frequently encountered in hedge bottoms or in old orchards. It is far removed from the modern hybrids which have perfectly symmetrical round flowers.

White petals

'Verona' 🏆 is pure white. **'Doctor Hugh'** 🏆 is glistening white with a green eye and a small flared orange cup. The colour bleeds into the petals. **'Vernal Prince'** 🏆 has a green eye and a yellow cup with a distinct deeper rim. **'Mint Julep'** 🏆 has a yellow cup and is slightly nodding; **'Purbeck'** 🏆 has very round

Narcissus 'Purbeck'.

Narcissus 'Angelito'.

flowers. The yellow cup has a pinkish red edge. **'Merlin'** 🏆 has a red-edged yellow cup; **'Royal Princess'** is similar.

Yellow petals

'Badbury Rings' 🏆 has bright yellow petals and a red-rimmed, deep yellow cup; **'Angelito'** 🏆 is similar.

Dwarf

'Segovia' 🏆 is a delightful dwarf daffodil with a small, round, white flower and a neat yellow cup. It looks like a jonquil that has escaped from Division 7 – which is probably where it should have been registered given that it has *N. rupicola* subsp. *watieri* as one of its parents. Height: 20cm.

Narcissus 'Segovia'.

Division 4

Double Daffodils

One or more heads where the flowers are fully or partly double.

In these both the perianth segments and the trumpet or cup are doubled up and in some the stamens are replaced by extra 'petals' as well, resulting in two sets of petals in the centre which are often of a different size and colour. Some of the older varieties have a rather uneven appearance but in modern cultivars the segments overlap evenly. Double forms occur in most of the Divisions; some have a bold single head whilst others, usually double forms of Division 8 (tazetta) are multi-headed with small, scented flowers. The large single-headed doubles are very bold but they tend to be top heavy, easily collapsing in wet or windy weather.

For ease of reference, they have been grouped into single and multi-headed.

Old single-headed cultivars

'Telamonius Plenus' (syn. 'Von Sion') is one of the oldest daffodil cultivars – it has been in cultivation for over 300 years. It has an iron constitution and can survive literally years or decades of neglect under brambles, for example. Once uncovered they apparently miraculously start to flower, seeming to appear from nowhere. The golden yellow flowers, often with a greenish cast, are very variable and can be fully double with narrow, uneven petals but sometimes only the trumpet is double. It is early flowering. Height: 35cm. **'Rip van Winkle'** is an old dwarf variety and possibly

Narcissus 'Telamonius plenus'.

Narcissus 'Unique'.

a double form of the early-flowering *N. minor*. The narrow yellow segments are very uneven and look as though they have not been combed for a hundred years. The heads are rather top heavy and it is best grown in part shade or grass. Height: 15cm. **'Eystettensis'** (Queen Anne's Double Daffodil) has been grown since the seventeenth century and is very similar but the lemon yellow segments neatly overlap. Sadly it is slow to increase, preferring a cool, shady position. Height: 15cm. **'Tamar Double White'** is sometimes known as the 'double poeticus'. This strongly scented daffodil has glistening white double flowers and the remains of the tiny red cup can sometimes be seen amongst them. It is one of the last to flower and prefers a border to grass. It may abort its flowers if it becomes too hot or dry. Height: 40cm.

Modern single-headed cultivars

'Golden Ducket' is a sport of King Alfred with bright yellow pointed flowers. It is vigorous but the flowers are rather top heavy. **'Tasgen'** has smooth yellow petals interspersed by slightly ruffled petals of a darker hue; **'Crackington'** 🏆 has neat round flowers of yellow interspersed with smaller orange petals; **'Irene Copeland'** is an old reliable variety with pale creamy-lemon petals interspersed with tiny apricot ones.

Narcissus 'Golden Ducket'.

It gradually fades to an even cream with age. **'Trendspotter'** is cream with a rim of petals outside a ruffled and frilled double cup. **'Unique'** 🏆 has white petals interspersed in the centre with smaller yellow ones. **'White Lion'** 🏆 is similar. **'Gay Kybo'** 🏆 has beautifully shaped round flowers of white with small orange petals. **'Pink Paradise'** 🏆 is one of a number of excellent white and pink doubles.

Multi-headed cultivars

These have up to five small flowers and are usually scented and make excellent long-lasting cut flowers. **'Abba'** 🏆 has up to three small scented flowers on stiff stems. These are round and creamy-white mixed with orange. **'Cheerfulness'** 🏆 is very similar but with yellow rather than orange mixed in. **'Yellow Cheerfulness'** has similar flowers that are pale yellow. **'Sir Winston Churchill'** 🏆 is a double form of 'Geranium'. This strongly scented daffodil has white petals interspersed with tiny orange-red ones in the centre. Although it is quite tall, 35cm, it is sturdy enough for pots and is good for cutting.

Narcissus 'Gay Kybo'.

Narcissus 'Cheerfulness'.

Narcissus 'Thalia' under a cherry tree.

Division 5

Triandrus cultivars

The characteristics of N. triandrus *are clearly evident with one or more nodding flowers to a stem. The petals are more or less reflexed.*

Once again this is a remarkably variable group of daffodils. The species *N. triandrus* has two or more small nodding flowers to a stem and requires an acid soil. This later characteristic has been inherited by some of the smaller cultivars such as 'Hawera'. The larger cultivars are much sturdier, only the twin, nodding flowers hinting at their often distant *N. triandrus* parentage and they are among the best for naturalizing in grass.

Narcissus 'Petrel'.

Narcissus 'Hawera'.

Dwarf

'Hawera' 🏆 has up to eight small nodding lemon-yellow flowers per stem and more than one stem per bulb and is an ideal daffodil for pots. It is late flowering. The short cup is slightly darker than the petals and in appearance is like a larger yellow version of its *N. triandrus* parent. It is named after a bay in New Zealand where it was bred towards the beginning of the twentieth century. On dry alkaline soils it will gradually disappear but it is long lived, forming large vigorous clumps, when grown on acid soil among shrubs. Height: 30cm. The pure white **'Petrel'** has a similar parentage but is slightly larger. It is perfect for pots but is prone to virus. Height: 35cm.

White

'Ice Wings' 🏆, a modern hybrid, has two or three nodding ivory-white flowers with relatively long trumpets and smooth petals. It is shorter than many and is excellent for growing in borders or can be grown in grass. Height: 30cm. **'Tresamble'** is a vigorous twin-headed cultivar with white petals and a slightly ruffled creamy cup. It naturalizes well. Height: 35cm. **'Thalia'** is an old cultivar, bred before the First World War, with twin heads of rather ragged white flowers. But although its form may be old-fashioned it is this simple shape, coupled with its longevity and vigour, that make it still so popular for naturalizing where it looks completely at home among buttercups and bluebells. **'Mission Bells'** 🏆 is shorter with two or three nodding white flowers. Height: 30cm.

Narcissus 'Ice Wings'.

Bicolor

'Tuesday's Child' 🏆 has one or two nodding flowers of white with a neat lemon-yellow cup. It can be grown in part shade. Height: 35cm. **'Dutch Lemon Drops'** 🏆 is similar but slightly smaller and shorter. Height: 30cm. **'Stint'** 🏆 is a short cultivar with two or three relatively large lemon-yellow flowers. Height: 30cm.

Narcissus 'Dutch Lemon Drops'.

Division 6

Cyclamineus cultivars

The characteristics of N. cyclamineus are clearly evident. Solitary flowers with conspicuously reflexed petals.

These are excellent all-round daffodils and are instantly recognizable. They have a unique charm with their nodding flowers and reflexed petals, which give them a windswept look as though they were heading into a stiff breeze. Most are remarkably vigorous, early flowering and not too tall, and are among the best for naturalizing in grass, happy in our damp climate and rapidly increasing to form extensive free-flowering and long-lived clumps. Unlike their parent *N. cyclamineus* which requires an acid soil, most of the hybrids are very tolerant of soil pH. They vary in height from 12–35cm.

All yellow

'February Gold' 🏆, although it does not always live up to its name and flower in February, is among the earliest. It has neat golden flowers with a bold trumpet and petals that are only slightly reflexed. It may not have the perfect shape of the newer cultivars but it is still one of the best for naturalizing in grass or growing among shrubs. It is very vigorous and long lived in the garden. Height: 30cm. **'Peeping Tom'** 🏆, an old variety, is still one of the best for naturalizing in grass, being vigorous and long lived. It has large golden-yellow flowers with well reflexed petals and an exceptionally long slightly darker golden trumpet which has a pronounced rolled rim. Height: 35cm.

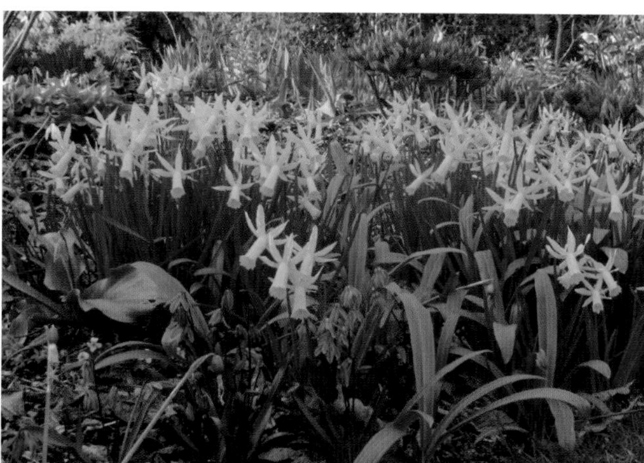

Narcissus 'Mite' with *Scilla sibirica*.

Narcissus 'February Gold'.

Narcissus 'Rapture'.

'Rapture' 🏆 is early flowering and has well-formed slender golden yellow flowers on sturdy stems. It increases well and is very floriferous. Height: 25cm. **'Swift Arrow'** 🏆 and **'The Alliance'** 🏆 are similar golden yellow cultivars. **'Lemon Silk'** is a superb new cultivar with well-formed clear lemon flowers and well-reflexed petals. The trumpet pales with age. Height: 35cm. **'Mite'** 🏆 is a tiny golden yellow cultivar rather like an overgrown version of the species. Like *N. cyclamineus* it prefers a neutral to acid soil and is very vigorous. It benefits from regular division otherwise the clumps can become too congested to flower. This can be done, like snowdrops, during or just after flowering without any ill effect. It is particularly useful as an edging plant for shrub borders. Height: 20cm. **'Snipe'** is a similar tiny daffodil but with creamy petals and a long narrow lemon yellow trumpet. Sadly it is not very vigorous, preferring a cool acid soil. Height: 20cm.

White with yellow trumpet

'February Silver' has slightly larger flowers than most of this Division with white petals which only slightly reflex from the bold lemon-yellow trumpet. It might not have the perfect shape to grant it an AGM 🏆 but it is exceptionally long lasting in flower and very long lived. Height: 33cm. **'Surfside'** 🏆 is like an improved 'February Silver'. It is a very vigorous cultivar with creamy-white, well-reflexed petals and a bold lemon-yellow trumpet. Height: 35cm. **'Wisley'** 🏆 is a very vigorous cultivar with large, bold flowers and a rather ruffled yellow trumpet and only slightly reflexed petals. It is probably in the wrong division and is rather too 'modern' for planting in grass. Height: 35cm. **'Dove Wings'** has neat white petals well reflexed from the lemon-yellow trumpet. Good for naturalizing or using at the back of a border but it can be prone to basal rot on wet soils. Height: 30cm. **'Jenny'** 🏆 is very similar but the cup gradually fades to cream with age. Sadly, it is also prone to basal rot, as is **'Trena**' 🏆 which has well-formed flowers of white with a large clear yellow trumpet. **'Jack Snipe'** 🏆 is a small, very vigorous

Narcissus 'Surfside'.

Narcissus 'Wisley'.

cultivar with reflexed white petals and a neat lemon-yellow cup, on sturdy stems. It is long lived, increasing well and it must be the first choice for naturalizing in grass. Height: 20cm. **'Tracey'** 🏆 is a neat cultivar with rather 'tubby' flowers. The pale yellow trumpet gradually fades to match the cream petals. Height: 25cm.

Yellow with orange trumpet

'Itzim' 🏆 is an elegant and vigorous daffodil with bright yellow petals swept back from a long, deep-orange cup. Height: 35cm. **'Jetfire'** is similar but the trumpet is shorter and fatter. Sadly many of the stocks available are infected with virus which shows as an uneven colour in the cup.

Narcissus 'Itzim'.

Narcissus 'Jack Snipe'.

White with pink trumpet

Pink in daffodils has gradually become more refined and more acceptable in the garden. **'Foundling'** was one of the earliest pinks to appear. The colour is rather muddy but it is a very pretty plant and vigorous. Height: 35cm. **'Reggae'** 🏆 is one of a group of similar white and pink daffodils raised by Brian Duncan of Northern Ireland. All have names pertaining to dances and this one is certainly out to dazzle with well-reflexed petals and a jaunty deep pink cup. Height: 30cm. **'Kaydee'** 🏆 and **'Bilbo'** are similar with weather-proof cups.

Narcissus 'Reggae'.

Division 7

Jonquilla cultivars

The characteristics of jonquils are clearly evident. 1–5 or more flowers to a stem.

These daffodils have round flowers with a small, flared cup. Many (but not all) are scented. They vary greatly in height, from 10–45cm and nearly all are yellow and late flowering. Many of the smallest are unsuitable for the open garden as they need a hotter, drier summer than is usually encountered in northern Europe. The larger cultivars are excellent in sunny borders or containers.

Yellow

'Rugulosus' *(odorus)* is a very old cultivar with twin yellow flowers and narrow leaves. The scented flowers have a rather ragged appearance, which lends them a particular charm, although they are rather too small for the height of the stem. Height: 40cm. **'Trevithian'** is still popular despite being an old hybrid. It is also scented, and is vigorous with twin soft lemon-yellow flowers. It is quite tall and is excellent at the back of the border or in grass. Height: 45cm. **'Quail'** 🏆 and **'Rosemoor Gold'** 🏆 are similar but with deep golden yellow flowers. Both are prolific growers and strongly scented. Height: 45cm.

'Stratosphere' 🏆 and **'Bunting'** 🏆 have neat yellow flowers with small orange cups.

Reversed bicolor

'Pipit' 🏆 is an excellent all-round daffodil. It is small and neat enough for borders or pots but is strong enough to grow in grass. It has two, sometimes three, flowers to a stem and multiple stems per bulb. The scented flowers open lemon-yellow and the cup gradually fades to white. Sadly some stocks have virus. Height: 35cm. **'Dickcissel'** 🏆 and **'Intrigue'** 🏆 are very similar but the lemon colour is more intense; they are excellent alternatives to 'Pipit'. Height: 35cm.

Small flowered or dwarf

'Sun Disc' 🏆 is a perfect miniature jonquil whose stature belies its vigour. The solitary flower is a perfect disc carried on a rather tall, stiff stem. It opens an even yellow but the petals gradually fade to creamy yellow. It is perfect for the rock garden or a dry sunny bank. It is late flowering and will grow in grass. Height: 20cm.

Narcissus 'Kokopelli'

'Sundial' is twin-headed and shorter. The heads tend to nod slightly. Neither of these is scented. Height: 18cm. **'Kokopelli'** 🏆 is like a multi-headed 'Sun Disc' with up to three perfect round golden flowers on rather tall stiff stems. It is too tall for the rock garden but is an excellent daffodil for pot culture as it is very upright. It also makes a superb cut flower. It is long lasting and vigorous enough to grow in grass. Height: 35cm. **'Bobbysoxer'** has twin heads of pale yellow with a flat orange cup. Height: 25cm. **'Chit Chat'** 🏆 looks like a dwarf *N. jonquilla* with five tiny bright yellow flowers per stem, thread-like leaves and a strong scent. It can be short lived in the open garden, preferring a warm position where it is dry in summer. **'Pixie's Sister'** 🏆 is very similar. Both are recommended for growing in pots under cold glass. Height: 20cm.

White

There are few white jonquil hybrids as the golden *N. jonquilla* has been the principal parent. The tiny hybrids derived from *N. rupicola* subsp. *watieri* are more suited to cold glass although **'Xit'** will survive in the shelter of trees. Height: 20cm. **'Bellsong'** is a delightful short jonquil hybrid with one or two small white flowers and neat pale pink cups. It is strongly scented and a good choice for large containers where it is particularly effective with blue hyacinths and the dwarf tulip 'Little Princess'. Height: 35cm. **'Tinhay'** is multi-stemmed with a neat, pure white flower. Height: 30cm. **'St Piran'** has two or three scented white flowers per stem with small, pale yellow cups. Height: 35cm.

Narcissus 'Geranium'.

Division 8

Tazetta Daffodils

These have the characteristics of tazettas clearly evident with between three and twenty small flowers to a stout stem with broad foliage.

The varieties in this division are mostly tall with thick stems and luxuriant foliage and fall into two distinct groups. Most, but not all, are scented. First, those that are based upon *N. tazetta*: these have up to fifteen small, scented flowers, which come into growth very early, making them susceptible to severe frost (although 'Compressus' came through -15°C undamaged). They like a warm, sunny position in a free-draining soil that is dry in the summer to ripen the bulbs. Our 'Compressus' are planted along the edge of a border where the canopy of *Crocosmia* 'Lucifer' planted behind them keeps them dry in summer. They flower profusely every year. The second group, which show a more marked *N. poeticus* influence, are just as strongly scented but have only two to four larger flowers. These are hardier than the above.

Narcissus 'Minnow'.

The Christmas-flowering **'Paperwhite'** is the classic tazetta. It is very early flowering and a full description can be found in *Chapter 2*. **'Avalanche'** 🏆 and the virtually identical **'Compressus'** are old cultivars from pre-1882. They have fifteen or more small white flowers with bright yellow cups on thick stems. Unfortunately, like many of this group, their very fleshy leaves are rather intrusive, but they make an outstanding cut flower, being strongly scented. Height: 35cm. **'Silver Chimes'** has similar fleshy leaves and up to seven small, creamy flowers. Height: 25cm. **'Soleil d'Or'** is the classic cut flower with up to seven tiny deep golden flowers and small orange cups. It is not fully hardy and flowers early in the year. Height: 45cm. **'Canaliculatus'** is a dwarf tazetta of unknown history, possibly originating in the south of France. It has narrow grey leaves and up to five tiny white flowers with deep gold cups. It is highly scented. It will increase freely but will only flower well if it has a warm, dry summer. We grow it at the edge of the canopy of a sequoiadendron where it has steadily increased and maintained flowering for many years. Height: 15cm. The unscented **'Minnow'** is another dwarf tazetta with two to four creamy yellow flowers per stem. The petals gradually fade with age. Again the leaves are slightly too large for the flowers and it tends to fade away after a few years, although we have naturalized it in grass. Height: 15cm. **'Pacific Coast'** 🏆 is the yellow-flowered form. **'Geranium'** 🏆 is an excellent all-round daffodil, strong and vigorous. It has up to four pure white flowers per stem, each with a small clear orange cup. It is strongly scented and perfect both for pots or general garden decoration. Height: 35cm.

'Falconet' 🏆 has up to three small deep-yellow flowers per stem with orange cups. Height: 35cm. **'Golden Dawn'** 🏆 and **'Hoopoe'** 🏆 are a similar colour.

Narcissus 'Hoopoe'.

Narcissus 'Actaea' naturalized in grass.

Division 9

Poeticus Daffodils

These have the characteristics of poeticus daffodils clearly present. The solitary very round flowers have pure white petals and a small flat red-rimmed cup. They are usually strongly fragrant.

This division is the most uniform, being made up of a small group of essentially identical bulbs.

'Actaea' 🏆 is unsurpassed as a late-flowering daffodil for naturalizing under trees. The large, flat, white flowers have a small red-rimmed cup. Height: 45cm. **'Cantabile'** 🏆 and **'Chesterton'** 🏆 are much smaller and are like perfect miniature *N. poeticus* with round white flowers and tiny red-rimmed cups. Both are equally good in the garden for the front of a sunny border where they flower very late. Height: 30cm.

Narcissus 'Cantabile'.

Division 10

Bulbocodium cultivars (hoop petticoat)

The characteristics of N. bulbocodium are clearly present with a widely flaring trumpet and insignificant petals.

Many of the bulbocodium hybrids are based upon the early-flowering white hoop petticoat daffodil of southern Spain and Morocco. These require a hot, dry summer dormancy and only flower well under glass. Recently there has been a rise in interest in golden bulbocodiums and new varieties with improved flowers are becoming available, but as many of these are based on *N. obesus* they also require a dry summer dormancy to flower well.

'Classic Gold' 🏆 is a vigorous small narcissus producing masses of deep gold flowers. These have the typical *N. bulbocodium* shape. Sadly it seems to be short lived in the open garden. Height: 15cm.

'Kenellis' is a little gem that will grow outside on a rock garden for a few years but tends to gradually fade. It has pale cream flowers with a wide trumpet and short petals. Height: 15cm.

Narcissus 'Classic Gold'.

Narcissus 'Kenellis'.

Narcissus 'Gunwalloe'.

Division 11

Split corona daffodils

The cup is split for more than half its length.
They are subdivided into:

11a) collar daffodil with overlapping segments

11b) papillon daffodils with alternate segments

This group of daffodils is the latest development in flower shape to make its way onto the show bench. The cup and the perianth segments are no longer separate but the cup is split and laid flat across the petals.

For many gardeners these are an aberration and a step too far, but some of the newer varieties have a refinement and brilliance of colour that make them garden-worthy. They have the advantage that the flowers are outward facing so 'look you in the eye'.

Narcissus 'Sunnyside Up'.

Division 11a

In this section the cup is split into three and each part is laid immediately on top of the corresponding petal so that the petal colour shows as a rim around it. Most are 40–45cm tall.

'Menehay' 🏆 and **'Boslowick'** 🏆 are similar cultivars with bright yellow petals and contrasting orange perianth segments. **'Jack Wood'** has the same colouring and was named after the indefatigable gardening journalist. It has the charming habit of reflexing three of the segments as though it were pinning its ears back for the latest news. The central petals of **'Sunnyside Up'** 🏆 are ruffled and less flattened than many. It opens yellow and fades to an attractive cream. Similarly the central petals of the white and pink **'Vanellus'** 🏆 and **'Trigonometry'** 🏆 are barely split. **'Lady Eve'** and **'Bossington'** have the same colour in a more classic split corona form. **'Tripartite'** 🏆 is smaller in all its parts with three small yellow heads that are only slightly split. Height: 40cm.

Narcissus 'Lady Eve'.

Division 11b

These daffodils look rather more like a ruffled Division 3, as the split cup remains in the centre rather than overlapping the petals. **'Jodi'** is white with a flat split corona of salmon pink. Height: 40cm.

Narcissus 'Jodi'.

Division 12

Other daffodil cultivars

Daffodil cultivars that do not fit the definition of any other division.

This group forms a curious mélange but includes some of the most vigorous daffodils ever produced. They usually have the characteristics of more than one Division, such as the twin-headed cyclamineus hybrid 'Tête-à-Tête'. It is here that the split corona daffodils resided until they found a home in a new division. These are some of the best daffodils for containers, being multi-headed and multi-scaped (producing more than one flower stem per bulb).

'Cornish Chuckles' 🏆 has sturdy stems with two or three relatively chunky flowers of cream with yellow cups. It is good in containers having true flower power. Height: 35cm. **'Eaton Song'** 🏆 is very similar but smaller overall. Height: 30cm.

'Tête-à-Tête' 🏆 needs no introduction. It is the most instantly recognizable of all daffodils. From its 1940s origin as a chance seedling raised in Cornwall by the great miniature daffodil breeder Alec Gray, it has risen to be the largest single organism grown today, principally as small pot plants. Some 70 million tons of it are produced annually. It is fantastically versatile – vigorous enough for grass, small enough for pots and rock gardens or it is good along the front of a border and especially among shrubs. It will even survive neglect on a roadside verge. It is early flowering, very hardy, foolproof and long lived as well as long lasting. Each bulb produces four or more stems each carrying a

Narcissus 'Cornish Chuckles'.

perfect golden miniature daffodil. Newly planted bulbs will be twin headed but this characteristic, inherited from its tazetta parentage, tends to disappear with time but the resultant plant is no less attractive. The leaves are short and upright, making it perfect for pot cultivation. It is associates well with blue-flowered bulbs such as *Anemone blanda*, chionodoxas or grape hyacinths, both in containers and in borders. It can readily be divided as the flowers fade. Height: 15cm. **'Jumblie'** 🏆 is a sister seedling where the slender flowers show more of the *N. cyclamineus* parentage. They are reliably twin headed and just as vigorous. Height: 20cm.

'Toto' 🏆 is a floriferous multi-headed variety with three to four nodding flowers of creamy white. The slender trumpets open pale lemon but fade to cream. Each bulb produces two to four stems and it is one of the best for using in containers. It flowers in the middle of spring and can also be grown in grass, although it is too new to assess its longevity. Height: 20cm.

Narcissus 'Tête-à-Tête'.

Narcissus 'Toto'.

Ornithalgum
(Star of Bethlehem)

There are many non-hardy members of this very disparate group of bulbs. Most have a spike of green-backed white flowers. Some have tall handsome spikes; others nestle at ground level hiding their flowers within the basal rosette of leaves, only revealing themselves when the sun opens the flowers wide. They have starry or tubular-shaped flowers with six petals. Some have an inner tube. Modern DNA testing has shown that the current classification is probably inaccurate and many are likely to change their name in the future, some moving into the genus *Albuca*.

Ornithalgum umbellatum.

Cultivation

The bulbs are planted 10cm deep in the autumn in a sunny, well-drained soil. Those listed below are fully hardy. With the exception of *O. nutans* all need full sun to open the flowers, otherwise they stay resolutely closed, only showing the dull green outer petals.

O. balansae

This is one of a group of very similar dwarf bulbs from southern Europe and the Middle East, which produce a low spike of green-backed white flowers that nestle deep within a rosette of basal leaves. They are more of a collector's plant. Height: 10–15cm.

O. nutans 🏆

This woodland bulb from Europe and southwest Asia is perfect for massing under shrubs or growing in grass mixed with late-flowering daffodils, such as *N. poeticus* or the slender blue *Camassia quamash*. It has a spike of nodding silvery-white open bells, each with a prominent green stripe on the outside, and it has a quiet charm. Height: 35cm.

O. pyrenaicum
(Bath Asparagus)

This British native is a curiosity rather than a good garden plant. The tiny pale yellow flowers are in a tall, insignificant spike that is easily overlooked. It has narrow basal leaves. Height: 60cm.

O. umbellatum
(Star of Bethlehem)

This small bulb is widespread throughout Europe to the Middle East, and is locally naturalized in Britain. It has a clump of long, narrow basal leaves with a central silver stripe reminiscent of a crocus, and a lose corymb (open spike) of up to twelve starry green-backed flowers in late spring. These are striking when the sun opens them wide to reveal their glistening white crystalline interiors – otherwise they are insignificant. They are suitable for light grass in full sun or even a gravel path but they are very invasive. The bulb splits into a myriad of tiny bulblets, which are almost impossible to eradicate. Height: 15cm.

Ornithalgum nutans.

Oxalis

Some very invasive members have given this genus a bad name but the little clump-forming bulbs listed below are very well behaved. The bulbs are planted in autumn, 7cm deep and 15cm apart in a sunny position or under cold glass.

O. adenophylla 🏆

This south Andean native has curious bulbs with a heavy netted tunic. It produces a mound of beautiful grey-green leaves that are like that of a superior clover but cut into many more segments. In mid-spring the lilac-pink flowers open from typical oxalis buds that are tightly furled like an umbrella. The flowers are veined with deeper purple and have a dark purple throat. It requires a well-drained soil in full sun. Height: 12cm.

O. enneaphylla 🏆

This looks similar to the above but it has small rhizomes rather than bulbs and the flowers have a white throat. They vary in colour from deep pink to white. It comes from the far south of South America including the Falkland Islands and although hardy can be temperamental in the open garden, disliking too much moisture. Height: 10cm.

Oxalis adenophylla.

Puschkinia libanotica.

Puschkinia

This charming mid-season bulb comes from eastern Turkey. Plant the bulbs 10cm deep in any well-drained soil in sun or part shade. It is useful for bedding or pots.

P. scilloides (syn. *P. libanoticum*)

This small bulb from the Middle East produces a compact spike of ice-blue flowers and two semi-erect leaves. This is one of a group of blue bulbs that are not particularly intrinsically attractive or dramatic but are very effective when used in large drifts, especially under spring-flowering shrubs or trees where they are excellent companion plants for blue grape hyacinths and the shorter daffodils. They are useful as underplanting for shorter tulips, both in the garden and in containers. Alternatively, they are small enough to be grown on a rock garden. Height: 10cm.

Romulea

These small bulbs are grown for their colourful crocus-like flowers. The leaves are very narrow and thread-like. Most come from South Africa and are not hardy, but the species below is suitable for outdoor cultivation in northern Europe. The corms are planted in the autumn in a well-drained gritty soil in full sun. They are easily raised from seed or by offsets.

R. bulbocodium

This tiny corm from the Mediterranean produces a mass of fine thread-like leaves and a succession of showy flowers in varying shades of lilac and purple. In warm sun these open wide to reveal a starry flower with pointed petals and a bold white or yellow centre. They are small enough for a trough where they flower in late spring. They are frost hardy to -5°C but excess water at any time is more of a problem. They are easy subjects for cold glass, seeding freely into neighbouring pots! Height: 7cm.

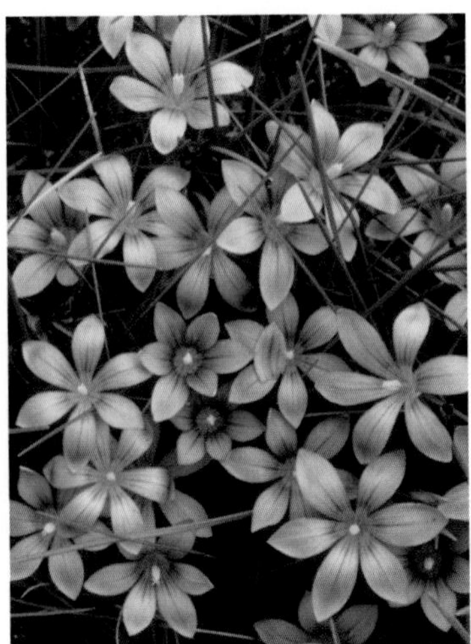

Romulea bulbocodium.

Scilla

Although this name is understood by most gardeners it is also a very confusing catch-all genus. Many of the most familiar members, especially the bluebells, have now been split off, leaving a rather disparate group of bulbs, most of which have racemes of blue, bell-shaped flowers and linear basal leaves. They vary in height from 2–40cm and are found in a wide variety of habitats, from mountains to seashore, in South Africa and Europe. Some are tender whilst others are very insignificant, but many make excellent garden plants. Most have a small round bulb, some with a shiny purple tunic resembling a tiny hyacinth, which are planted 10cm deep and 5–10cm apart in the autumn. The huge bulb of *S. peruviana*, and the smaller one of *S. lilio-hyacinthus,* look more like that of a lily and are almost evergreen. These bulbs are planted just below the surface with at least 15cm between them. Propagation is by seed, offsets or by breaking up the large clusters of bulbs in the clump-forming varieties.

Scilla bithynica alba.

Scilla bithynica naturalized with hellebores.

S. bifolia 🏆

This is a precocious bulb that is definitely spring-flowering but first appears as the snowdrops fade. It has racemes of intense blue starry flowers. It is too small to make an impact by itself but is delightful dotted in the grass or massed under shrubs where it is a good foil for white snowdrops or cream crocus. (*See* also *Chapter 2.*) Height: 10cm.

Scilla bithynica.

S. bithynica

This central and southern European bulb is a prolific seeder and a weed of the first order, but in the right place it makes a fantastic display; the small racemes of bright blue flowers and the apple-green leaves totally covering the ground in a blue sea. Although they are dramatic in full flower they can be a problem as they fade: the leaves and seed heads fall over to form an impenetrable blanket smothering any but the most vigorous of neighbours. However, they are so dynamic it seems impossible to kill them and the leaves, and unripe seed heads, can be pulled off once the flowers have finished. They are perfect for adding early colour to the wilder parts of the garden or carpeting the ground around the base of winter-flowering shrubs such as *Hamamelis*. They will happily fill the gaps between hellebores and will even tackle light grass. There is also a white-flowered form *S. bithynica alba*. Height: 12cm. *S. amoena* is virtually identical.

Scilla lilio-hyacinthus.

Scilla sibirica.

S. lilio-hyacinthus

This scilla has a quiet charm of its own. The large bulb, looking more like that of a lily, is clump-forming, spreading to form a compact patch. The dense clear blue spikes rise up rather like candles from the rosette of bright green basal leaves. It replaces our bluebells in the woods of the Pyrenees and northern Spain where it flowers alongside wild daffodils before the leaves appear on the trees. It is perfect for planting in a cool position under shrubs. There is a white-flowered form. Height: 18cm.

S. peruviana

This exotic Spanish and North African bulb has nothing to do with Peru – this mis-naming was a classic example of Chinese whispers. It produces a very large, virtually evergreen bulb that looks more like that of a lily with a cluster of scales. It is clump-forming, spreading to form a compact patch which needs regular division. If they are left undivided the individual bulbs become so congested that they become too small to flower. Deep planting may control this tendency. The leaves, which appear early in the autumn, form a basal rosette from which rises a huge, 15cm-wide, rather flat pyramidal spike of starry flowers in late spring. These are an intense blue with conspicuous yellow anthers and are neatly arranged in concentric circles. The flowers achieve heroic proportions when grown under glass but are more modest outdoors. Although they are native to southern Europe they appreciate a high level of moisture when they are growing (I have seen them flowering well in a damp Spanish ditch), followed by a dry summer. Height: 30cm. *Forma alba* has white flowers.

S. sibirica 🏆

This very hardy small bulb comes from north Iran through to the Ukraine. The basal leaves are upright and each bulb, which resembles a miniature hyacinth, produces a number of stems which gradually elongate over time. Each of these stems has up to four intense blue, nodding, open cup-shaped flowers with a darker central vein. It flowers early in the spring and has an exceptionally long flowering period. They are very tolerant of many situations in the garden and can even be grown in grass, but to my mind they are perfect for massing around the base of a spring-flowering shrub or small tree such as a magnolia, where they mix well with blue *Anemone blanda*. They are also very effective when used to fill the narrow gap between a clipped box hedge and a path. Height: 10–20cm. **'Spring Beauty'** supposedly has deeper blue flowers; **'Alba'** has white flowers but is rather a waste of time as it is not especially attractive.

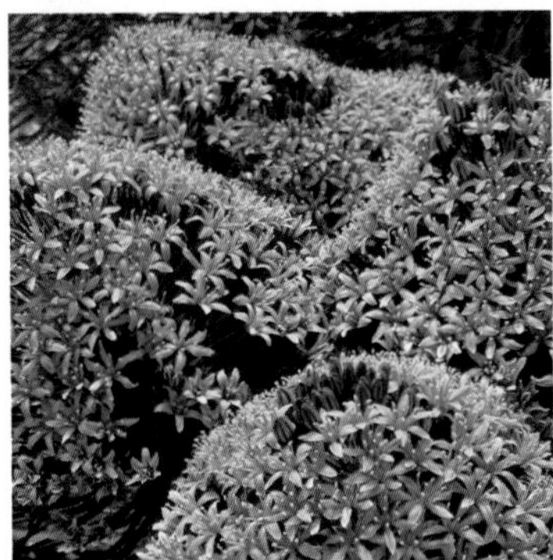

Scilla peruviana.

S. verna

The spring squill is found growing in the short turf on sea cliffs from Portugal to Scotland. It has tiny spikes of up to fifteen relatively large deep-blue flowers. It is more a curiosity for a trough than an effective garden plant. Height: 5cm.

Trillium
(Wake-Robin)

These rhizomatous plants grow in the deep woodland soils of North America and East Asia including Japan. They flower in late spring. There are many species in the wild but only a few are readily available in cultivation and these are very muddled. The fat rhizome produces a single stem topped by three leaves. The three-petalled flower nestles directly onto the leaves, or it may be carried on a short stalk above or hang down below them. The large bracts are very obvious and are one of the distinguishing features between species. They are plants that require considerable patience on the part of the gardener. Like all rhizomes they resent disturbance and commercially bought plants may take two or more years to re-establish their root system and start to grow. When growing well they can make sizeable clumps but on thin, dry soils they will be considerably smaller. In growth they need ample moisture and part shade otherwise they may abort their buds, leaving a sad brown offering instead of the dramatic flower you had expected.

Cultivation

Plant the rhizomes in the winter when dormant or as potted plants at any time. They do best in a rich soil with plenty of leaf mould in part shade and where there is ample water when they are growing. They must not become waterlogged, however, or they will rot. They do not grow well in containers. The rhizomes can be carefully divided as the leaves fade. Some species will self-seed.

Trilliums can be split into two types – those where the flower is on a short stalk (pedicellate) and those where the flower sits directly on the leaves (sessile).

Trillium cuneatum.

Sessile Trilliums

The nomenclature of the sessile trilliums is very confused, especially in commerce. All have more or less mottled leaves and are the first to flower.

T. cuneatum from southeast USA has flowers in shades of brownish maroon with large 7cm flowers. It is frequently sold as *T. sessile,* which is a much smaller plant with rather small, 'fat' flowers. ***T. chloropetalum*** from California is similar in appearance and is very variable in colour. It can be white, brown, greenish or maroon. Some forms of the white-flowered ***T. albidum*** from California and Oregon can be confused with it although it has only slightly mottled leaves. The best forms of *T. albidum* have wide-petalled flowers of much substance. Where the populations overlap they will hybridize. The largest flowering of all is another Californian, ***T. kurabayashii***, which has exceptionally large reddish-maroon flowers. A particularly fine form was distributed from the Royal Botanic Gardens in Edinburgh. It is very vigorous, growing into huge clumps and freely setting seed. Height: 60cm.

Trillium chloropetalum.

Trillium luteum.

T. luteum 🏆

This handsome trillium from southeast USA has beautifully clear yellow-green 5cm flowers and mottled leaves. It is easily grown but can be confused with green-flowered forms of other sessile trilliums. Height: 30cm.

Pedicellate Trilliums

T. erectum 🏆

To my mind this is not the most showy of the trilliums but it has a quiet charm. In the wild it is very variable but the plant in cultivation has deep reddish-maroon flowers held at an angle on a small stalk above the plain green leaves. The petals are slightly reflexed with the green sepals filling the gaps between them. It can grow into large clumps. var. *albiflorum* has white flowers and a very distinct dark ovary.

T. erectum will hybridize with the similar ***T. flexipes***, which has large creamy-white flowers of much substance. Height: 35cm.

T. grandiflorum 🏆

The best known of all the trilliums, the White Wake-Robin is the national flower of Ontario, Canada. It has plain green leaves which sometimes have a purplish tint when they first emerge. The large, glistening white flowers framed by the neat green sepals have distinctly indented veins and are held above the leaves at an angle.

T. grandiflorum is one of the last to flower. Its leaves are only just starting to show when the sessile trilliums are in full flower. Emerging so late, they are particularly vulnerable to a period of dry weather. When growing well they can form prodigious clumps. As the flowers fade they take on a rosy hue; however, there are some forms that have pink flowers from the outset. These usually have darker leaves as well. *f. polymerum (flore pleno)* has tight double white flowers like miniature roses and is very beautiful when growing well. Sadly it is slow to increase and prone to abort its flowers if it becomes too warm or dry. Height: 35cm.

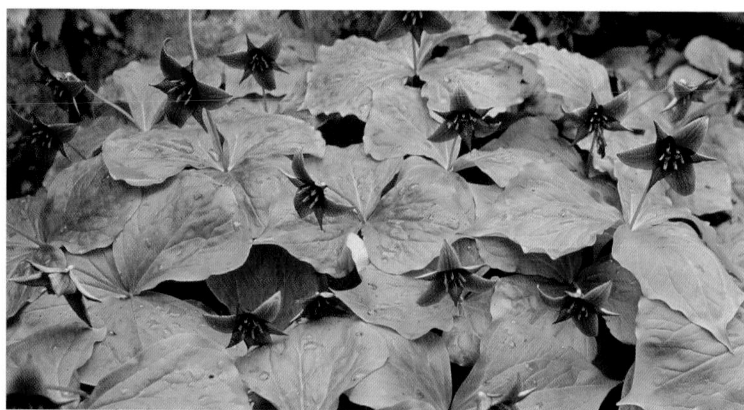

Trillium erectum.

T. rivale 🏆

This tiny trillium is remarkably easy to grow but its small stature means that it should be given a select spot such as a raised bed in part shade. It is also prone to slug damage. However, when growing well, it can form extensive colonies, freely seeding around. Its name means 'stream loving' – it grows in west USA and it seems to do best in the cooler, wetter parts of the country. The small deep green leaves are carried on short stalks. The flowers are white or pinkish and heavily spotted with purple towards the middle. Height: 10cm.

T. rugelii (white) and ***T. vaseyi*** (red) have relatively large flowers that are carried below the leaves.

Trillium grandiflorum.

Trillium rivale.

Tulips

The tulip, in all its infinite variety, needs little introduction. There are over a hundred species but it is the colourful hybrids, the result of many centuries of careful breeding, which dominate the spring garden. The pointed bulb, usually more or less covered in a tough, brown outer tunic, varies in size from less than 1cm in the tiny species to 7cm for a modern hybrid. The flower is carried at the top of the stem. The leaves, usually broad and grey in colour, clasp the stem, although in some species they are narrow and held close to ground. Some are attractively striped or variegated. Most tulips are single-flowered with the six petals (more accurately perianth segments or tepals) arranged in two layers: the outer three protect the bud and the inner three are revealed only when the flower opens. There may be a significant difference in colour between the inner and the outer petals and the base of the flower is often a contrasting colour, especially in the species. Although a single flower is the norm there are some that have double flowers and others that are multi-headed.

Although all tulips have a broadly cup-shaped flower they are remarkably variable. Some have well rounded flowers whilst others are slender and pointed. In some the edges are fringed like a Victorian scarf whilst others are curled and twisted like crushed tissue paper. Of all the spring-flowering bulbs tulips are the most varied in colour and when it comes to the taller hybrids, the sky – or your imagination – is the limit. They are so rainbow hued that using them in the garden is often more like decorating than gardening. With the exception of true blue every shade is represented. Many are also splashed or shaded with another colour, sometimes in a subtle way like a watercolour wash but in others there is a bold contrast between the two colours.

Tulips have conventionally been grouped into fifteen Cultivar Groups according to their parentage but a revision of this classification is long overdue as many of the newest cultivars can no longer be easily allocated to the existing groups. Some catalogues group tulips by flowering time but many still list them by type – 'Triumph', etc. However, the *Plantfinder* has allocated a number to these groups so this is included as well.

Unlike most bulbs, tulip varieties have a relatively short life. As a particular cultivar gradually loses vigour and dwindles, so well-loved names disappear, but there are always new varieties in similar colours to replace them. There are many hundreds of tulips and there follows only a basic selection to illustrate the enormous range available.

Tulip 'White Triumphator'.

Using tulips in the garden

The tulip is the quintessential bedding bulb, seen on every roundabout rising through a carpet of wallflowers or forget-me-nots. In the garden they bring strong colours to a border that may have little colour once the daffodils fade, filling the gap between them and the summer herbaceous plants.

The showy hybrid tulips can be extremely frustrating, flowering magnificently in the first year then only producing a few straggling leaves and a handful of pathetic flowers the subsequent year or even disap-

A narrow bed beside a wall filled with pink tulips.

pearing completely without a trace. The tulip bulb is not a permanent structure but is replaced every year and it frequently only produces small, non-flowering bulbs. All tulips need a good moist growing period followed by a dry summer dormancy to ripen the bulb in order to flower the following season. The problems caused by our rather damp northern European summers can be overcome by lifting the bulbs, leaves and all, as they fade after flowering. They are then stored in a dry mouse-proof place, such as a net suspended from the ceiling of the garage. In late autumn the bulbs are cleaned and the largest ones replanted in the garden. Bulbs planted under deciduous trees may well benefit from the umbrella effect of the canopy and may maintain flowering for at least a few years. Tulips seem to prefer heavier soils and on light ones the bulbs may quickly split into small non-flowering bulblets. Deep planting, at least 20cm, may slow this annoying habit. This is particularly recommended if the bulbs are to be left *in situ* in a mixed border as they will then be well below a weeding fork! The annual addition of a few new bulbs each autumn will maintain the display and any non-flowering ones can easily and quickly be removed in the spring. Some varieties seem more perennial on some soils than others but only experimentation will find the right one for your garden.

If the bulbs are to be massed in a border they must be planted close enough to give a bold display. Thin planting dissipates the effect and looks pathetic. An alternative is to use a few bold clumps of around 7–15 bulbs at regular intervals. Unlike with daffodils, mixed colours can be surprisingly effective, particularly if a few contrasting colours are used to give an accent. I mix a scattering of the lily-flowered 'Marietta' and 'China Pink' through a bold planting of 'Greenland' with a few 'Queen of Night' for contrast. Another classic combination is a mix of the scarlet 'Couleur Cardinal' with the flamed orange 'Prinses Irene', which I use under my bronze *Amelanchier*, along with a handful of the mad parrot tulip 'Rococo'.

As well as the conventional use in bedding or borders it is worth experimenting with growing tulips in other parts of the garden. They like the same hot and dry conditions as bearded iris and make good companions for them. 'Queen of Night' flowers at the same time and is the same colour as Iris 'Langport Wren'. Tulips will push up though the soft carpet of leaves of the bulbous *Geranium malviflorum* which flowers at a similar time and can be used as an underplanting for them, perhaps in front of a stand of *Nerine bowdenii* under a sunny wall. Dramatic effects can be created by planting strong-coloured tulips such as the vivid orange 'Ballerina', with the deep purple young growth of *Lysimachia ciliata* 'Firecracker' 🏆 or purple heuchera, and they look stunning floating above the fluffy pony tails of *Stipa tenuissima*, particularly when the light catches them both. The mounds of lime-yellow bracts of *Euphorbia polychroma* make a good backdrop to 'Spring Green' and its yellow counterpart.

The shade-loving Lenten rose – *Helleborus* × *hybridus* (*H. orientalis*) – can be an effective, albeit unlikely, companion plant for tulips. The removal of the fading hellebore flowers in early April leaves an undulating carpet of fresh green foliage which is the perfect supporting plant for tulips, especially the long-lasting lily-flowered varieties. As they mature, the flowers open wide like a cloud of butterflies floating above the hellebores. The bulbs can be left *in situ* as the canopy of both the hellebores and any shrubs above will ensure a dry summer for them. There are many other emerging herbaceous perennials with similar fresh green leaves which will complement tulips. 'Spring Green' mixed with 'West Point' rising through the spikes of crocosmia leaves is another example. Or try pink tulips and the grey ferny leaves of *Dicentra oregonum*. Fresh bulbs can be added in subsequent years to maintain the display.

The smaller species not only have a particular charm of their own; they often belie their delicate appearance by proving themselves as vigorous and long-lived garden plants. Their small stature hides their greatest asset – they are much more perennial than many of the larger hybrids and do not need to be lifted once planted. Provided that they are given a dry sunny situation and planted reasonably deeply they will reward the gardener with many years of display for no further effort. Traditionally they are planted on rock gardens and similar open sunny situations or tucked along the front of a border, but they are much more versatile than that. *Tulip batalinii* hybrids can be used to underplant herbaceous peonies, for example, where their creamy flowers are a perfect contrast to the reddish new foliage of the peonies. For a perfect spring succession they can follow on from *Anemone blanda* 'White Splendour'. *Tulipa sprengeri* is one of the few tulips to seed freely in Britain and these will naturalize in light grass. Cultural details for the species vary and will be found under the individual entry.

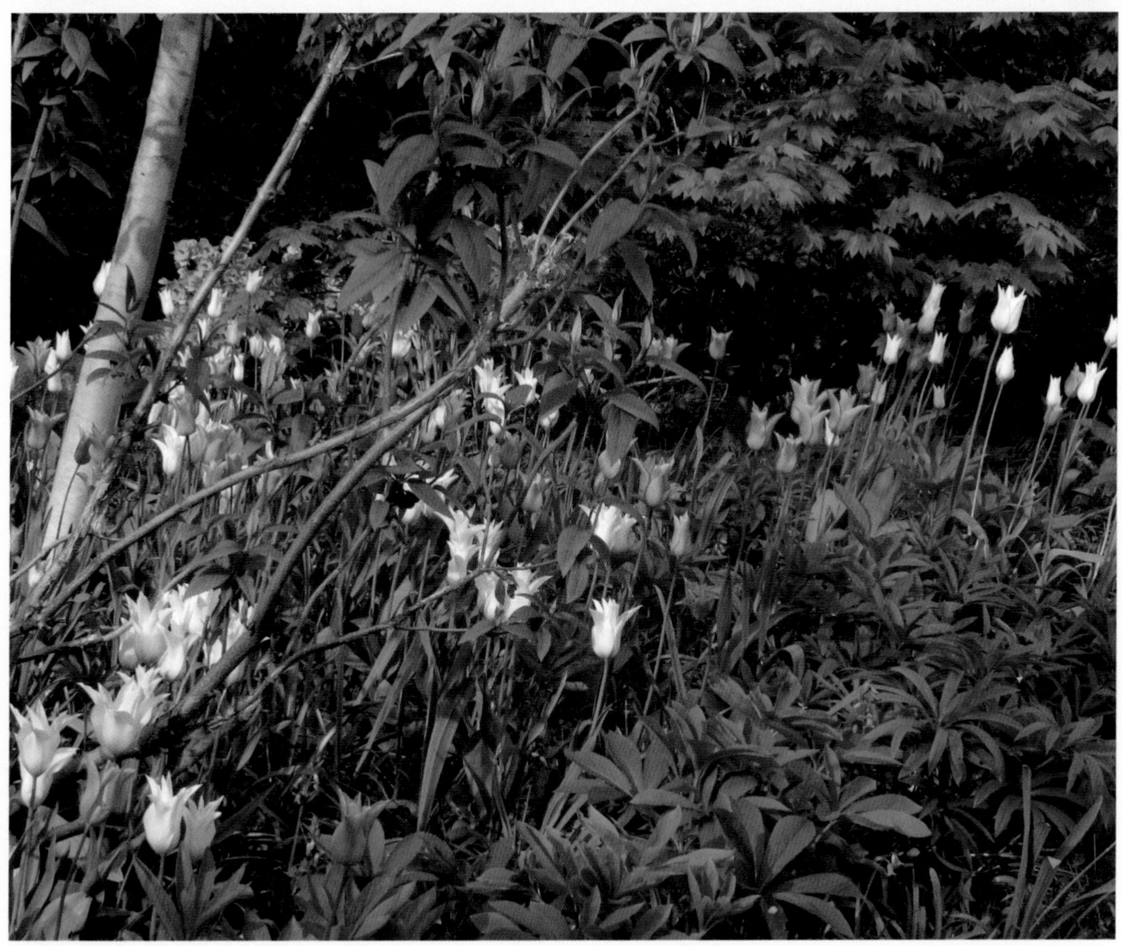

Massed lily-flowered tulips with hellebores.

Tulip 'Ballerina' lightens a dark corner.

Although tulips are relatively neat and die back standing to attention, not flopping in the unattractive way of daffodils, their flower heads should be removed as soon as they fade. A mature tulip flower is a thing of beauty: the petals opened wide in the sun to reveal contrasting colours and the central geometric boss of anthers and style. A few days later this beauty is sadly bedraggled, the dying petals hanging on in a sad parody of their former glory and inevitably drawing the eye and thus attention to them.

Using tulips in containers

Tulips are ideal for all shapes and sizes of container. They are so varied both in size and colour that there is a tulip to match every situation. With virtually every colour except blue available to choose from, it is more a case of interior design than garden design. One of my great pleasures is to experiment with colour and shape combinations. Other spring bulbs, especially *Anemone blanda*, hyacinths and muscari, are perfect companions for tulips. Tulips prefer to be planted in a loam-based compost with at least 10cm of soil on top of them.

Cultivation

Tulips prefer to be planted into a cold soil in the late autumn. The spacing of the bulbs in the garden is dependent upon the size of the flower head and the nature of the display wanted but they look best in tightly packed clumps. Unless they are to be lifted after flowering they should be planted 15–20cm deep. The tunic which covers the bulb to protect it during the summer can easily become dislodged during handling prior to sale and planting. Provided the exposed bulb shows no sign of any fungal infection (a bluish mold, not the brown discolouration that follows the outline of the split tunic) this is of no significance and tunic-less bulbs need not be rejected. Indeed, many growers of exhibition tulips will actually peel the tunics away as they fear it may harbour the spores of fungal infection. Whether this is true or not, the removal of the tunic has no detrimental effect upon the subsequent flowering.

Pests and diseases

Mice, badgers and squirrels all find newly planted tulips irresistible. The fungal infection Tulip Fire can affect tulips where the foliage has been damaged by bad weather.

Species and near-species hybrids

Miscellaneous (15)

Although this is the last of the classification groups, the species tulips form the building blocks from which the modern tulip was bred so they are listed first. This group includes some of the most beautiful and the most distinctive tulips. These are the delicate wild tulips that are found from southern Europe right through to Central Asia. They grow in a variety of habitats – from snowy mountain hillside to scorched dry deserts. Many of them make surprisingly easy and long-lasting garden plants, needing little more than deep planting in a well-drained, gritty soil in full sun to give years of trouble-free pleasure. Many are small and delicate enough for a rock garden or even trough, while others will spread to form a carpet under deciduous trees.

T. acuminata
(Horned Tulip)

Despite its name, which suggests this is a species in its own right, this extraordinary and immediately recognizable tulip is in fact a hybrid originating in Turkey from where it made its way into western Europe some 250 years ago. Unlike most tulips this has remarkably long, narrow petals that twist and turn at bizarre angles, like the tulips seen on Turkish tiles. The flower is essentially yellow but it is streaked to a lesser or greater extent with a fiery red. Sadly it is not one of the easiest to keep from year to year in the open garden as it requires a free-draining soil in full sun followed by a dry summer dormancy, and is prone to fungal attack. Late flowering. Height: 15cm.

T. aucheriana

This is one of the tiniest tulip species with 3cm soft pink flowers nestling in the centre of a rosette of glaucous leaves. It comes from Iran and is probably happiest in a bulb frame but will grow outside in a gritty soil in full sun and is small enough for a trough, although it will dwindle following wet summers. Late flowering. Height: 10cm.

Tulipa aucheriana.

T. bakeri

This Cretan tulip is similar to *T. saxatilis* and there has been much confusion over whether they are two distinct species. Current botanical thinking says they are. **'Lilac Wonder'** is the form usually encountered in commerce

Tulipa acuminata.

Tulipa bakeri 'Lilac Wonder'.

Tulipa biflora.

Tulipa clusiana.

and is a very vigorous selection with up to three buds per stem, although a single flower tends to be the norm. It has well-formed flowers of rich pinkish-purple with a clearly defined yellow centre colour. It can be less reliable in the long term than *T. saxatilis*. Mid-season. Height: 15cm.

T. biflora

This tiny species has one of the widest distributions of all tulips, from eastern Turkey eastwards to Tajikistan where it flowers as soon as the snow melts. The typical plant in commerce has neat healthy foliage, and three to six 4cm white flowers, stained bluish-green on the outside. Although not showy there is a good balance between flowers and leaves. It is an attractive and long-lived subject for a trough or scree where its early flowering is a bonus. Height: 10cm.

T. clusiana 🏆

The lady tulip of Central Asia is probably one of the most beautiful and graceful of all species with small, slender flowers held well above the leaves on stiff stems. The white flowers are heavily stained maroon on the outside and open to reveal striking black anthers above a dark maroon base. It needs a dry, gritty soil in full sun and does not enjoy wet weather in summer, which will cause it to dwindle. It is stoloniferous but the young bulbs will take some years to start flowering. Our large colony has only a scattering of flowers each year. Height: 20cm. There are many selections and cultivars with similar elegant flowers which seem to be more vigorous: var. *chrysantha* 🏆 comes from north Afghanistan. The flowers are deep yellow with the outer three being entirely red, without the usual lighter edge; **'Cynthia'** 🏆 has pale cream flowers with a red mark on the outer three petals; **'Sheila'** has small flowers that open pale yellow with a reddish exterior, the whole flower gradually deepening to apricot with age. **'Lady Jane'** 🏆 has large, elegant flowers of glistening ivory white, with the outer three petals stained clear pink on the outside. It is a tall, vigorous variety with attractive grey foliage. Height: 35cm.

Tulipa clusiana 'Cynthia'.

'Peppermintstick' 🏆 has similar flowers of a more intense colour, like a seaside stick of rock.

T. greigii

This tulip from Central Asia is one of the few that is instantly recognizable even out of flower as the broad grey-green leaves are vividly striped with purple. In the wild it grows on dry open hillsides, the large flowers varying in colour from scarlet to yellow, often with a darker mark on the petals. Although the species requires a dry summer dormancy and is best grown in a bulb frame, its cultivars make excellent garden flowers. Mid-season. Height: 25cm.

T. humilis

A well-known and popular tulip with up to three pale pink flowers and neat grey leaves. It comes from the mountains of east Turkey and north Iran and seems reasonably tolerant of our damp summers, growing well in a raised bed or trough. Early flowering. Height: 10cm. There are many similarly named clones with slightly differing shades of pink flowers. **'Liliput'** is a vigorous cultivar with clusters of well-shaped deep ruby pink flowers which open to reveal a striking blue base. The stunning dwarf ***T. humilis* var. *pulchella* 'Albocaerulea Oculata Group'** has a name that is almost larger than its tiny blue-based glistening white flowers. It can be grown outside in a trough or scree bed but is probably best protected in a pot. Height: 8cm.

T. kaufmanniana

The waterlily tulip comes from the Tien Shan mountains where it grows under trees or in open mountain meadows. In the wild it is rather variable but the basic colour is white or cream, more or less flushed with rose on the outer three petals. In Kazakhstan, where it grows alongside *T. greigii* with which it hybridizes, I have seen the occasional pure scarlet ones. It is earlier flowering than *T. greigii* and the large flower is more slender with plain, unmarked leaves. Although its cultivars are much brighter in colour this species has a quiet charm and is long lived in a sunny, free-draining soil.
Early flowering. Height: 20cm.

Tulipa greigii dotting the dry slopes in Kazakhstan.

Tulipa 'Albocaerulea Oculata'.

T. kolpakowskiana 🏆

The tulip in cultivation under this name is very similar in shape and colour to *T. clusiana chrysantha* with yellow flowers stained red on the outside. It does reasonably well in a well-drained gritty soil. Mid-season. Height: 18cm.

T. linifolia 🏆

This is one of the most dramatic of the dwarf tulips especially when the brilliant sealing wax red flowers open flat in the sun. The relatively

Tulipa kaufmanniana.

Tulipa linfolia.

Tulip 'Little Beauty'.

large flowers smother the plant. It grows well in gritty soil in a raised bed, or under a dwarf shrub. We tucked them in a huge tub of hostas, where they happily poke out through the variegated leaves as they first open. Late flowering. Height: 15cm. The vigorous **'Red Hunter'** 🏆 has similar rich red flowers of much substance.

T. linifolia Batalinii Group *(T. batalinii)*

This delightful pale primrose-yellow tulip was the first of the coloured forms of *T. linifolia* to be collected and described and until recently was treated as a separate species although it is almost certainly the albino form. It is rather delicate with small, creamy flowers. Sadly it is not long lived in the garden. The more vigorous and very long-lived **Batalinii Group** tulips are the result of crossing it with *T. linifolia*. They are among the best small tulips for the garden, being very perennial, the clumps increasing in size every year. They are perfect for a sunny rock garden (mine are still flowering well after nearly forty years), and they are very effective as an underplanting for peonies where their pale colour is a perfect foil for the purplish new growth of the peonies. **'Bright Gem'** 🏆 has golden yellow flowers, held only just above the leaves, gradually fading to an even yellow. It is very vigorous, increasing rapidly and flowering well. Height: 15cm. **'Apricot Jewel'** is slightly taller with neat yellow flowers that open suffused with rich apricot but, like all this group, they tend to fade with age to a uniform creamy yellow. We find this the best. Pots of seven bulbs that were used in our Chelsea Flower Show exhibits were planted out on our rock garden and now have more than twenty flowers. Height: 20cm.

Tulip 'Bright Gem'.

'Little Beauty' 🏆

This and the next are two outstanding new tulips with a complex parentage. Each bulb produces four to six flowers of rich pink with a dramatic blue base. It makes an excellent companion plant for the pink-flowered *Narcissus* 'Bellsong' in containers. Vigorous and increasing well, they can be naturalized with fritillaries in light grass under trees or are perfect for a sunny rock garden. Mid-season. Height: 10cm.

'Little Princess' 🏆

This is similar in appearance to 'Little Beauty' with masses of brick-red flowers, each with a conspicuous yellow-rimmed black centre. It increases well and is vigorous enough to be naturalized in light grass. Mid-season. Height: 10cm.

T. marjolettii

This small tulip is not known in the wild and may be of hybrid origin. It has neat flowers of classic tulip shape and stands up stiffly to attention in the garden like a miniature Darwin hybrid. The flowers are pale primrose yellow with the outer edges feathered

Tulip 'Little Princess'.

Tulipa marjoletti.

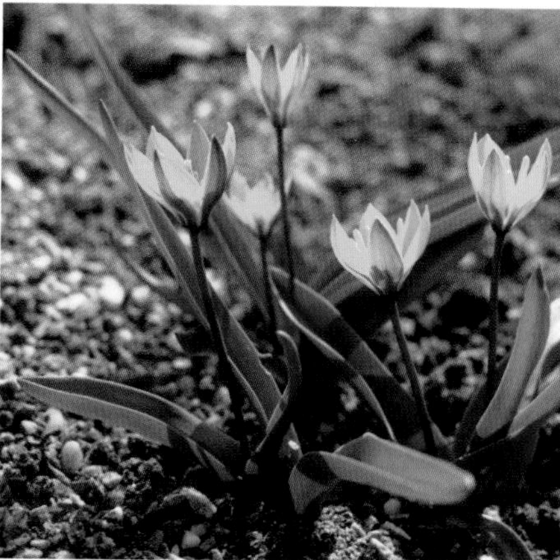
Tulipa neustruevae.

with red. It is perfect for small clumps on a large rock garden or the front of a sunny border. Late flowering. Height: 15cm.

T. neustruevae

Despite its tiny stature this little tulip increases well in a dry, gritty soil although bad weather will damage the flowers. It has an unfortunate habit of holding its small brown-backed golden flowers within the deep green leaves rather than above them but when growing well is utterly charming and is small enough for a trough. It is excellent under cold glass. Mid-season. Height: 8cm.

T. orphanidea

This yellowish-orange flowered tulip from eastern Europe is usually encountered in the more vigorous tetraploid form ***T. orphanidea* 'Whittallii Group'** (*T. whittallii*) 🏆 named after Edward Whittall, whose family traded in dried fruit in Smyrna and who caught the bulb bug and introduced many Turkish bulbs to cultivation. It has slightly nodding flowers of rich orange-red, the outer three tepals being stained greenish. It usually produces a single flower per stem but it may be multi-headed. It is very vigorous and if happy will spread by stolons but needs a dry summer to maintain vigour. It is a delightful weed in one of our tunnels where a rogue bulb has spread to form an impressive patch. Outside it is more reticent. Late flowering. Height: 30cm.

T. polychroma

Some confusion exists regarding the correct name of this plant, which is sometimes listed as a synonym of *T. biflora,* though it looks nothing like any *T. biflora* I have seen in the wild. The bulbs available under this name in commerce are very distinct with three or four large, round (rather than pointed) white flowers held above the clean glaucous foliage. Mid-season. Height: 10cm.

Tulipa whittallii.

T. praestans

The bulb of this tulip from Central Asia is unmistakable, being large and covered in a solid dark brown leathery tunic. Various collections have been given clonal names but all are multi-flowered with mid-sized, bright red flowers and stem-clasping leaves. Mid-season. Height: 15–25cm. **'Fusilier'** 🏆 is one of the best and most reliable of the smaller tulips with up to five blooms per stem.

Tulipa polychroma.

Tulipa saxatilis.

Tulipa sprengeri seeding in a sunny border.

It is very long lived in the garden, although the number of flowers per bulb tends to gradually decline each season, especially after damp summers. Although the light cream variegated leaves of 'Unicum' are not to every taste, this variety performs well.

T. saxatilis

This extremely vigorous, strongly stoloniferous tulip grows on rocky ledges in Crete where it spreads to form impressive patches. Given a similar well-drained position in the garden it is very long lived and can be almost too invasive, spreading in my garden from a handful of bulbs to a $2m^2$ patch of many thousands of bulbs over thirty years. One problem with this tulip is that its mass of bright green leaves appear in the autumn but it does not flower until mid-spring so it cannot really be mixed with any other bulbs. In any patch there will be a number of small non-flowering leaves. They need a well-drained position and patience but once growing well they are spectacular in flower. They can even be naturalized in grass under trees such as cherry although you must remember to cut the grass early in the autumn before the leaves appear or you will have to wait until the following May. The rather lax stems carry up to four pink flowers with a distinct bright yellow centre which is revealed when the flowers open flat in the sun. The flowers are a shade paler and taller than *T. bakeri* 'Lilac Wonder'. Mid-season. Height: 35cm.

T. sprengeri 🏆

This gem is the last tulip to flower and although it is one of the easiest to grow it is rather scarce in commerce. Unlike most tulips it increases by seed, which makes commercial production less easy and therefore less attractive. It is one of the most persistent of all species tulips. Self-sown seedlings seem to perform best and it is tolerant of a range of conditions, but possibly preferring soil that is not too dry, even cropping up in the middle of a clump of hostas. It is as happy in part shade as it is on my sunny rock garden. It originated in north Turkey but is thought to be extinct in the wild. The slender flowers are a brilliant orange-red with biscuit-backed outer petals and narrow, stem-clasping green leaves. Very late – the last to flower. Height: 30cm.

Tulipa sylvestris.

Tulipa tarda.

Tulipa turkestanica.

T. sylvestris

This distinctive tulip has been in cultivation throughout Europe, the Middle East, Central Asia and North Africa for many centuries where it is naturalized in cultivated or waste ground. There is uncertainty over whether it is a British native, although there are some extensive and apparently ancient colonies, but these only produce a handful of flowers in a normal summer. It is very variable but the plant in commerce is a stoloniferous form with large lemon-yellow flowers, stained green on the back, at the top of slender stems. The buds nod at first, gradually turning upright as the flower opens. The tips of the petals often reflex back, even from half-open flowers. Although it is called the 'wood' tulip it flowers best in an open, sunny position and after warm summers, preferring the fertile soil of a border to grass. In cooler, shadier sites there may only be a scattering of flowers among the mass of slender leaves. It prefers a continental climate. Mid-season. Height: 40cm.

T. tarda 🏆

This is an easy dwarf tulip for a well-drained soil on a rock garden or the front of a sunny border. It is perfect to mass in a dry bed under a wall with bulbs such as nerine or sternbergia or the winter-flowering *Iris unguicularis*, which like similar warm conditions. The narrow, bright green leaves make a rosette on the ground with up to eight small flowers clustered in the centre. The open, starry flowers are white but the central bright yellow mark extends almost to the tips of the petals so that they appear to be almost entirely yellow. It is perfect for containers, *Muscari* 'Blue Spike' being a good companion bulb. Late flowering. Height: 10cm.

T. turkestanica 🏆

This Central Asian tulip is very variable in the wild but is always a very dwarf tulip with one to three small flowers. The clone in commerce is very vigorous with up to ten small, starry flowers per stem and two narrow basal leaves, and is almost certainly a form of *T. bifloriformis*, not *T. turkestanica*. The buds are a dull greyish-green but in the sun they open wide to reveal a pyramid of bright, creamy white flowers, each with pointed petals and a bold yellow centre. It is rather straggling in overall appearance but is vigorous and long lived in a sunny border, flowering remarkably early, often accompanying *iris reticulata*. It makes a surprising companion for late snowdrops, cyclamen, *hederifolium* leaves and small ferns on the sunny side of the canopy of a large tree. Early flowering. Height: 30cm.

T. urumiensis

This well-known bulb is similar to *T. tarda* but with flowers that are entirely yellow. It requires a hot summer to persist in the open garden. It is an excellent subject for a pot, mixed with small daffodils and blue grape hyacinths. Late flowering. Height: 10cm.

Tulipa urumiensis.

Single Tulips

Early (1)

This is a group of tulips with classic, elegantly shaped flowers on relatively short stems. These gradually elongate from 30–45cm and the flowers are very long lasting. They are the first of the standard tulips to flower and are invaluable for pots or the front of the border. **'Apricot Beauty'** 🏆 is the classic tulip for containers with well-shaped flowers of soft pinkish apricot; **'Christmas Dream'** is a deep rose pink with slightly paler edges to the petals; **'Candy Prince'** is a soft bluish lilac; **'Prins Carnaval'** 🏆 is yellow, flamed red.

Triumph (3)

These are the result of crossing early tulips with late-flowering varieties to produce vigorous mid-season tulips which are perfect for borders or bedding. This is by far the largest group of tulips and I have given only a tiny selection. They vary in height from 30–60cm.

White

'Wildhof' 🏆 (45cm) and **'White Dream'** (35cm) have well-formed white flowers. **'Calgary'** 🏆 and **'Don Quichotte'** 🏆 are very short with well-shaped white flowers, perfect for pots. Height: 20cm. **'Shirley'** is one of the best-known tulips. The white flowers are delicately edged in purple and they have a dusting of small purple spots. Height: 60cm.

Tulip 'Couleur Cardinal'.

Tulip 'White Dream'.

Tulip 'Apricot Beauty'.

Yellow

'Yellow Flight' has good shaped flowers of a clear yellow with a paler edge to the petals. Height: 35cm. **'Sunny Prince'** is a sport of 'Purple Prince' and has large, clear lemon flowers on short stems which gradually lengthen. It is excellent in pots with grape hyacinths; I have used it to cheer up a patch of Spanish bluebells round the base of a birch tree. Height: 35cm.

Tulip 'Yellow Flight'.

Tulip 'Abu Hassan'.

Red/Orange

'Couleur Cardinal' has dramatic red flowers with a purplish bloom on the outside and dark-hued leaves. Being compact they are perfect for pots or the front of a border. I mass them with 'Prinses Irene' and 'Rococo' under a bronze-hued *Amelanchier*. Height: 30cm. **'Prinses Irene'** (Princess Irene) 🏆 is of similar stature and has rich orange flowers suffused with mahogany red on short, very stiff stems. Height: 30cm. **'Fidelio'** 🏆 is a rich salmon with deep rose shading on the outer petals. Height: 45cm. **'National Velvet'** 🏆 has flowers of an intense burnt crimson. Height: 40cm. **'Abu Hassan'** has flowers of a bronze-red and is a perfect foil for gold wallflowers or polyanthus. Height: 45cm.

Pink/Purple

'Ronaldo' has intense purple, almost black flowers that are the perfect companion plant for the purplish new foliage of many roses. It is exceptionally long lasting. Height: 45cm. **'Purple Prince'** is indispensable for pots or early bedding with long-lasting rich purple flowers on short stems. Height: 30cm. **'Purple Flag'** is similar. Height: 45cm. **'Attila'** has well-shaped flowers of an even violet. Height: 50cm. **'Passionale'** 🏆 is a rich pinkish purple and good in pots. Height: 40cm. **'Valentine'** is a soft rose with paler edges to the petals. Height: 40cm.

Tulip 'Helmar'.

Multi-coloured

Many of this group have strongly contrasting marking in two or more colours. **'Gavota'** 🏆 has deep, almost brownish, red flowers with a crisp yellow rim to the petals. At first glance this tulip appears to be in the wrong section as the flowers are slightly lily-flowered in shape, the yellow rim exaggerating this impression. Height: 45cm. **'Helmar'** is a dramatic mix of strong yellow with red feathering. **'Jackpot'** is white with violet feathers. **'Grand Perfection'** looks like an escapee from a Dutch Old Master painting with blood-red feathering on the white flowers. Height: 40cm. **'Hot Pants'** is a clear violet with a bold white central stripe. Height: 50cm.

Tulip 'Purple Prince'.

Tulip 'Hemisphere'.

'Hemisphere' looks as though it was painted by Seurat and saves you the problem of buying a mix. It varies from pinkish red suffused with tiny white spots to white with a haze of red spots and every shade in between. No two flowers are identical. They are best planted in bold drifts. Height: 45cm.

Darwin Hybrid (4)

These tulips have classic large bowl-shaped flowers on tall, stiff stems. They flower mid- to late season. Although they are too tall for all but the largest containers they are perfect to add to a border, being vigorous and long lived. Height: 45–60cm.

White

'Ivory Floradale' 🏆 has large, creamy-white flowers more or less specked with rose.

Yellow/Orange

'Daydream' 🏆 is a clear yellow that darkens to apricot with age. **'Olympic Flame'** 🏆 has large flowers of clear yellow and bold red feathering. We have grown it in a border clustered round the base of a small tree for many years without any diminution of its flower size or number. **'Gudoschnik'** has a similar colour combination but in each flower the feathering is very variable. **'Golden Apeldoorn'** has large, clear yellow flowers with a black base. **'Apeldoorn Elite'** 🏆 is the same intense yellow but shaded with orange-red on the outside.

Tulip 'Olympic Flame'.

Tulip 'Ivory Floradale'.

Tulip 'Golden Apeldoorn'.

Red

'Apeldoorn' has the perfect neat bowl shape with a bold black base. It is the classic red tulip that is seen in so many gardens. It is long lived, the flowers just reducing in size after the first year. **'Red Impression'** 🏆 is a very similar, more modern cultivar, which is probably more vigorous. **'Parade'** 🏆 has deep crimson pointed flowers; **'Big Chief'** 🏆 has neat rose-red flowers on sturdy stems; **'Holland's Glory'** 🏆 is another classic red tulip; **'World's Favourite'** 🏆 is clear red with a yellow edge.

Tulip 'Apeldoorn'.

Tulip 'Menton'.

Tulip 'Pink Diamond'.

Pink
'Pink Impression' is pale rose with a deeper central band. **'Ollioules'** 🏆 is pale pink with a deep pink stripe on each petal.

Single Late (Darwin and Cottage) (5)

These are the standard roundabout tulips whose stiff stems and bright colours are often seen rising above a sea of wallflowers or forget-me-nots. The flowers tend to be compact and smaller than many. They are the last to flower. Height: 50–60cm.

White
'Maureen' 🏆 is probably the best of the late white-flowered tulips. **'Alabaster'** is similar. **'Sorbet'** 🏆 is white with rose feathering.

Tulip 'Queen of the Night'.

Tulip 'Recreado'.

Yellow
'Mrs John T. Scheepers' 🏆 has elegant canary yellow pointed flowers but is sadly no longer available. **'Roi du Midi'** is a good alternative. **'Sweet Harmony'** 🏆 has soft yellow flowers with a cream edge to the petals. **'World Expression'** 🏆 opens yellow but gradually fades to a uniform cream with a red base and feathering. It is long lasting. **'Big Smile'** and **'Helmar'** – yellow and red.

Orange/Red
'Temple of Beauty' 🏆 has exceptionally large salmon-red flowers. **'Menton'** 🏆 is a subtle mix of pink with orange tones on the outside. **'Dordogne'** 🏆 is a sport of it with similar colouring.

Pink/Purple
'Pink Diamond' is rose with paler edges; **'Recreado'** is a rich purple; **'Rems Favourite'** is purple and white and one of the best to add a touch of drama to a border; **'Queen of Night'** is still the darkest of the tulips although the flowers are relatively small. It is such an intense dark plum-violet it is best planted with paler tulips. **'Bleu Aimable'** is a soft lavender mauve.

Tulip 'Rems Favourite'.

Multi-flowered Tulips

These are a relatively new and distinct group of tulips with three to six heads per stem. They are very good as a bedding variety or in containers. They are sports from other groups and are listed here for convenience as they do not have their own section as yet. Height: 45–50cm.

'Weisse Berliner' has two or three heads of creamy-white flowers giving a bold display. **'White Bouquet'** is similar. **'Orange Bouquet'** 🏆 has up to four clear orange flowers. **'Georgette'** has up to four pointed flowers of pale yellow with a striking red feathered edge. **'Red Georgette'** 🏆 has up to four flowers of clear red. **'Happy Family'** has three to four heads of deep pink with paler margins to the petals.

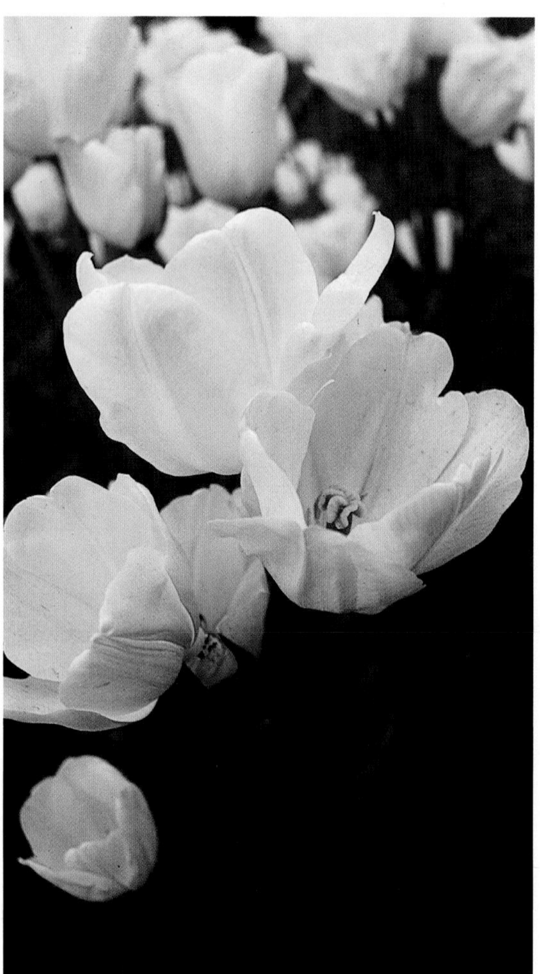

The multi-flowered tulip 'Weisse Berliner'.

The classic open flowers of the double early tulip 'Monte Carlo'.

Double Tulips

Double Early (2)

These tulips have 'fat' flowers that gradually open wide to reveal a rather muddled centre that is more or less filled with smaller petals. They are exceptionally long lasting and make an ideal subject for containers. Most are 40–45cm tall.

'Cardinal Mindszenty' is white flowered; **'Monte Carlo'** 🏆 has very compact double flowers of bright yellow, and is long lasting and scented. **'Oranje Nassau'** 🏆 is a dramatic mix of orange and cherry-red and very dwarf. Height: 25cm. **'Montreux'** is an unusual combination of delicate creamy yellow with a pink tinge; **'Carlton'** is a deep carmine; **'Garanza'** is strong cherry pink; **'Double Dazzle'** has very large flowers of rich purple; **'David Teniers'** is deep ruby red; **'Peach blossom'** is true pink.

Tulip 'Montreux'.

Double Late (11) (peony tulips)

These are more fully double and cup-shaped, and are sometimes called peony-flowered tulips. The flowers can be a little too heavy and fall over in an exposed situation. Height: 40–45cm.

White

'Mount Tacoma' has pure white flowers with a greenish outside. It is excellent both for pots and bedding, standing up well in a border.

Yellow/Orange/Red

'Yellow Mountain' has very large blooms of a clear yellow. **'Orange Princess'** 🏆 is a sport of **'Prinses Irene'** with similar mix of rich orange and flame red. **'Golden Nizza'** is a similar shape to **'Carnaval de Nice'** but the base colour is yellow. **'Uncle Tom'** is deep blood red.

Pink/Purple

'Angélique' 🏆 is a very popular bedding variety. It is compact and in shades of pink deepening with age with a cream centre. **'Drumline'** 🏆 is the perfect peony shape with blood red petals that merge from pink to white. **'Carnaval de Nice'** 🏆 has a similar colouring with beautifully shaped flowers with incurved petals. They are white flamed with raspberry red. It has a narrow white edge to the leaves. **'May Wonder'** 🏆 has very full flowers of a rich deep pink. **'Antraciet'** is a deep purplish-red. **'Black Hero'** has fully double flowers of intense purple. **'Ice Cream'** is one of those new varieties that you either love or hate: it has a pointed mound of white petals arising out of a deep raspberry-red and green cone formed by the outer petals and in bud is just like a vanilla ice cream cone! It is more of a curiosity than a thing of beauty to my mind. **'Horizon'** has the same strong colouring but in a classic peony tulip shape.

Tulip 'Orange Princess'.

Tulip 'Mount Tacomoa' with muscari.

Tulip 'Drumline'.

Tulip 'White Triumphator' with peonies.

Lily-flowered (6)

These elegant tulips have the distinctive vase shape of the early oriental tulips seen on Iznik tiles. They are slender in outline and the tips of the petals are strongly recurved even when they are closed. They are mid-season and are an excellent all-round tulip for massed planting or grouping in borders. Most of them are too tall for all but the largest containers. They all flower at the same time and can be combined. Height: 50–70cm.

White

'White Triumphator' 🏆 is still the best white; the perfect bedding tulip. I use it with peonies in my parterre. At dusk they are almost luminous, hovering above the box hedges. **'Elegant Lady'** is creamy white with a narrow violet edge which spreads over the petals as a smattering of spots. **'Marilyn'** is pure white with a bright cerise flash on each petal. **'Holland Chic'** is similar but the flash is pale rose.

Yellow

'West Point' is well known and not too tall with deep-yellow flowers but is prone to tulip fire. The more vigorous **'Moonlight Girl'** 🏆 is a good alternative with paler lemon-yellow flowers. **'Sapporo'** is shorter than many and has pale lemon flowers with a blue base which fades to cream as it ages. **'Mona Lisa'** is clear yellow with a rose red flash on slender flowers.

Tulip 'West Point' with 'Queen of the Night'.

Tulip 'Burgundy'.

Tulip 'Aladdin's Record'.

Orange/Red

'Aladdin's Record' has slender flowers in a strong orange-red with a yellow edge to the petal. It is a good replacement for 'Queen of Sheba', which is no longer available. **'Synaeda King'** 🏆 is similar. **'Ballerina'** 🏆 is probably the best orange tulip. It doesn't seem to matter where you plant it; I find it particularly useful to lighten a dark corner. It is strongly-scented. **'Red Shine'** 🏆 has long-lasting flowers of an intense true red. The flowers open to reveal a striking blue base. **'Lily Fire'** is deep apricot gold shading to orange at the edges.

Pink/Purple

'Ballade' 🏆 is purple-pink with a neat white rim; **'Burgundy'** is deep reddish purple and an old favourite; **'China Pink'** 🏆 is a true pink but can be a weak grower; **'Marietta'** has an elegant shape and is a strong salmon pink. It is tall and very long lasting. **'Jonina'** is a very distinctive variety of soft salmon pink shading to paler pink at the edges and with a blue base. It is shorter than most and good in containers.

Tulip 'Burgundy Lance'.

Fringed (7)

The upper edges of the petals are strikingly dissected as though they had been shredded by a strong wind. They are vigorous and long lived and make excellent cut flowers. Height: 45–60cm.

White

'Honeymoon' is a compact variety with heavily frilled pure white, rather fat flowers. **'Swan Wings'** is similar; **'Aria Card'** has neat white flowers with an extravagant pink fringe.

Yellow/Orange

'Hamilton' 🏆 has neat, strong yellow flowers delicately frilled, and stands well; **'Maya'** is a paler shade. **'Lambada'**: the deep red centre of the petals fades

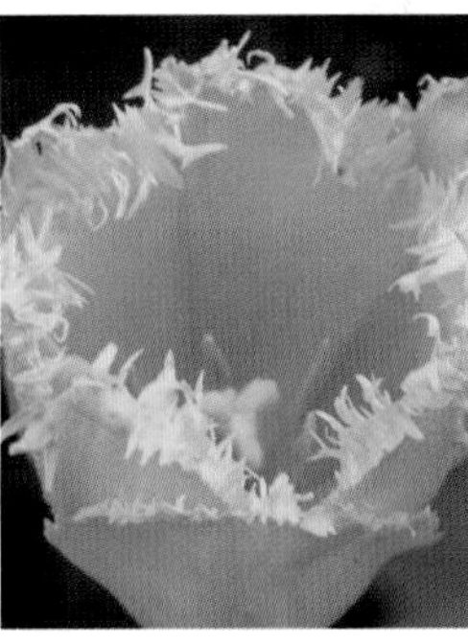

Tulip 'Hamilton'.

Tulip 'Sensual Touch'.

Tulip 'Red Hat'.

through salmon to an apricot orange edge and frill; **'Sensual Touch'** 🏆 is one of a new group of double fringed tulips. It is a mix of apricot, orange and yellow.

Red

'Barbados' has rather open glowing crimson flowers with neat fringed edges; **'Red Hat'** has neat, deep-red flowers shaded purple on the outside; **'Davenport'** has neat red flowers with a bold yellow fringe.

Pink/Purple

'Blue Heron' is deep violet, shading to lilac at the edges. **'Burgundy Lace'** is the colour of a good red wine. It has proved to be very long lived in our border where it is especially fine in front of a blue *Centauria* and the purple of honesty flowers. **'Fancy Frills'** 🏆 is a delicate mix of rose and pale pink which opens to a white inside. It is heavily fringed. **'Fringed Beauty'** is pink with a white base. **'Cummins'** is a unique shade of lavender-mauve with a creamy-white frill.

Tulip 'Cummins'.

Viridiflora (8)

Apart from the prominent green band up the middle of each petal this is a very variable group. They are late flowering and long lasting, opening predominantly green with the base colour only gradually appearing. They are very variable in height: 40–50cm.

'Spring Green' 🏆 is the classic viridiflora tulip with elegant flowers of creamy white. It is good planted in clumps in a border or among the spikes of variegated iris. **'Flaming Spring Green'** 🏆 is a sport of 'Spring Green' where tongues of scarlet have been added to each petal. **'Yellow Spring Green'** has citrus yellow flowers which contrast well with the bright green stripe. **'Red Spring Green'** has neat red flowers with only subtle green shading. **'Groenland'** opens with an overall greenish cast. The petals then gradually turn pink. It is exceptionally long lasting and mixes well with pink lily-flowered tulips.

'Artist' 🏆 is a short flowered variety with flowers in a curious mix of salmon and rose. The green band is lighter than in most of this group. **'China Town'** 🏆 has short, pale pink and green flowers with white margins to the leaves. **'Esperanto'** 🏆 is similar but the colour is a deep rose.

Tulip 'Spring Green' with *Euphorbia polychroma*.

Tulip 'Flaming Spring Green'.

Tulip 'Groenland'.

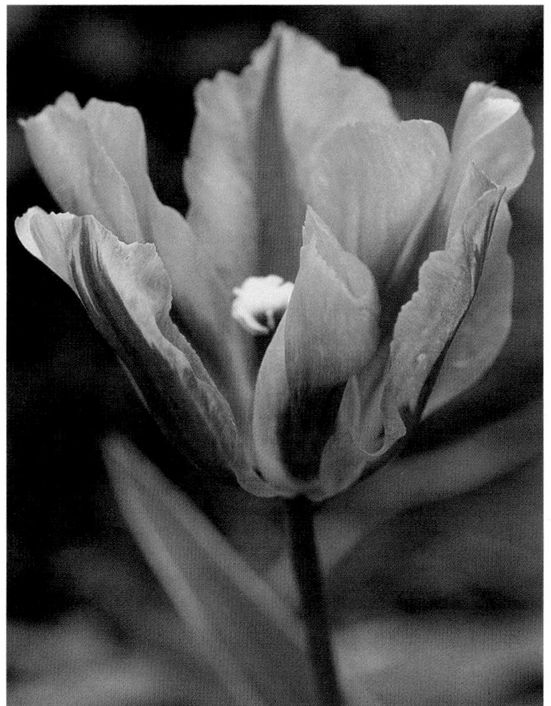
Tulip 'Esperanto'.

Rembrandt (9)

This is the best known of the classification groups. These are the exotic tulips seen bursting from Old Master paintings of flowers: extravagantly striped and mottled in wild colours. Tulips are genetically unstable, regularly 'sporting' (mutating) to give another colour form of the same variety (hence all the related names like Apeldoorn, Golden Apeldoorn, Apeldoorn Elite, etc.). Therefore these exotic colour 'breaks' were seen as natural and greatly prized. What had not been realized until relatively recently is that this attractive marbling was the result of a virus – they are basically diseased! For a while they were sold in mixes until the growers realized that the virus was infecting other stocks and they have now all been destroyed. However, their form lives on in modern, healthy striped varieties found in other groups such as 'Rems Favourite' and 'Helmar' and groups of these are sometimes sold as Rembrandt tulips. The English Florist tulip gives us an idea of what they looked like in their prime.

THE ENGLISH FLORIST TULIP

Since the introduction of the tulip into western Europe in the sixteenth century, people have been fascinated by its ability to transform itself from a flower of a single colour to one with magical markings. Now known to be caused by Tulip Breaking Virus, affected bulbs changed hands for enormous sums in Holland during 'Tulipomania' in the first part of the seventeenth century.

In the United Kingdom, enthusiasts, given the name Florists, bred new varieties and held over a hundred competitive flower shows annually in inns and public houses throughout the UK in the nineteenth century. Standards were set with three different colour groups: bizarres with a yellow base, roses with a white base and pink/red colouring, and bybloemens with a white base and lilac to purple colouring. Only the best marked flowers received approval.

Since 1936, the Wakefield and North of England Tulip Society has been the last UK's remaining tulip society. In 2010 it held its 175th annual show, never having missed a year even during the two world wars.

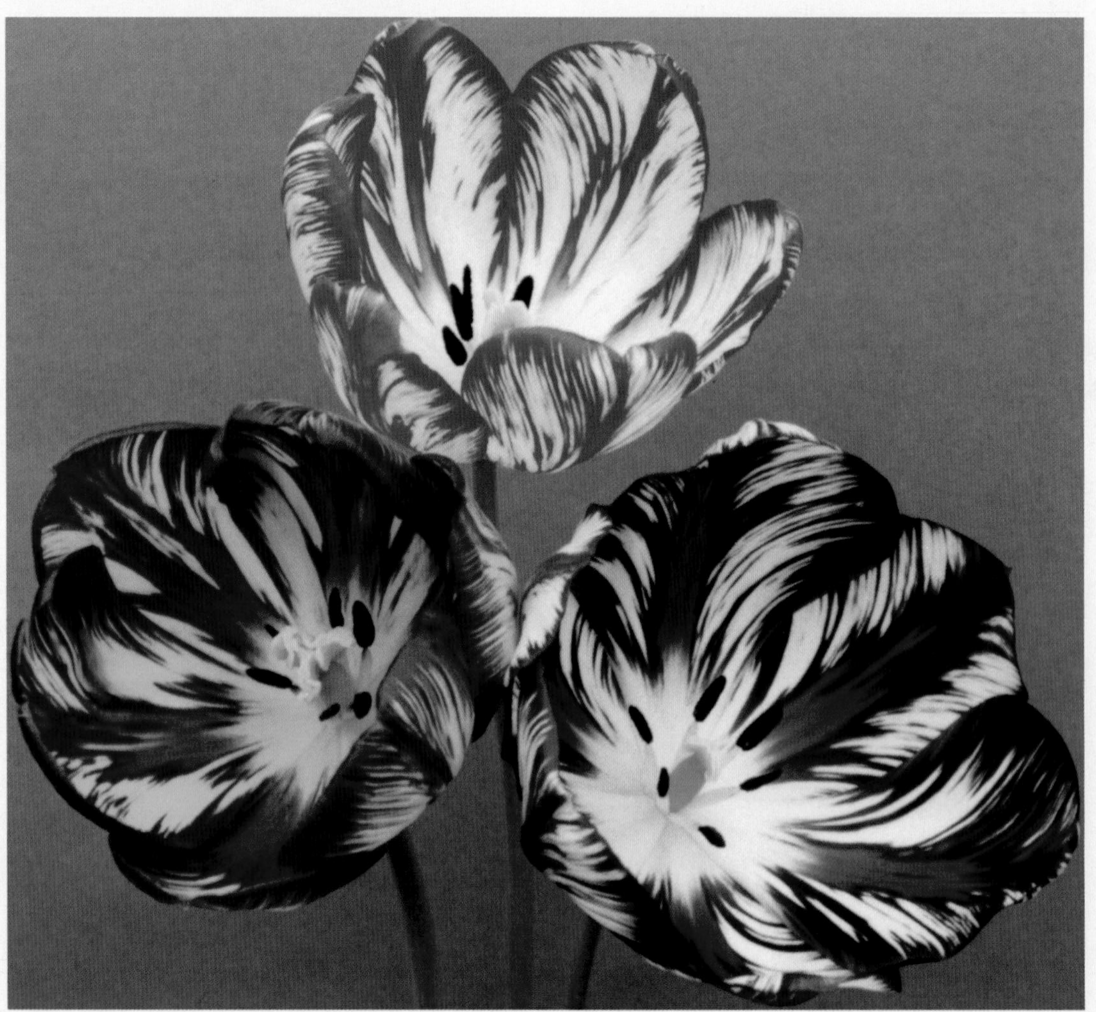

English Florist Tulips. *(Courtesy of Wakefield Tulip Society)*

Parrot (10)

The margins of the petals of this group are twisted and distorted ('laciniated' is the correct term) in an often amazing manner, resulting in some quite extraordinary outlines. The flowers usually open flat with age. Height: 40–50cm.

'Apricot Parrot' 🏆 is a subtle mix of apricot, cream and rose; **'Black Parrot'** 🏆 is such a very dark purple-black that it needs a paler colour to show it up; **'Fantasy'** 🏆 is less distorted than some and has pink flowers with green feathering; **'Blue Parrot'** is a clear violet-blue. **'Estella Rijnveldt'** is less distorted than many, and the white flowers are flamed with deep red; **'Flaming Parrot'** is a wild mix of yellow and red; **'Rococo'** is a sport of 'Couleur Cardinal' and has similar purple flushed red flowers with green veining on short stems. I mix it with 'Prinses Irene' for a very dramatic and long-lasting pot. **'White Parrot'** has pure white flowers and complements 'Black Parrot' perfectly. **'Silver Parrot'** is a gentle mix of pale pink, lilac and white with white-edged leaves.

Tulip 'Apricot Parrot'.

Tulip 'Flaming Parrot'.

Tulip 'Silver Parrot'.

Tulip 'Rococo'.

Kaufmanniana tulip cultivars.

Kaufmanniana (12)

These colourful dwarf tulips are bred from *T. kaufmanniana*, *T. greigii* and *T. fosteriana* and have large heads on short stems which nestle just above the broad grey-green leaves. They are early flowering, often as the snowdrops fade, and are perfect for pots or edging. Known as the 'water lily tulips', they open flat in the sun to reveal a striking central mark. Most have strong colours, often with a contrasting shade down the centre of the outer petals, and are long lived in a dry, sunny position. The flower size will reduce over time but they are still attractive. Height: 15–20cm.

Tulip 'Heart's Delight'.

White

'Ancilla' 🏆 has white flowers with a soft pink shading on the outside which open wide to reveal glistening white inside with a yellow centre bordered by red. It is

Tulip 'Ancilla'.

Tulip 'Stresa' with Narcissus 'Jumblie'.

excellent in pots. **'Heart's Delight'** has slender white flowers heavily suffused with rose which open wide to reveal a pure white interior. It has grown happily with *Anemone blanda* on our dry rock garden for many years.

Yellow

'Stresa' 🏆 has round, golden yellow flowers with a neat red flame up the centre of each petal. I grow it in pots mixed with *Narcissus* 'Tête-à-Tête' and *Anemone blanda*. **'Early Harvest'** 🏆 is a similar yellow with red markings on the outside. The inside is stained orange.

Red

'Shakespeare' 🏆 is a blend of salmon, apricot and orange. It is paler inside than out. **'Alfred Cortot'** 🏆 has elegant flowers in shades of scarlet. **'Showwinner'** 🏆 has large flowers of glowing red which open wide to reveal a yellow base. **'Pink Dwarf'** is magenta with a paler inside.

Fosteriana (13)

This group of early-flowering tulips has distinctive broad grey leaves and large well-shaped flowers in shades of white, red and yellow. They vary in height from 20–45cm and flower before most of the other large hybrids. They are excellent for borders where they are long lived especially tucked in among iris or similar sun lovers at the base of pleached fruit trees on a sunny wall. The shorter varieties are ideal for containers.

White

'Purissima' 🏆 (White Emperor) opens primrose and gradually fades to pure white. At 45cm it is the perfect choice for an early display. They are very long lived in the garden, surviving for many years in my herbaceous border where they are particularly good with yellow and white hyacinths. I actually plant them in the same hole – the tulips at 20cm deep with the hyacinths above them at 12cm. **'Concerto'** is a short creamy white with large flowers that open flat in the sun. Height: 30cm. **'Flaming Purissima'** has cream flowers heavily feathered in rose. Height: 45cm. **'Exotic Emperor'** is one of the new tulips that defies the classification

Tulip 'Purissima'.

Tulip 'Concerto'.

Tulip 'Orange Emperor'.

system: it is a semi-double white and green and is a mix of 'Spring Green' with 'Purissima'.

Yellow/Orange

'Candela' (Yellow Emperor) 🏆 is a rich, egg-yolk yellow. Height: 45cm. **'Sweetheart'** has white-edged lemon yellow flowers. Height: 45cm.

'Yellow Purissima' 🏆 is a pale canary yellow. Height: 45cm. **'Orange Emperor'** 🏆 has large, well-shaped orange flowers. Height: 45cm.

Red

'Juan' 🏆 is orange-red with a yellow base. Height: 40cm. **'Pirand'** 🏆 is scarlet with a bold white edge to the petals. Height: 40cm. **'Princeps'** is very dwarf with red flowers. It is ideal for pots. Height: 25cm. **'Madame Lefeber'** was formerly known as 'Red Emperor' before she underwent a sex change and was demoted. As the old name implies it has a large scarlet flower. At the same height and flowering at a similar time, it is the perfect companion for 'Purissima' for a bold and dramatic planting of scarlet and white.

Tulip 'Juan'.

Tulips 'Purissima', 'Madame Lefeber', and 'Pinocchio' with white hyacinths.

Greigii (14)

These share the same genetic mix as the Kaufmanniana hybrids (12) and have similar large flowers on short stems in shades of red and yellow but are much later flowering. Most of their leaves are beautifully striped with maroon. They make perfect subjects for containers, as attractive out of flower as in. Height: 25–35cm.

White/Pink

'Albion Star' is a multi-headed variety with pink, flushed white, flowers. **'Addis'** 🏆 is pale apricot with red tips to the petals. **'Czar Peter'** 🏆 has white flowers heavily splashed with rose.

Yellow

'Buttercup' 🏆 is compact with yellow flowers, each with a pale orange mark on the outer petals. **'Cape Cod'** is very distinct. The flowers are yellow with a red flame which appears as a stripe on the inner petals when it opens wide. **'Easter Surprise'** 🏆 is lemon yellow with a bronze flush. **'Oriental Splendour'** 🏆 has a rose-red flame up each petal and a pale yellow edge. The base is black.

Red

'Red Riding Hood' 🏆 is probably the best known of this group with good red flowers and well-marked leaves. Virtually indistinguishable from the species, **'Pinocchio'** has long red flowers with a narrow white edge, and is a good choice for pots. In **'Plaisir'** 🏆 the outer colouring of red edged with cream is repeated on the inner petals. It is a very dramatic variety. **'Princess Charmante'** 🏆 is a clear red. **'Toronto'** 🏆 is multi-headed with pinkish-red flowers.

Tulip 'Pinocchio'.

CHAPTER 4

BULBS FOR THE SUMMER

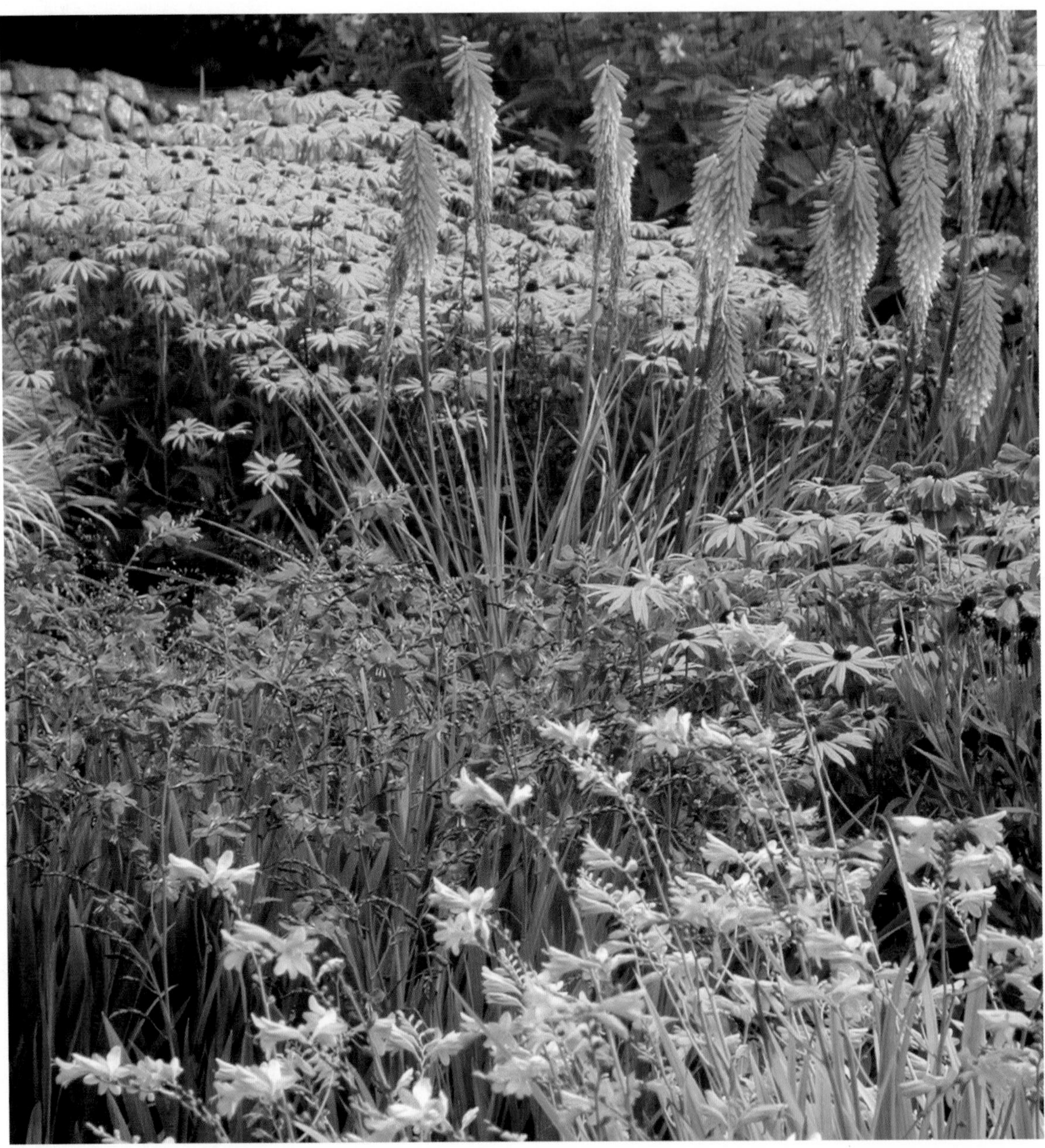

Clumps of Crocosmia add colour to a late summer border.

Although most gardeners associate bulbs with spring, a remarkable number do flower during the summer months. Early in summer there are those that fill that awkward gap between late spring and early summer when the spring bulbs finish flowering and the garden has a temporary green hiatus before the herbaceous plants really begin their display. Early alliums and camassias are especially useful here as they start flowering just as the last of the true spring bulbs like tulips fade, thus maintaining an unbroken display.

Later on, in the height of summer, bulbs must compete with the more exuberant herbaceous perennials and tend to be overlooked. However, although they might not be the star turn, as their flowering period is often relatively brief compared to that of a herbaceous perennial, used carefully they can certainly add impact. Many, such as camassias, gladioli, galtonias and some lilies, produce their flowers along an erect spike which are a good foil for the often flat-headed mounds of herbaceous perennials. To be most effective these should be planted towards the middle or front of the border, so that they can rise through and above the border herbaceous, rather than at the back as might be indicated by their ultimate flowering height. Their dying stems can then be easily removed.

Many summer-flowering bulbs come from areas where moisture is only available in the spring, which is when they produce their leaves; they then delay flowering until the temperature rises so that the seeds can be dispersed under dry conditions. Consequently these bulbs have fading foliage at the same time as their flowers are at their peak, but planted in the middle of a border these unattractive leaves are hidden by other plants.

One other problem encountered by gardeners is balancing the water requirements of the herbaceous plants with the need for a dry dormancy for some early summer-flowering bulbs like alliums. The overhanging foliage of the neighbouring plants may give them sufficient dryness under normal conditions but some automatic watering systems like trickle hoses, which deliver water to the roots, may induce rot in the dormant bulbs. If this is a problem they may need to be grown in another part of the garden. Alliums associate particularly well with ornamental grasses that like similar open sunny and dry conditions. Lilies on the other hand revel in a constant availability of moisture. Excessive dryness is more likely to be a problem with them, inducing blindness and premature die-back.

Many of the most colourful summer-flowering bulbs, such as dahlias and the large-flowered gladiolus, are excluded from this book as they are not reliably hardy.

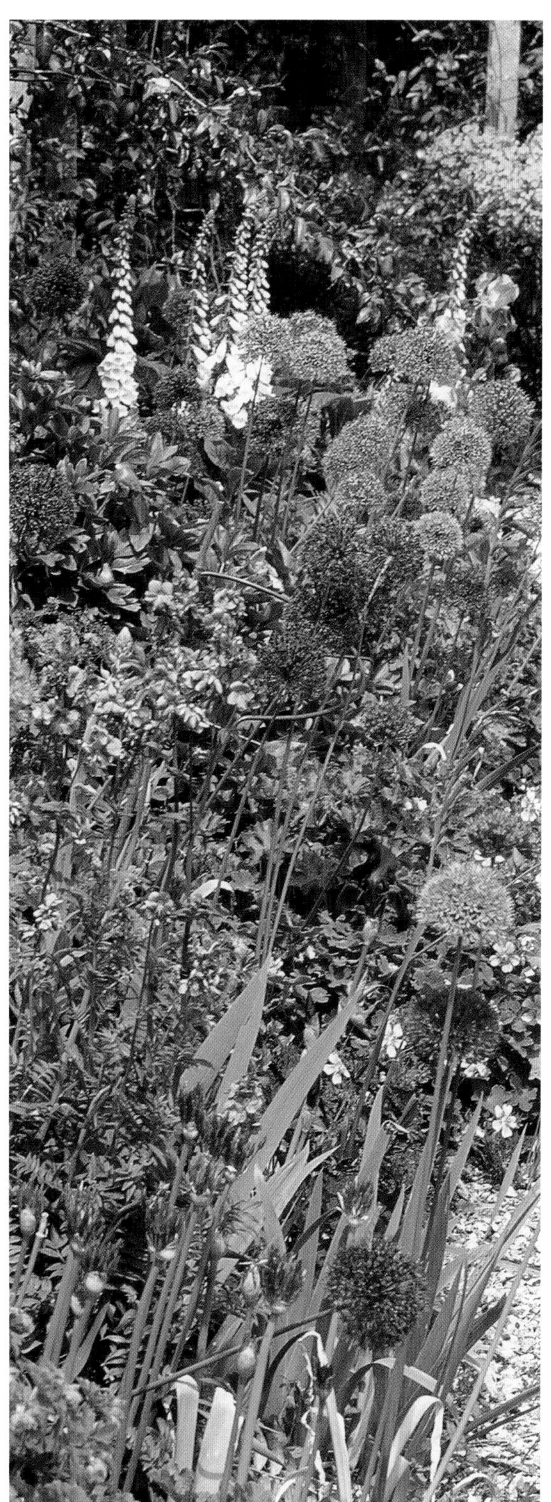

Drumstick alliums in early summer.

Allium
(ornamental onion)

The tall drumstick alliums are synonymous with early summer, when their tight purple pompom heads on tall stems dominate many sunny borders. But although these are the most dramatic and well-known members of the onion family it is an extremely variable genus, varying in size, shape, height and flowering time. It is possible to have an allium in flower throughout summer to early autumn.

In a sunny border the tulips will segue without a break into the tall alliums. Their season starts with the soft purple *A. × hollandicum* (often encountered under the species name *A. aflatunense* but it has been in cultivation for so long it is almost certainly of hybrid origin) and its rich purple form, 'Purple Sensation'. These are perfect massed in a border where the first flowers will coincide with late tulips such as 'Burgundy Lace' or 'Groenland'. Alliums will then continue to flower throughout May into June and are excellent with early-flowering perennials such as blue polemonium and the feathery purple flowers of *Thalictrum aquilegifolium* or planted among ornamental grasses. Shorter midsummer-flowering species can be tucked in along the front of a sunny border or used to add colour to rock gardens or raised beds.

The onion family contains over 700 species and is amazingly disparate with plants varying in height from a few centimetres to well over a metre. They are primarily found in dry mountainous areas of the northern hemisphere. Many, but not all, allium species have a classic round bulb which varies in size from 1–12cm in diameter. Each bulb produces a single flower head. Others have an elongated bulb attached to a fleshy rhizome and are clump-forming and are virtually evergreen, e.g. chives. The flowers of an allium are held in a cluster called an umbel on the top of a leafless stem. The umbel can be few- or many-flowered, round, flat or nodding. The basal leaves are usually long and strap shaped; some are cylindrical, thread-like and stem clasping; a few have broad, short leaves.

The drumstick alliums are native to dry areas of the Middle East. They naturally produce their fleshy leaves early in spring when there is ample water, then, as the water dries up in early summer, so the leaves fade and the flowers appear ready for seed dispersal during the dry summer months. This is the natural appearance of the bulbs but it can cause a headache for the gardener as the dying leaves are very unsightly. However, they

Allium 'Ambassador' in a dry border with grasses and Iris sibrica.

can be successfully hidden behind later-flowering herbaceous perennials. Low mound-forming plants like geraniums and astrantia are good companions. Alliums are perfect for adding colour to a bed of grasses as both like the same dry sunny conditions, or for planting in bold swathes through box parterres. They are also at home in the modern prairie-style plantings. It is best to avoid borders that have irrigation systems as the bulbs can easily rot after flowering if they are too wet, although it is possible to treat them as annuals and replace the bulbs each autumn. As with their height, so there is considerable disparity in the size of their flower heads, from 2–35cm. Contrary to intuition, those with the largest heads are always on shorter stems. (This is not really surprising as they are natives of exposed steppes where there is a danger that, if they were on taller stems, the wind might blow the heads over before the seeds were ripe.) The species usually have rather open, sparsely flowered heads but there are now many cultivars and hybrids with longer-lasting, much denser heads of flowers.

One of the joys of the drumstick alliums is their seed heads. These will remain on the plant provided that it is not too windy, gradually fading to a soft khaki regardless of their initial colour. Alternatively the heads can be cut and dried or sprayed for indoor decoration. The denser heads of many modern hybrids are usually sterile and do not dry as well.

All alliums are members of the onion family and share the distinct aromatic foliage of the culinary varieties. However, the aroma is only present if the leaves are bruised and most of the flowers are strongly honey scented and many make excellent cut flowers. On a warm, sunny day a border with alliums will hum with the quiet contented drone of bees, which adore them, often chasing us into an exhibition tent as we carry potted alliums in.

The smaller, rhizomatous alliums are suitable for the very front of a border or a sunny rock garden.

Cultivation

The native habitats of most alliums are dry, mountainous regions where rainfall occurs in the spring, often in the form of snow melt, followed by a dry, hot summer. In the garden they need a well-drained soil in full sun, although they can tolerate some shade for part of the day. Once dormant they should be kept reasonably dry. This is particularly important for those from hotter climates in order to ripen the bulb for flowering the following year. Too much water in the summer, either in the form of natural rainfall, heavy wet soils, or irrigation can cause the bulbs to rot. Bulbs should be planted 10–15cm deep, the distance apart being dictated by the size of the flower head. Small-flowered varieties such as *A. caeruleum* and *A. sphaerocephalum* are best clustered together but those with large heads such as *A. christophii* should be given room to 'breathe' or else the heads will lean away from each other and break off. Alliums with rhizomatous roots should be planted with the rhizomes just below the surface. The small Himalayan species prefer a damp humus-rich soil in part shade.

Alliums and wild flowers fill a central reservation in Sheffield.

Propagation

Most alliums increase by offsets; this may be a slow process with some of the larger cultivars, which only slowly divide. The drumstick species can be raised from seed which should be sown under cold glass in the autumn. Seedlings may take up to seven years to flower. Some, such as *A. christophii*, may seed around in the garden if the conditions are favourable. Some of the smaller species, such as the native *A. ursinum* (wild garlic) or *A. moly* (golden garlic), can be invasive and the seed heads should be removed once the flowers have faded unless they are wanted for naturalizing in wild places. Rhizomatous varieties can be divided in the spring. Alliums are vulnerable to white onion rot and should not be planted in infected soils.

Tall alliums for the border

These varieties are tall enough for the middle of a sunny border and are excellent with grasses and other sun lovers. Their seed heads gradually dry to an attractive pale khaki colour. The temptation is to plant them at the back of the border among other tall flowers but they are more effective planted in the middle where they can punctuate the other planting, the slender stems of the alliums rising above the mounds of shorter herbaceous foliage.

A. atropurpureum

This eastern European allium is not a showy species, having rather small, flat heads of intense purple starry flowers in midsummer. It has been crossed with other species to produce some excellent dark-coloured hybrids such as **'Firmament'**, **'Gabrielle'** and **'Spider'**. Height: 75cm.

A. christophii 🏆

This is a dramatic but relatively short allium for planting in groups at the front of a border or it can be scattered through low perennials. It is one of the few that looks at home with its flowers virtually at the same level as its neighbours. Deep purple astrantias and the spiky blue *Eryngium bourgatii* are good companion plants. The allium flowers first in early summer and then as its colour fades so the purple flowers of the astrantia take over. *A. christophii* is a rich purple-pink with a metallic sheen and is one of the best for drying, the seed heads surviving in the garden for many weeks. Sprayed silver they make dramatic indoor decorations. Height: 60cm. **'Firmament'** is a hybrid between *A. christophii* and *A. atropurpureum*. It has rather flat 10cm-diameter heads with the deep purple colour of one parent and the metallic sheen of the other. Height: 75cm.

Dried heads of *Allium christophii* among grasses at Wisley.

Allium 'Firmament'.

A. giganteum 🏆

Its name implies that it will be large but it is tall rather than exceptionally large flowered. It has dense 15cm heads of deep purple flowers on sturdy 1.3m stems with rather wide basal leaves. On well-drained sunny soils it is a very dramatic bulb for midsummer, towering above the surrounding plants. It hates waterlogged soils and is slightly tender and can disappear in hard winters. **'Ambassador'** is a dramatic *A. giganteum* cultivar with dense 15cm heads packed with intense purple flowers on tall sturdy stems. The individual flowers gradually open over a long period. It is one of the tallest, flowering in late June. Height: 1.3m.

A. hollandicum 🏆 *(A.atlatunense)*

This popular allium has round heads of starry purplish-pink flowers 10cm across. Although the flowers are only in their perfect state for about two weeks they only gradually lose their colour. They are amongst the best for massing in a sunny border. They will self-seed if the seed heads

Allium 'Ambassador'.

Allium nigrum.

are left on. They seem impervious to summer rainfall so can be incorporated into herbaceous borders that are irrigated in the summer provided they are not waterlogged. **'Purple Sensation'** 🏆 in its best form should be an intense royal purple but it is often raised from seed with consequential mixed and often indifferent shades. It is excellent mixed with *Astrantia* 'Ruby Wedding' where the strong purples complement each other. Early summer. Height: 75cm.

Allium 'Purple Sensation'.

A. nigrum
(A. multibulbosum)

This Mediterranean bulb really lives up to its former name. Each bulb produces a mass of small offsets which could become a nuisance but provided the clumps are left undisturbed they are not an embarrassment. The off-white heads with their prominent dark central ovary are flat rather than round and more fleshy than the drumstick types. It is useful for lightening a dark corner in part shade. Height: 75cm.

A. schubertii

This is a true sparkler with spectacular heads that can be 30–40cm across. Each individual flower stem is of a different length so rather than a neat round ball it is a real explosion of a flower. It is hardy but it comes from the eastern Mediterranean and flowers best in a warm, sunny position in well-drained soil. This allium might have the

Allium schubertii.

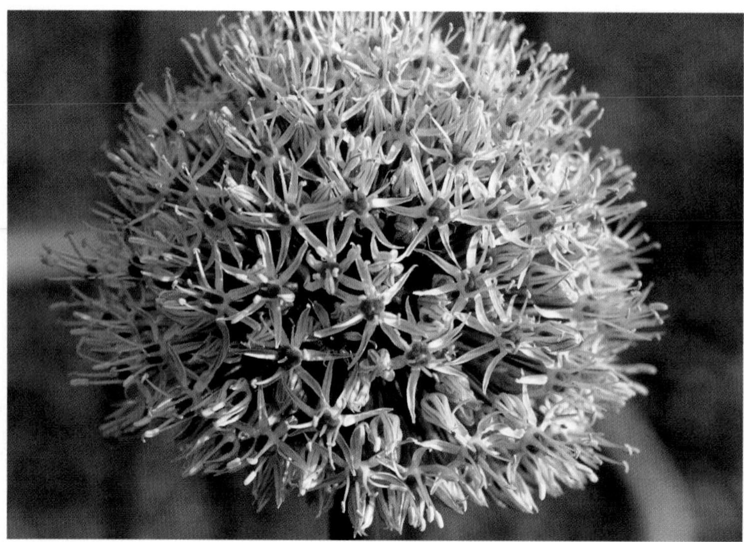

Allium 'Mount Everest'.

largest heads of all but it is only 60cm tall so the heads are only just held off the ground. It is therefore suitable for planting against a wall. The seed heads are amongst the best for drying.

A. rosenbachianum
(A. jesdianum, misapplied)

This allium's nomenclature has had a chequered history but it now seems to have settled as *A. rosenbachianum*. It is often confused with *A. stipitatum* but the true plant could never be mistaken for anything else. This is the earliest of the drumstick alliums to flower. It comes from Central Asia and has a 12cm round head of purple flowers with very conspicuous white anthers. Height 70cm. **'Early Emperor'** is a good coloured selection and **'White Empress'** is a pure white form with larger flowers.

A. stipitatum

This tall allium has tightly packed, rather small (7cm) heads of purple flowers and is one of the first to flower. The white form 'Album' has tall, rather 'bendy' stems but it has produced some excellent hybrids with stiffer, more upright stems. 1–1.2m; **'Mount Everest'** and the similar **'Mont Blanc'** are white-flowered hybrids with sturdier stems that are less inclined to bend and twist. Both have dense heads of off-white flowers. Height: 75cm.

Allium 'Early Emperor' and 'White Empress'.

Hybrids

In recent years there has been an upsurge in interest in the tall purple alliums, and ever more hybrids appear each year. Most have more flowers per head, producing a denser and longer flowering head than the species, but many are very similar. They are often sterile so the seed head is less effective for drying. These are among the best purples:

'Beau Regard' 🏆 has pale purple flowers in a very large head, medium height; **'Gladiator'** 🏆 has mid-purple flowers; **'Globe Master'** 🏆 has large (14cm) very full heads of mid-purple flowers and is a good doer; **'Pinball Wizard'** is very similar but it is earlier flowering and has slightly darker flowers in a larger umbel; **'His Excellence'** is another tall allium with deep purple flowers; **'Round and Purple'** has large purple heads and is mid-height. **'Spider'** is a new, late-flowering hybrid between *A. schubertii* and *A. atropurpureum*.

Allium 'Pinball Wizard'.

Allium 'Silver Spring'.

It has a large (20cm) open umbel of deep purple flowers all on pedicels of different lengths. Height: 60cm.

'Forelock'

This is a curiosity rather than a good garden plant as the height of the stem is out of proportion to the size of the flower. It is reminiscent of an overgrown *A. sphaerocephalum*, and the pointed flower heads rise curved over like a shepherd's crook before straightening out to flower. It needs to be planted among other tall sun-lovers such as grasses. However, it makes an excellent and long lasting, if unusual, cut flower. The 6cm round heads are densely packed with small flowers of an intense brownish-mauve with conspicuous white stamens. As they fade so the paler seed heads push up through the centre of the flower to give an overall pear-shape. Height: 1.5m.

'Silver Spring'

This is a new, very distinct cultivar selected in Israel from a stock of *A. nigrum*. It has similar domed heads of white flowers but with conspicuous deep rose rather than green centres. It is also sweetly scented. Sadly, it starts into growth early in the year and seems not to be very hardy, although it thrives in the dry conditions in one of our tunnels, so excess moisture might be the problem rather than temperature as *A. nigrum* grows freely with us. Height: 1m.

Allium 'Forelock'.

Allium beesianum.

The shorter alliums

A. beesianum 🏆

This is a tiny alpine gem from the Himalayas. It is virtually evergreen, producing clumps of slender, grassy leaves and small, nodding deep blue or white flowers. It is best grown in cool conditions in part shade. It is intolerant of drought. Height: 15cm. ***A. cyaneum*** 🏆 and ***A. sikkimense*** are very similar and are often confused with it.

A. caeruleum 🏆
(A. azureum)

This slender June-flowering bulb has small 3cm heads of clear blue flowers and slender, stem clasping leaves. It comes from the dry steppes of Central Asia and can be frustrating to grow as it is very susceptible to excessive water. When growing well in a very dry, sunny position it will form quite large clumps. The individual flowers are small so the bulbs should be planted in dense groups to make any effect, at the front of a border, or preferably on a raised bed or bank where they are a good foil for yellow pansies or the sun-loving prostrate *Oenothera speciosa* 'Siskiyou'. The heads have an annoying habit of sometimes producing bulbils rather than flowers. Height: 60cm.

A. carinatum subsp. *pulchellum*

This clump-forming, late summer-flowering bulb from southern Europe and Turkey has very erect stems and rather curious open heads of bell-shaped purple flowers which seem undecided whether to be erect or nodding. The thin thread-like leaves are stem-clasping. It is easy to grow but can be over-enthusiastic with its seedlings, especially in a dry soil in full sun. Placed carefully it is a useful plant for brightening up the edge of a shrub border. Vigorous and regular deadheading will control its spread beyond the confines of the clumps. Height: 50cm. **subsp. *album*** 🏆 is pure white and less invasive.

Allium carinatum subsp. *pulchellum*.

Allium cernuum.

A. cernuum 🏆

This is a vigorous clump-forming allium from North America that is virtually evergreen. It has rather open heads of nodding pinkish-purple flowers in midsummer. It is very easy to grow but scrupulous deadheading is needed or it can be rather too enthusiastic with its offspring. Height: 40cm.

A. cyathophorum var. *farreri*

This short, clump-forming Chinese allium flowers in midsummer. It has narrow tufts of leaves and small heads of deep purple nodding flowers. It is easily grown in any sunny position and is very vigorous. Height: 12cm.

A. flavum 🏆

This attractive clump-forming European allium is very variable. The best forms have heads of up to fifty deep lemon-yellow flowers with prominent stamens and narrow, grassy leaves. The buds start upright but then bend down to open in late summer, returning to the vertical as the seed is set. We grow it on a sunny raised bed. Height: 10–40cm.

Allium cyathophorum var. *farreri*.

A. insubricum 🏆

This small, clump-forming allium from Italy is often confused with ***A. narcissiflorum*** but instead of erect seed pods they remain pendent. Both have a few-flowered umbel of purple-pink nodding flowers and are perfect for a dry, sunny rock garden. Height: 20cm.

Allium flavum.

Allium karataviense on the screes of the Karatan mountains, Kakakhstan.

A. karataviense 🏆

This Central Asian allium grows naturally among the boulders of screes in the Karatau mountains where it is perfectly disguised: the pinkish flowers are the exact shade of the stones and are of a similar size. It can not be confused with any other allium. Rather than its flowers it is grown for its handsome broad grey-green leaves that are reminiscent of a hosta but appear in spring long before any hosta is through the ground. They are perfect to edge a sunny border and look good inter-planted with purple-leaved heucheras. The rather disappointing, muddy pink flowers appear in early summer as the leaves fade. Low geraniums such as *G. cinereum* 'Ballerina' are good companion plants, spreading to fill the gaps left when the bulbs are dormant in the summer. **'Ivory Queen'** is a great improvement with wide leaves that are more conspicuously ribbed. The tight pompoms of clear white flowers sit just above them. Height: 20cm. **'Red Giant'** is a new hybrid with large intense red flowers. Height: 35cm.

A. moly (Golden Garlic)

The golden garlic is a vigorous bulb, increasing rapidly both by offsets and seed and is really only suitable for the wild garden, under trees, where it can be allowed to spread. The deep golden yellow flowers, which gradually fade to a papery white, are produced in early summer. Height: 25cm. **'Jeannine'** 🏆 is a much-improved form. It is taller, with larger heads, but its big advantage is that it is virtually sterile so it can be planted at the front of a sunny border where it will gradually form a clump without becoming a nuisance by seeding everywhere. It is especially useful as yellow is rather scarce in the garden in early summer. Height: 35cm.

Allium karataviense 'Ivory Queen'.

A. neapolitanum (*A. cowanii*)

This small, white-flowered allium is perfect for the front of a border. It is native to southern Europe and revels in a dry sunny position and is slightly tender. It has narrow leaves that wither as the flowers open. The heads, a loose 5cm umbel of bright white starry flowers, are held on rather lax, often contorted stems and it needs to be grown en masse as each single bulb is rather insignificant. In Italy they are massed in the box parterres of formal gardens. They make good cut flowers. Midsummer. Height: 40cm.

A. obliquum

This midsummer-flowering allium comes from eastern Europe through to Siberia and its yellow is a

Allium obliquum.

welcome break from the normal pink-white colour range. It has small bulbs attached to slender rhizomes which gradually make small clumps. It has thread-like, grey-green stem-clasping leaves. The 5cm tightly packed pompom heads of lemon flowers have fluffy stamens and look rather like powder puffs on tall stems. The stems start curled over, gradually becoming erect as the buds open. Height: 60cm.

A. oreophilum 🏆
(A. ostrowskianum)

This tiny, midsummer-flowering Central Asian allium is perfect for a sunny rock garden. The individual bright pink flowers are in a rather open umbel and are most effective when the small bulbs are massed together. They retain their strong colouring for many weeks, only gradually fading to the standard khaki. Height: 12cm. **'Zwanenburg'** 🏆 is supposedly a darker carmine.

Allium oreophilum.

Allium sphaerocephalum.

A. roseum (Rosy Garlic)

In its best forms this is a pretty plant for a sunny border with open heads of delicate pink flowers in early summer. Sadly, many forms have a tendency to produce only a few flowers, replacing them instead with a mass of bulbils which can spread prodigiously. Height: 45cm.

A. schoenoprasum 'Forescate' (Chives)

The clump-forming culinary chives need little introduction but this form has deeper pink flowers than the standard. Regular deadheading will encourage a further crop of flowers and prevent self-seeding of inferior-coloured plants. **'Silver Chimes'** has white flowers and is attractive enough to escape the confines of the herb garden and make a pretty edging to a sunny path. Height: 20cm.

A. senescens

This is a very variable clump-forming allium that flowers throughout the summer. It has short, narrow grey-green leaves and is easily grown in any sunny position. The small soft purple pompom heads are carried on stiff stems and vary from 10–40cm tall. ***A. angulosum*** is very similar.

A. sphaerocephalum

These small bulbs have long, willowy stems topped by shuttlecock-shaped green buds that gradually become suffused with intense purple. Individually they are insignificant but are very effective when planted *en masse*. It must be dry and sunny or they will gradually disappear but when happy, such as among grasses,

Allium senescens.

Allium tuberosum.

the display just improves as the bulbs settle down. Even the faded heads are attractive waving among the grasses. Although they would appear too tall they are also remarkably attractive planted in dry beds on the top of a wall as their overall impression is light and airy. Height: 75cm.

THE 'THUGS'

- ***A. triquetrum:*** this bulb is occasionally offered for sale and is only included so that it can be avoided: on no account should it be let loose in the garden. It is incredibly invasive and virtually impossible to eradicate once it has escaped. It comes from southern Europe and is naturalized in the hedgerows of the southwest of England and should stay there! It produces its long and untidy leaves, which are triangular in cross section, in late autumn and this is the best time to attempt to remove them when the majority of the myriad of tiny bulblets are still attached to the parent bulb. The whole clump, soil and all, should be lifted and disposed of. The small, nodding, insignificant white flowers appear at any time between winter and spring. It is also a vigorous seeder.
- The British native ***A. ursinum*** (wild garlic) falls into the same category although this is a much neater plant with broad basal leaves and a showy head of white flowers. It is suitable for naturalizing in wild areas such as damp woodlands but again it is very difficult to eradicate once established. It is another vigorous seeder.
- **'Hair'**: you may be seduced by vases of this curiosity at flower shows but just admire it; do not be tempted to buy it for it is only an exaggerated form of ***A. vineale***, which is a common weed in gardens. It has a slender stem with narrow, stem-clasping grey leaves and instead of flowers it produces heads of bulbils, each with a long grassy shoot.

A. tuberosum
(Chinese Chives)

This clump-forming allium has narrow upright leaves and small, flat, white flowers which appear from late summer to early autumn. These have a strong honey scent which attracts masses of butterflies. Chinese chives are fully edible and are popular in cooking in Sichuan and Yunnan where you see great bundles for sale on every vegetable stall. Everything from the bulb to the flower is chopped and added to the ubiquitous stir fry. In the garden they can be used as a flowering edible border to the vegetable garden but they are sufficiently decorative to plant in clumps at the front of the border where their late flowering is a bonus. Height: 60cm.

Allium unifolium.

A. unifolium 🏆

This has a small true bulb with slender stem-clasping leaves and is another useful one to mass in groups at the edge of a sunny border. The rich pink flowers form a rather open, upward-facing head. It flowers in early summer and should be packed into tight groups for the best effect. Height: 35cm.

Camassia

These useful bulbs fill the 'May gap' between the last of the tulips and the main display of the herbaceous perennials, although in early seasons their flowering may overlap. Although they are native to the mountains of western America, where they flower as the snow melts, they are very easy garden plants in almost any soil in full sun or part shade. Here on our dry, sandy soil we must religiously remove the seed heads if we are not to be overrun with seedlings. They vary in height from 30cm–1m with long basal leaves and a showy raceme (spike) of six-petalled, star-shaped flowers. The stamens are often conspicuous and in a contrasting colour. All will naturalize in grass but many are really too tall for all but the largest gardens, especially as the grass must be left uncut until the leaves completely fade in June or later if you want them to seed. They can be particularly effective around the base of apple trees in orchards. At the RHS Wisley garden in Surrey the short silvery blue *C. cusickii* and a taller darker blue form of *C. leichtlinii* have been planted together to follow on from daffodils planted in grass.

Like many summer-flowering bulbs the leaves take advantage of the spring moisture to grow but are fading and rather unsightly when they flower. They are therefore best planted towards the middle of a border where herbaceous perennials such as geraniums or day lilies provide a good screen. They will tolerate part shade and can be planted to come through hellebore leaves to add late colour to a shrub bed.

Cultivation

The bulbs are planted in the autumn 10cm deep and 10cm apart. They are easy and trouble-free, quickly forming large clumps which should be lifted and replanted every few years to maintain vigour and flower size. They are propagated by offsets or they can be easily raised from ripe seed sown either in seed trays or directly into a seed bed. Seedlings can flower in four years. In some gardens self-sown seedlings can be a nuisance so we recommend cutting the stems as soon as the flowers fade.

Camassia cusickii.

Camassia cusickii and *Camassia leichtlinii* following on from daffodils in grass at Wisley.

C. cusickii

This is the earliest to flower with racemes of pale ice-blue flowers on tall stems. Sadly it is rather fleeting in flower but very pretty with pale tulips such as *T. viridiflora* 'Spring Green' or as an underplanting to the taller dark blue cultivars of *C. leichtlinii*. It can be naturalized in long grass. It is useful as it will coincide with late-flowering daffodils. There is a fine planting of it below the house at the National Trust's Knightshayes Court in Devon where it flourishes with 'White Lady' daffodils. Height: 45cm.

C. leichtlinii 🏆

This is a very variable species from western USA, flowering in late spring to early summer. The type, often erroneously referred to as **'Alba'** by nurserymen, has a rather open spike of creamy white, star-shaped flowers with greenish

Camassia leichtlinii.

backs. It will seed freely in well-drained soils. Height: 60cm. **subsp. *suksdorfii*** is the correct name of the taller blue-flowered forms. These come in shades of blue to violet. **'Blau Donau'** ('Blue Danube') has deep blue flowers and is probably the correct name for the identical clone often listed as **'Caerulea'**. **'Electra'**, raised by Eric Smith, is one of the newer cultivars with truly electric blue flowers, shot through with turquoise. Seed-raised cultivars are now appearing on the market with more or less pink or purple flowers; true whites are also occurring. Height: 70cm. **'Semiplena'** is the tallest of the group, the last to flower and being sterile is very long lasting in flower. It has a stiff spike of up to forty semi-double, creamy flowers. These open in a random fashion up the spike, some of the upper ones opening before the lower ones so that there is always a mix of bud, open and faded flowers on any one spike. They also have an annoying habit of producing more buds than will ever mature so the top is always crowned by a slightly unsightly cluster of brown, unformed buds. They are magnificent in a border, only slowly clumping up and are never an embarrassment. Like all this group their large leaves are dying back as they start flowering and are best hidden. They are particularly good planted behind early-flowering daylilies such as *Hemerocallis lilio-asphodelus* or *H. dumortieri*. Height: 1.3m.

Camassia leichtlinii subsp. *suksdorfii*.

Camassia 'Semi plena'.

C. quamash (C.esculenta)

This is the smallest of the camassias and is perfect for naturalizing in grass where its slender spikes of intense blue flowers coincide with the pure white of *N. poeticus recurvus* (Pheasant's Eye) and cowslips. The open, starry flowers have conspicuous bright yellow stamens. It is rather like an upright bluebell when viewed *en masse* from a distance. It is too vigorous and insufficiently showy for a border. Height: 35cm. **'Orion'** is taller with larger flowers. **'Blue Melody'** has cream-edged leaves which is a doubtful improvement.

Cardiocrinum
(Giant Lily)

These giant monocarpic (dying once it has flowered) bulbs have a single stiff stem topped by a number of long, tubular, scented flowers. The large, heart-shaped leaves form a basal rosette and are scattered up the stem. It comes from the Himalayan foothills where the heavy monsoon rainfall dominates the growing conditions. The poor gardener must struggle to mimic this. Consequently they thrive best in the wetter and cooler parts of the UK where they appreciate a semi-shaded situation. On light, dry soil they may only be a pathetic 1m rather than the spectacular 3m they can achieve under more favourable conditions. Unless they are growing happily the bulb quickly deteriorates, becoming smaller rather than larger as the years pass. The other consequence of the monsoon is that plant material quickly rots down under the hot, humid conditions, providing the bulbs with a deep, highly fertile soil with a high humus content. Thus they appreciate additional compost or even well-rotted farmyard manure under them. A Scottish colleague plants hers on the compost heap. Their towering seed heads are an attractive bonus lasting well into the winter.

Cardiocrinum giganteum.

Cultivation

The huge bulbs are usually planted in autumn or early spring with the neck just below the surface in a fertile, moist, yet well-drained soil in part shade. Newly planted bulbs are prone to basal rot and should be watered sparingly until growth is established. In cold areas a winter mulch of leaves or bracken is beneficial. Once growing well they require regular moisture. Although the main bulb dies after flowering, offsets will usually form around the base which can be grown on. These should not be left *in situ*, as the soil will be exhausted by the parent bulb, but should be moved to a new position. In nature these giants increase by seed, the tall stems scattering the seed well away from the parent, and seed-raised plants often out-perform offsets. The seed should be sown as soon as it is ripe in a fertile, humus-rich compost. The seedlings should be lined out – the vegetable garden is ideal – as soon as they are large enough to handle. Watering must be regular at all times. When the bulbs reach a diameter of 5cm they can be planted into their final flowering position. It is possible to have seedlings in flower within four years.

C. cordatum

This bulb comes from north Japan and neighbouring Russia and has up to fifteen tubular cream flowers, each 15cm long, clustered at the top of the 2m flower spike in midsummer.

C. giganteum 🏆

When growing well this really lives up to its name. It has up to twenty huge white tubular flowers, each 30cm long, with a red throat. The flowers point downwards, funnelling the heady scent to the passerby. The dramatic seed heads with their elongated capsules, rising among the shrubs, are long lasting and an attractive bonus. Up to 3m.

Var. *yunnanensis* from Central China is shorter with smaller, green-tinted flowers on maroon stems and bronzed young growth. The seed capsule is also squatter. They will hybridize with each other.

Cardiocrinum giganteum var. *yunnanensis.*

Crinum

The long-necked bulbs of these South African late summer-flowering subjects are amongst the largest of all. Each of these huge bulbs produces very long, strap-like leaves and an umbel of trumpet flowers on stiff stems. Some are sweetly scented. At the end of summer the leaves turn into a soggy mess but it is best to leave these attached to the plant and resist the temptation to tidy them up. The faded foliage then acts as a blanket, protecting the neck of the bulb during the winter. It has even been suggested that they contain a form of antifreeze. The whole plant can be tidied up once the regrowth starts in spring. Despite their soft, luxuriant appearance they are remarkably hardy. Each flower stem produces up to twelve flowers which open in succession but once the first are successfully pollinated they have an annoying habit of going on strike and switching from flower to seed production, aborting the rest of the buds which can be seen abandoned in the centre of the umbel. I learnt a valuable lesson about these from a great French gardener. We were late for lunch and this *grande dame* was irately standing in the drive waiting for us. While she did so she was carefully cutting out the faded flowers from her impressive bed of *Crinum moorei*. If the faded flowers are carefully removed at regular intervals all the buds will continue to mature and open. This is time-consuming but a pleasant job on a warm afternoon and will almost double the flowering period.

Cultivation

They should be planted in early spring with only the rounded basal half of the bulb below the surface. They require a well-drained site in full sun and can become exceptionally large clumps. Propagation is by division in the early spring just as they start into growth.

C. moorei

This large bulb is reputedly to be not fully hardy but will survive even low temperatures in sheltered gardens and has survived -15°C here in a very well-drained soil in our walled garden. It forms much smaller, lower clumps than its hybrid *C.* × *powellii* and has fewer and less-intrusive leaves. The flower stems arise from the side of the bulb rather than from the middle of the leaves. The heads have four or sometimes more large, open trumpet flowers of a delicate pale pink. These suddenly appear in the late summer or early autumn and are strongly fragrant, being capable of scenting a whole garden and, unlike *C.* × *powellii*, stand about 60cm clear of the leaves. Like most of this group, established clumps flower best, especially after a warm summer. Height: 80cm.

Crinum x powellii.

C. × *powellii* 🏆

This hardy hybrid between *C. bulbispermum* and *C. moorei* has a huge bulb some 30cm long and certainly needs space in the garden as it will increase to form large, congested clumps, as much as 1.5m or more across. In the spring the bulbs produce fleshy mid-green leaves which can be as long as 1.7m and which will quickly swamp any injudicious nearby planting. In mid- to late summer they suddenly erupt into flower, producing stiff stems topped by up to ten nodding trumpet-shaped pink flowers. Dead-heading the individual flowers as they fade will extend the season and mature clumps flower best. Height: 1.7m. **'Album'** 🏆 has large, glistening white flowers.

Crinum x powellii 'Album'.

Crocosmia

These easily grown South African corms are extremely useful for adding colour to the garden just as the main show of the herbaceous perennials is going past its best. They have fans of leaves, usually mid-green but occasionally bronzed, and a spike of tubular yellow, orange or red flowers. Unlike most corms where the old one disappears as the new season's is formed these retain their previous corms – building into veritable Tower-of-Pisa structures. This causes the corms to gradually diminish in size and vigour, resulting in a loss of flower display and they become a mass of non-flowering leaves. This has given these attractive and useful plants a bad reputation. However, regular division of the clumps will maintain the vigour of the bulbs and their flower-to-leaf ratio will remain acceptable. They are hardy but their habit of coming into growth early in the year leaves the new foliage vulnerable to late frost.

Most of the cultivars grown today have a very confused and confusing parentage, which is of little interest to the average gardener. For garden use they can be split into two broad types: those that are clump-forming and have spikes of relatively small more or less tubular flowers that open in a rush; and those that have much larger, flatter flowers that open singly along well-branched stems. These flower over a much longer period and tend to be more stoloniferous, forming open patches rather than congested clumps.

C. × *crocosmiiflora*, better known as montbretia, is really too vigorous and this proclivity has given the whole genus a bad reputation. It is the crocosmia found naturalized along road and stream sides in upland areas of Britain where it is a thug of the first order. Most modern hybrids are not only better behaved: they also have much larger and brighter flowers and are perfect to extend the flowering season of the garden. Kniphofias (red hot pokers) and late-flowering yellow and orange daisies such as rudbeckia and helenium are perfect companions for them, sharing the same colour spectrum and liking similar growing conditions. Or you can be bold and try a daring mix of orange crocosmia, yellow rudbeckias and pink *Echinacea purpurea* for something completely different.

Crocosmias need a humus-rich soil that is not too dry. They do not like too much sun directly on their corms as this seems to encourage rust. However, too much shade will result in poor flowering and 'floppy' clumps. They do well in sunny glades in a woodland garden where they receive sun for much but not all of the day, or on the east-facing side of an open sunny border. Most are short enough to be self-supporting but some of the taller varieties will require discreet staking.

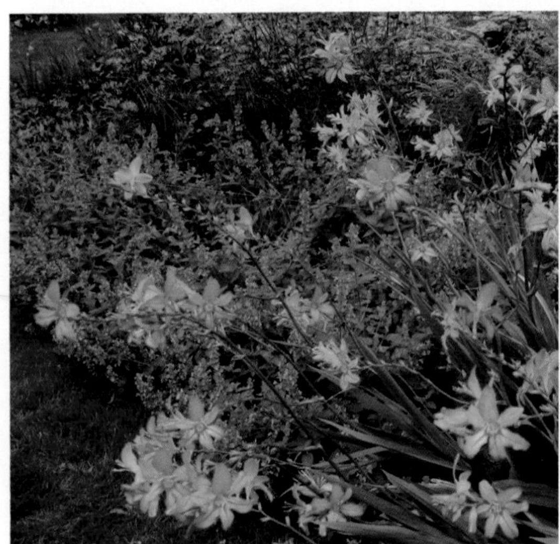

Crocosmia 'Zambesi'.

Cultivation

The corms are planted 5cm deep, 12cm apart in the spring. Established clumps should be divided every three years to maintain vigour and flowering. This can be done after flowering in the autumn in mild districts but is probably best left until the early spring in colder areas. The faded foliage can then be left on the plants throughout the winter to act as a protective mulch. This must be removed in the spring before the new leaves appear. When the corms are lifted the top two of each stack should be removed for replanting and the old, exhausted corms discarded.

A glance at the RHS *Plantfinder* shows a very large number of different crocosmia, many masquerading under different names, of which a number are very similar indeed. This is not surprising, considering the limited range of colours available. There has been an upsurge in interest in them recently and there are now some good new hybrids with very distinctive flowers.

Crocosmia with echinacea and helenium.

Crocosmia 'Rowallane Yellow'.

C × crocosmiiflora
(Montbretia)

This easy and overly vigorous thug needs little introduction. The large clumps of narrow, spear-shaped leaves are topped by branched stems of bright orange flowers with paler centres. It is too vigorous for all but the largest gardens. Height: 75cm.

C. masoniorum 🏆

This early-flowering crocosmia has arching sprays of upward-facing large tubular flowers that open wide to give a bold display above the fans of mid-green leaves. They must be divided regularly to maintain flowering. **'Rowallane Yellow'** 🏆 with bold, deep yellow flowers on outward-facing arching stems, and the similar **'Paul's Best Yellow'** are among the very best of all the crocosmias, being distinctive, dramatic and above all, well behaved; **'Spitfire'** is a vigorous clump-forming cultivar with arching stems of small fiery orange-red flowers. Height: 60–80cm.

C. paniculata

This is a vigorous species with huge fans of attractively pleated leaves and large showy branched spikes of deep orange-red flowers on tall stems. It is rather too vigorous for small gardens and quickly stops flowering, although regular splitting of the clumps should help maintain flowering. Height: 1.2–1.4m. Its cultivar **'Lucifer'** 🏆 is more free-flowering with large orange-red flowers on well branched stems. It is the earliest to flower and the tallest

Crocosmia paniculata.

Crocosmia 'Lucifer'.

Crocosmia 'Canary Bird' and 'Saracen' (behind).

and is particularly useful to add height to a sunny border. They are good behind clumps of *Helenium* 'Moorheim Beauty' which has similar orange-red tones, or arching above a gently waving sea of *Stipa tenuissima*. They are very vigorous and may need supporting and will certainly need to be divided regularly. The similar **'Hellfire'** is a darker red.

Smaller flowered, clump-forming hybrids

(all c. 60cm tall)

Orange/Red

'Carmin Brillant' 🏆 is of French origin and is relatively short with masses of deep orange-red flowers on dark stems. It is a good foil for golden kniphofias or red dahlias such as 'The Bishop of Llandaff'. **'Okovango'** has relatively large, open flowers of a distinct peachy apricot carried well above the leaves and makes bold, very showy clumps. **'Severn Sunrise'** 🏆 opens orange with a yellow centre but the flowers take on a distinct pinkish hue with age.

Yellow

'Canary Bird' is one of the many free flowering hybrids with deep yellow flowers – definitely on the golden side of yellow but very useful as the colour really seems to glow in overcast days and they are a good foil for the many other orange and yellow shades in the garden in late summer; **'George Davidson'**, who was a notable breeder of crocosmias ('Star of the East' was his finest) and **'Norwich Canary'** are very similar golden yellow varieties. **'Citronella'** is very distinct with pale green leaves and sprays of clear lemon-yellow flowers. It is very vigorous, quickly forming huge non-flowering clumps which require regular division, but it looks especially good with blue agapanthus.

Crocosmia 'Citronella'.

Bronze foliage

All these have the bonus of forming clumps of attractive dark, bronzed leaves during the summer before they flower but they are prone to rust and can look very sick in hot, dry soils. **'Dusky Maiden'** has dark burnt orange flowers and very dark leaves. Sadly it can be shy to grow or flower well; **'Saracen'** is very vigorous, quickly forming large clumps of dark leaves with sprays of good sized orange-centred red flowers; **'Solfatare'** 🏆 (syn. 'Solfaterre') is another French hybrid with soft apricot flowers and lightly bronzed leaves. It is a good border plant. Try it behind the black grass *Ophiopogon planiscapus nigrescens*.

Crocosmia 'Star of the East'.

Large-flowered hybrids

These produce large flowers on branched stems from late summer into autumn. **'Emily McKenzie'** has very large, slightly nodding flowers 6cm across, which are carried on well branched stems and open gradually over a two-month period. They are a deep orange with a dark maroon ring around the paler centre and have dark spots in the very middle. It is not clump forming and makes a good cut flower. Height: 50cm. **'Babylon'** has bold spikes of 6cm-diameter deep red flowers with a dark maroon ring in the centre. It is clump forming. Height: 70cm. **'Constance'** is a similar size and type with dramatic bi-coloured flowers of orange and yellow; **'Star of the East'** 🏆 has the largest of all the flowers, 10cm across, carried on well-branched stems. They are a clear golden orange which pales towards the centre. It is not clump forming and mixes well with peachy *Echinacea* and pale blue *Agapanthus* 'Blue Moon'. Height: 80cm. **'Zambesi'** is one of the attractive new cultivars. It has tall stems with large, open reflexed flowers which are produced over a long period. The flowers are clear orange with a dark red central ring and have red markings on the petals. Height: 70cm.

Crocosmia 'Zambesi'.

Crocosmia 'Emily McKenzie'.

Cyclamen

See *Chapter 1* for notes on cultivation and pests.

C. purpurascens *(C. europaeum)*

One of the unexpected delights of walking in the Alps in high summer is encountering the intense fragrance of *C. purpurascens* wafting on the air. Unfortunately this cyclamen is rather temperamental as a garden plant, although it is easily grown under cold glass. It prefers dry, humus-rich soil under spreading shrubs such as *Viburnum* 'Lanarth'. Unlike other cyclamen it never makes a dramatic display, producing only a few deep carmine flowers at a time throughout the summer months. The leaves are normally lightly marbled, or very occasionally heavily silvered. Height: 10cm.

Cyclamen purpurascens.

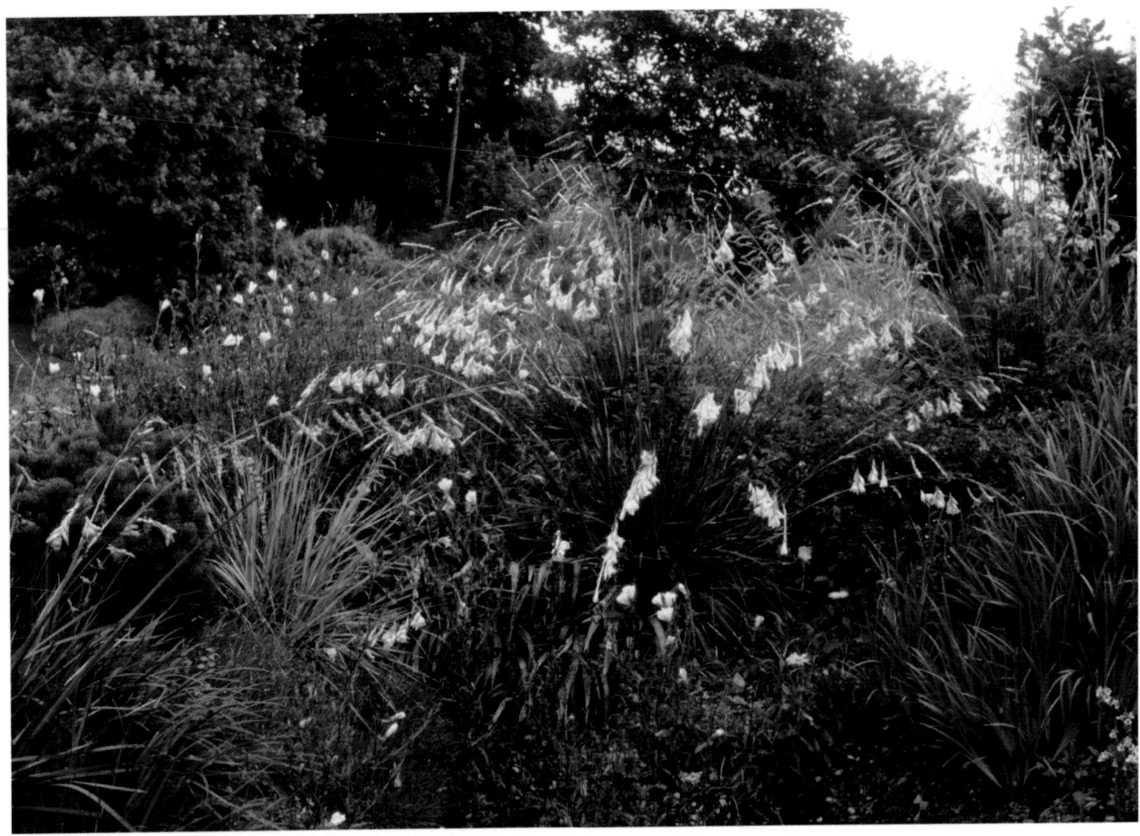

Established clumps of dierama in a Devon garden.

Dierama

(Angel's Fishing Rod; Wandflower)

These early summer-flowering corms are native to South Africa. They are clump forming, producing a mound of narrow evergreen leaves, although they may become deciduous in cold winters. The pendent tubular flowers, in shades of pink and white, are held in clusters along thin, wand-like stems which vary in length from 30cm–2m. Although they are often called angel's fishing rods, and indeed are very attractive arching over a pond, they will not tolerate the waterlogged soils of a bog garden which will cause the corms to rot. They are perfect for the middle of a bed of low-growing plants where the flowers seem to float above them, or arching out across a path. The smaller species are suitable for a rock garden. The species are distinguished by rather subtle differences in flower shape and the internal patterns around the ovaries. However, many plants offered for sale, regardless of the name, are garden hybrids rather than true species but are none the less attractive for that.

Cultivation

The corms should be planted in early spring just below the surface of a humus-rich, well-drained soil in full sun. Dieramas are normally evergreen but in hard winters or when transplanted the old leaves will die off completely, new growth only slowly appearing. They must be kept well watered at this stage. It may take a long time but once established they are trouble-free, slowly growing into very large clumps. Mature, established plants flower best.

Propagation

They are easily raised from seed but all will hybridize freely and named clones must be raised by division or tissue culture. Established clumps can be divided in early spring.

D. dracomantanum
(D. pumilum)

This is a dwarf species with relatively upright flower stems and flared salmon-pink to purple-pink flowers. Height: 60cm.

D. igneum

This compact dierama forms large clumps of narrow, grey-green leaves and is later flowering than most. Established plants are covered by masses of arching stems of small salmon pink flared flowers in midsummer, seemingly arriving overnight. It is a graceful plant both in and out of flower and should be planted on its own where it can be appreciated. It is less likely to produce self-sown seedlings. Height: 70cm.

D. pendulum

This is a mid-sized dierama with long arching stems of relatively large, flared flowers in shades of pink or white. It is useful as it is not as tall as *D. pulcherrimum* and more suited to smaller gardens. Height: 1.2m.

Dierama dracomontanum.

Dierama igneum.

D. pulcherrimum

This is the giant of the group with relatively broad leaves and towering 1.7m stems. The flowers are also the largest and of a distinct tubular bell shape, tending to curve in at the base rather than flare outwards. They may be any shade of pink, magenta or white. It is tall enough to be incorporated into a border although it is very dramatic arching out over a path or beside steps.

Many hybrids have been named but they are frequently seed-raised and not true to name: **'Guinevere'** is medium-sized with white flowers; **'Merlin'** is deep wine red, as is **'Blackbird'**.

Dierama pendulum.

Eucomis
(Pineapple Flower)

The common name for this late summer-flowering South African bulb derives from the tuft of leafy bracts that are carried above the stout flower spike, making it look rather like a pineapple. They have large bulbs producing a basal rosette of leaves which can be rather long and floppy. Although mid-green is the normal colour for the leaves there are cultivars now available with purple, bronzed or spotted leaves. The individual flowers are relatively small and are carried in a tightly packed raceme on stiff stems. They have the rather pungent smell common to many insect-pollinated plants – likened by one young visitor at a flower show to the smell of her brother's bedroom. The showy, inflated seed heads are just as attractive, or even more so, than the flowers and continue the interest until the first frost collapses the stems in late autumn. This is the indicator that the bulbs in pots should be brought under cover. They vary in height from a few centimetres to more than 1m.

Eucomis are useful to add an exotic touch to a sunny border. Their bold flower spikes associate well with half-hardy perennials such as argyranthemum in one of the new flame colours or the colourful spathes of *Zantedeschia elliotiana*. They flower in late summer. The larger cultivars can be planted in borders and the smaller ones make excellent pot plants. Despite their exotic appearance they are easy and undemanding bulbs. At first they were presumed to be borderline hardy and planting against a sunny wall was recommended, but a recent increase in interest and popularity has shown that most are fully hardy. Certainly overlooked bulbs that were left *in situ* in our nursery have survived temperatures to -15°C. Excess winter wet seems to do more damage than cold. The one thing they do require is an adequate supply of water when in growth and a fertile soil or regular feeding if in containers. Under-potting and lack of water will lead to blindness.

Seed head of *Eucomis* 'Joy's Purple'.

Eucomis comosa against a sunny wall.

Cultivation

Eucomis are easy bulbs for a well-drained soil with few pests other than slugs – though an excessively wet winter may cause the bulbs to rot. The bulbs are planted in the spring.

In the open garden they should be planted with at least 10–15cm of soil above them and with 30cm between bulbs to allow for the large leaves.

In containers the bulbs are planted towards the top of a pot but with at least 10–15cm of root run below the bulb. Lightly water them, preferably from the base, until they come into full growth; then water regularly. Large varieties will need daily watering. Feed once a week with a low nitrogen fertilizer. When the bulb starts to die back naturally in the autumn allow the pots to dry off and keep them unwatered in a garage or shed until growth starts again in mid-spring when they should be repotted.

The bulbs are propagated by carefully cutting off the offsets when they are large enough to be detached, or by seed.

E. autumnalis

This is one of the smaller species with bright green wavy-edged leaves and an 18cm raceme of small white flowers. There is often confusion between this and *E. zambesiaca*, which is very similar but has slightly larger racemes. Both are excellent subjects for shallow pans, needing little attention other than water and regular feeding. It is one of the most vigorous, rapidly producing offsets. It flowers in late summer.

E. bicolor 🏆

This easily grown South African bulb has compact heads of purple-edged waxy green flowers with a very obvious tuft of bracts above. The flowers have a quiet charm but are followed by extravagantly inflated seed capsules which remain throughout the autumn. They have wide bright green basal leaves. Although they are easily grown in a sunny border, even seeding around in milder districts, they really are one of the best for containers where their display lasts from midsummer through to the first frost of late autumn. **'Alba'** is a similar size and shape but with pale green flowers. Height: 45–60cm.

Eucomis bicolor.

Eucomis autumnalis.

E. comosa

This handsome bulb is very variable, producing a 60cm flower spike in shades of cream and green, often with a faint purple hue. Many have an obvious dark ovary. The long basal leaves are often bronzed but can be a nuisance, especially in pot-grown subjects. It is a vigorous grower and will rapidly increase. It makes a striking plant against a sunny wall but the flowers can flop; they will grow in light shade as well. Height: 60–90cm.

'Joys Purple' was bred in New Zealand and is one of the best coloured forms with deep wine-red flowers and green leaves. It is also shorter and more compact. Height: 50cm. **'Sparkling Burgundy'** has bronze foliage and stout spikes of white-centred, purple-backed flowers on purple stems. Height: 90cm. **'Zeal Bronze'** is similar.

Eucomis 'Sparkling Burgundy'.

Eucomis 'Joy's Purple'.

E. montana

This is a very distinct species with much shorter wavy edged green leaves and a stiff spike of creamy flowers on a dark purple stem. Each of the flowers has a bold dark ovary and dark anthers. Sadly they hybridize freely with the other species and many commercial stocks are mixed. Height: 40cm.

E. pole-evansii
(Giant Pineapple Flower)

This is the giant of the genus with huge 'fat' heads of pale green flowers on 1.5m stems. For best results it should be planted very deeply and kept well watered and fed although it can be grown in large pots. There seems to be much confusion between *E. pole-evansii* and ***E. pallidiflora*** 𝚼. Some authorities list them as synonyms, some as subspecies and others as separate species. Many of the plants in commerce are seed-raised and have become tainted with *E. comosa* which has added to the confusion. However, in their best forms they are truly magnificent and look spectacular in the middle of summer bedding. We overlooked a bulb in one of our nursery beds which survived winter temperatures of -15°C and flowered magnificently.

Eucomis vandermerwei.

Eucomis montana.

E. vandermerwei

This very distinct species has short, almost prostrate leaves that are heavily mottled and a compact spike of rusty red flowers. It is sometimes encountered under the curious cultivar name 'Octopus', which is indistinguishable from the species but probably sells better as it is easier to pronounce! It is relatively new to cultivation and although hardy its small stature makes it difficult to use in the open garden. It is excellent massed in a shallow pan and grown in full sun and then given winter protection. Height: 15cm.

Galtonia
(Summer Hyacinth)

This South African bulb produces a cluster of long, strap-shaped basal leaves and a spike of hanging tubular flowers in mid- to late summer. Like many summer-flowering bulbs the leaves are already dying away when the blooms appear but they can be disguised by planting them towards the centre of a border. Current DNA analysis suggests that these bulbs are closely related to the genus *Albuca* and they may well change their name at some future date.

Cultivation

The bulbs are planted 15cm deep and 10cm apart in the early spring in a well-drained soil in full sun. In cold, damp soils they are prone to

Galtonia princeps.

Galtonia candicans with agapanthus and crinum.

rot in winter and they are caviar for slugs. They are perfect for a sunny border where they provide an excellent vertical foil for the mounds of herbaceous perennials, especially the flat heads of sedum; or they could be mixed with the ethereal flowers of gypsophylla. They are vigorous enough to be self-supporting. They do not like borders that are heavily mulched with manure or irrigated, and grow best with other sun lovers such as daylilies, crinum or agapanthus. Galtonias are propagated by seed.

G. candicans 🏆

This summer-flowering bulb is one of those curious subjects that love one garden, seeding rapidly to form extensive patches, but hate the next, gradually dwindling away – so much so that some authors even recommend annual planting. Warmth and good drainage is the key to successful growing but the source of the initial bulbs plays an important part as many stocks are infected with the fungus 'basal rot'. They have long basal leaves and a stout spike of hanging waxy white tubular bells. Midsummer. Height: 1.2m.

The two greenish-flowered species seem to have a rather confused nomenclature in commerce with the two names being interchangeable. According to *The Flora of South Africa*, the correct name for the short, deep green-flowered plant on rather arching stems is *G. viridiflora* (70–90cm) while *G. princeps*, which comes from the cliffs of the Drakensberg Mountains, is very similar to *G. candicans* but with green tinted flowers. Height: 1.2m.

Gladiolus

The flat corms of gladiolus produce a fan of sword-like leaves and a one-sided spike of open funnel-shaped flowers. There are a few small-flowered species found in the Mediterranean area that are reasonably hardy but the majority of this family comes from South Africa and they do not tolerate frost. The best known of the northern species is *G. communis* ssp. *byzantinus* which is naturalized in southwest England. Most of the showy large-flowered gladiolus cultivars are not included here as they are not reliably frost hardy, needing to be lifted in the autumn, and they can also be tricky to incorporate successfully into a border as they have an annoying habit of falling over as soon as the flower spike extends beyond the first few flowers. They are also rather unattractive when the spike is half open (or half over depending upon how you view them) unless you assiduously remove the faded flowers. At Hyde Hall, the RHS garden in Essex, the deep burgundy 'Plum Tart' is particularly effective planted among a mass of the wiry stemmed *Gaura linheimeri,* where it has survived for some winters unprotected. Similarly the striking *primulinus* or butterfly gladiolus 'Atom', which has white-edged, brilliant orange-scarlet flowers, has survived some winters here in an open border where it is grown with crocosmia. The primulinus group all have smallish flowers with a distinctly flat upper petal that gives the individual flower a hooded appearance.

Gladiolus 'Plum Tart' with gaura.

The smaller-flowered and shorter *colvillei* and *nanus* hybrids are more in keeping with the scale of most sunny borders and are suitable for sheltered gardens where they will survive all but the coldest winters; alternatively they can be lifted in the autumn and stored frost-free like the larger hybrids.

Gladiolus murielae planted in the gaps left by tulips.

Cultivation

The corms are planted 10–15cm deep in the autumn (European species or small hybrids for mild areas) or in the spring. They like a deep, fertile soil in full sun with plenty of moisture available when they are in active growth. Autumn-planted corms flower from late April to June; spring-planted ones in July and August.

G. murielae *(G. callianthus)* 🏆 (Acidanthera)

Although this is not hardy and it is usually treated as an annual, the acidanthera, to give it its common name, is a very popular bulb for the late summer border with its great curved spikes of large scented flowers. These are pure white with a deep maroon centre. The corms are planted in the spring either directly into the border or they can be grown in pots to be added later to fill any gaps. Acidantheras are a perfect foil for late-flowering pale blue agapanthus such as 'Blue Moon' and burgundy penstemons. They are equally effective planted in large pots, scenting the whole garden in the evening. As the corms are relatively small it is easy to forget that they should achieve 1m or more in growth and there is a danger of using too small a pot. They need a large container for stability and a plentiful and regular supply of water or they may not produce any flowers. Although it is tempting to grow them on after flowering they will need a warm growing period rather than the cool autumn they experience in the northern hemisphere, so it is probably easier to discard the corms and start again the following season.

G. communis subsp. *byzantinus* 🏆

Better known as Whistling Jack, this striking gladiolus is a feature of West Country gardens and hedgerows where it has become naturalized. Whereas *G. communis* from southern Europe has spikes of well-spaced small purplish-red flowers and is often supplied in error, subsp. *byzantinus* as understood by gardeners has bold spikes of large carmine flowers, each with a pale flash on the lower three petals. There is some discussion as to whether the plant in cultivation is a true subspecies or a garden hybrid. In my experience it appears to set a small amount of viable seed (which would appear to be borne out by its wide distribution and movement around a garden) although it also produces many tiny cormlets. It is early flowering and mixes well with *Allium christophii* and deep blue aquilegias. Height: 75cm.

G. tristis

This delicate, pale lemon-flowered South African gladiolus flowers in April and is hardy only in very sheltered gardens. Like many moth-pollinated plants it has an almost overpowering scent but only at night. It is easily raised from seed, flowering in three years. Height: 90cm. Along with *G. cardinalis* it is one of the parents of a group of smaller-flowered gladiolus known as *colvillei* or *nanus* hybrids: **'Prins Claus'** (Prince Claus) has arching sprays of white flowers with a bold carmine streak on the petals; **'Impressive'** ('Good Luck') is similar but with salmon-pink flowers; **'Charm'** has an upright spike of clear pink flowers; **'The Bride'** has an upright spike of pure white flowers with a faint creamy green mark on the petals and is very popular for flower arranging. Height: 60cm.

Gladiolus communis subsp. *byzantinus* in a border with *Allium christopii.*

G. papilio *(G. purpureoauratus)*

This strange stoloniferous South African gladiolus is fully hardy provided the soil is well-drained in winter. It has slender grey leaves and in late summer to autumn produces a succession of arching stems of curious greenish-yellow nodding tubular flowers. These have a darker maroon centre. This gladiolus is rather reticent in flower and can easily be overlooked in the garden, although their offspring will not as they are enthusiastic spreaders. My parents moved some plants out of a border into the rose bed before giving them to us but twenty years later they were still removing corms from among the roses. They need a fertile soil to give a decent display of flowers and are best when seen against the backdrop of other colours, especially yellows. Height: 65cm. The New Zealand cultivar **'Ruby'** has much larger dramatic ruby-red flowers on tall stems and is just as easy. It is a wonderful foil for toning penstemons or growing through grasses. The only problem is the quantity of non-flowering stems it produces. Height: 1m.

Gladiolus 'Prins Claus'.

Iris

The florist iris, usually known as Dutch and English iris, are bulbs that can flower either in late spring or early summer depending upon the season or when the bulbs were planted. See *Chapter 3* for details.

Lilies in a shady border.

Lilium

(Lily)

Lilies are another extraordinarily disparate family of summer-flowering bulbs. The only unifying feature is their bulb, which is made up of a cluster of segments (scales) more or less loosely attached to the basal plate. These can be single or clump-forming and vary in size from 3–8cm in diameter. The bulbs produce a single unbranched flower stem carrying one or more showy flowers. Each of the flowers has six tepals (petals) and can be trumpet-shaped, cup-shaped, recurved like a turk's cap or almost flat. They are usually carried in a spike of two to forty flowers. The individual flower varies in size from 3cm to a mammoth 20cm and they can nod, point upwards or face outwards. They also vary in height from 30cm to a towering 1.8m. Some have the bonus of a magnificent scent than can permeate a whole garden. The narrow, pointed leaves are stem clasping and are either scattered up the stem or arranged in whorls.

Lilies are found in northern temperate latitudes, usually in cool soil in a woodland habitat although some inhabit more open situations. Many of the species and consequently their offspring have strong soil preferences; the scented Asiatic group in particular need an acid soil, but those like *L. regale* that come from limestone cliffs do equally well on acid soils. Most of the lilies grown today are garden hybrids or more accurately cut flower hybrids.

Lilies make excellent cut flowers although one of the risks is staining from the pollen, which is almost indelible. Florists will often remove the stamens and pollen-free varieties are now appearing. The popularity of lilies as a cut flower has caused a huge expansion in the lily market and an unexpected problem for the gardener. Most growers and breeders today concentrate on varieties with upward facing buds which are easy to slip into a cellophane sleeve for the myriad of cut-flower outlets, from florist to garage forecourt or supermarket. New 'improved' varieties are being bred all the time – one grower/breeder trials 500 new hybrids every year. Being seed-raised these are virus-free with the concentration being on 'shelf-life' and indoor decoration. This leads to a very limited palette of colours and a huge turnover in varieties with few being available for more than a few years before they are superseded. Consequently fewer people are growing the species or the well-known garden hybrids which can now be quite hard to track down.

Borders

Tall-flowered lilies can be incorporated into sunny borders. Lilies have a complex and rather muddled flower head and are best planted toward the middle of a border so that they can flower above the rest of the plants. They can easily be overlooked if planted among herbaceous plants of a similar height.

Woodland

If a lily has a turk's cap flower it is a candidate for the cooler part of the garden where it should be planted in open glades among shrubs. Here they will receive some sunshine and such water as is available. In a dry spring adding a bucket of water is recommended. Some, such as *L. martagon*, will seed themselves around.

Containers

Lilies are perfect for growing in pots. Many have a strong fragrance and there are many dwarf varieties specially bred for pot culture. An individual lily bulb is relatively small when compared to the ultimate height of the plant in full flower – this obvious fact is very easy to forget when planting lilies in containers. It is best to err on the side of caution and use a larger size rather than one that is too small. A large pot has enough compost to retain moisture from one watering to the next; small pots can dry out very quickly with the danger that the buds then abort and the whole plant goes into premature dormancy. Pots for lilies need a depth of at least 30cm. A large pot also adds stability to the plant when in flower. I always liken a tall lily in a small pot to a 2m-high man teetering in his wife's size 4 shoes instead of the size 11 wellingtons he would be happier in.

Like all bulbs the display in the next season is dependent upon adequate growing conditions in the current one. It is all too tempting to ignore the pots once they have flowered and forgo the chore of watering them but this will not allow the bulb to replenish itself. Watering and a weekly feed of a low nitrogen fertilizer should continue until mid-autumn when the leaves should naturally start to wither. If the leaves die back before this then they have not received enough water. Placing the pots in the shade will lighten the burden. In this way bulbs will continue to give a good display for many years. Ideally they should be repotted or at least top dressed with fresh compost in November before they produce their new roots. However, my huge pot of 'Casa Blanca' is still flowering magnificently after twelve years without repotting. Feeding and watering is the secret.

One of the dwarf Pixie lilies.

Cultivation

There are three basic rules for growing lilies:

1 Lilies prefer to have their heads in the sun but their feet in the shade – in other words they need a cool root run.
2 All lilies are greedy feeders and require a deep, fertile soil (check for those that are calcifuge – lime haters).
3 Despite the universal fear of bulb rot, lack of water is more likely to be a problem. Virtually all lilies require copious amounts of water when in growth otherwise the buds will abort and a promising clump will quickly turn into a grave disappointment. This is as true of bulbs in the open garden as it is of those in containers. I rarely have any flowers on my large clump of *L. pardalinum* as it is growing under the canopy of a small birch which takes all the moisture in late spring when it comes into leaf, causing the lily to go into premature dormancy.

With the exception of *L. candidum*, which should be planted at soil level, lilies are best planted with at least 10–15cm of soil above them. This will take them below the top layers of the soil with its fluctuating moisture content, give them stability and allow room for stem roots to develop on certain varieties.

Pests

In recent years the scarlet lily beetle from China (or rather its grubs) have munched their way across the UK. These are capable of destroying the foliage of a mature lily in a matter of days. As yet there is no biological control for them but I remember photographing *L. duchartrei* in China and being amazed at seeing a lily beetle looking back up the lens from the undamaged plants, so there is hope of a predator. Until then you must either catch as many of the beetles as you can, and pick off the disgusting grubs in their coat of excrement, or resort to chemical control. The beetle also attacks fritillaries and it is on these that they will first appear in the garden. Vigilance and early control here will prevent a scouting party turning into a full battalion. Lilies are also prone to virus infections and attack by vine weevil, aphids and slugs.

Lilium martagon.

Propagation

Despite their exotic appearance many lilies are remarkably simple to propagate. The species are simple if slow to grow from seed but the easiest method is to grow them from the scales that make up the bulb. They should be carefully detached from the bulb, dusted or dipped in fungicide and then put into a polythene bag with damp, not wet, vermiculite and placed in a warm, dark place. The airing cupboard is the usual choice. In time tiny bulbils will form along the edge of the scale. These are then potted up and grown on. Some lilies, notably *L. martagon*, will do it themselves if the bulbs are disturbed. We find masses of tiny bulblets formed on the scales that are dislodged when we lift the bulbs for sale. I have a curious mixed planting of lilies in a new woodland bed, all of which arrived as dislodged scales left in the bulb storage medium which I then threw out into the garden.

Some lilies such as *L. lancifolium* produce stem bulbils in the leaf axils. These can be removed and treated in the same way as seedlings or just dibbled into the soil at the base of the parents. Clump-forming lilies like *L. pardalinum* can be lifted and the clumps carefully split in late autumn. Most cultivars are micro-propagated commercially.

Like daffodils and tulips lilies are divided into nine divisions (written using roman numerals) based upon their parentage. These are further divided into twenty subsections which I propose to ignore as they are purely visual and do not assist the gardener. I am only listing a few examples of the more commonly available varieties as many of those available today will almost certainly have disappeared within a few years.

Species (Division IX)

Although numerically the species are the last of the classification groups I will list them first as all hybrids are based on them and their characteristics are used to define the groups. Although there are around a hundred species, many of them are not in cultivation or not suitable for the open garden. This list only includes species that are sometimes available.

L. auratum

(Golden-rayed lily of Japan)

This stunning and highly-scented lily from Japan is not easy to satisfy, needing rather poor soil in full sun, but ample moisture. It grows well on the rock garden at Royal Botanic Gardens, Kew, but seems to dwindle in dry woodland. It produces five or more large outward-facing almost flat white flowers recurved at the tip with a yellow central band to each petal in late summer. In some forms the flowers have a scattering of small crimson spots.

L. auratum requires an acid soil and is one of the parents of the Oriental hybrids, many of which have inherited their large open flowers. Sadly many of the commercial stocks are badly infected by virus. Height: up to 1.5m, though frequently shorter.

Lilium auratum.

L. canadensis

This beautiful midsummer-flowering North American rhizomatous lily can be very difficult to satisfy. It requires a well-drained acid soil where there is plenty of moisture available in the summer. In the wild it grows near streams. We grew it successfully for some years in a raised acid bed that was irrigated in summer. When growing well it produces a sturdy stem with whorls of up to twenty slender nodding bell-shaped flowers which are usually golden yellow and heavily spotted with deep maroon. There are red-flowered forms although these are rarely encountered in cultivation. Height: up to 2m but usually considerably less in the garden.

Lilium canadense.

L. candidum 🏆

(Madonna Lily)

The white Madonna lily of Renaissance paintings needs little introduction. Great stands of it still edge many Italian vegetable gardens where they jostle with the spikes of gladiolus. *L. candidum* probably originates in the eastern Mediterranean area where it can be found on dry mountain slopes, but it has long been grown for its medicinal properties as a wound herb. It has been in cultivation for at least 3,000 years with illustrations of it appearing in Minoan and Egyptian art. Unlike most lilies this one really does need a dry sunny spot to do well. Try and be clever with plant associations and it will just give up – as I know to my cost when my large colony was invaded and overshadowed by grasses and golden rod. One of the largest stands I ever saw was in the corner of a neglected cottage garden which was growing little else other than broken bicycles, old fridges and rough grass.

The bulbs are almost evergreen and should be planted just below

Lilium candicum.

the surface during August, which is the only time they are reasonably dormant. Once planted they quickly produce a basal rosette of overwintering leaves. The stiff spike of up to twelve funnel-shaped pure white flowers (the Latin word *candidum* means glistening white) appears in early summer, after which the whole plant slowly dies back. Some authorities suggest that they require or at least do best on a limey soil but this is not true in my experience where some of the finest and tallest clumps I have seen were on acid soil. Excellent drainage seems to be a more important requirement. One of the most attractive displays I have seen was filling a narrow bed circling a sundial in the middle of a sunken lawn. Height: 1.2–2m.

Lilium davidii.

L. davidii

This is a tall Chinese species with up to twenty deep orange turk's cap flowers lightly spotted with maroon on hairy stalks. It needs an acid soil. Height: 1.5m.

L. duchartrei
(Farrer's Marble Martagon)

This lily comes from north China and has, to quote E.H. Wilson, up to twelve 'reflexed marble-white flowers more or less spotted and striated with vineous purple.' This is one of my personal favourites, being

Lilium duchartrei.

Lilium hansonii.

remarkably tolerant of neglect and never ceasing to surprise us with its beautiful flowers clustered at the top of a stiff stem which appears in midsummer. Although it is stoloniferous we find that it rarely makes new bulbs under our conditions, although I have seen a large colony in a much wetter Scottish garden. However, it is easy to raise from seed. It needs a humus-rich, but not necessarily acid soil. I saw it growing in profusion in the amazing tufu region of Jiuzhaigou in China but it does like plenty of water when it is growing. Height: 80cm.

L. formosana var. *pricei*

The tall Taiwanese lily is not suitable for the open in cool northern gardens as it flowers too late in the year and is not fully hardy. However, this dwarf form from the mountains of Taiwan makes an easy and rather unexpected late summer-flowering bulb for the rock garden. Its full-sized reddish-brown backed white trumpet flowers are only 40cm high. It tends to be short lived but is quick and easy to flower from seed. Height: 30–60cm.

L. hansonii 🏆

This is an early and easily grown summer-flowering turk's cap lily from east Siberia and Japan. The distinctive 'fat' buds open to reveal up to twelve rather small waxy egg-yolk yellow flowers with a light dusting of purple spots. It is easy in any good soil in light shade and is long lived but like most lilies needs plenty of moisture when it is in growth or it will quickly abort its flowers. Height: 1.5m.

L. henryi 🏆

This vigorous lily from southwest China requires a neutral or limey soil and is an easy and long-lived plant. In midsummer the tall stem, which may be as much as 2m but is usually less, carries ten, or rarely twenty, large orange turk's cap flowers that pale towards the edge and have dark spots in the centre. Height: 1.5m.

Lilium henryi.

Lilium leichtlinii.

L. lancifolium

(L. tigrinum) **(Tiger Lily)**

The well-known tiger lily of the Far East with its large dark spotted deep orange turk's cap flowers needs little introduction. Sadly botanical rules have meant that it has had to change its name and revert to its earlier one. It has been in cultivation, as a food plant – the bulb scales are stir fried – for hundreds if not thousands of years. It is very vigorous, long lived and easily grown in any soil in part shade. Each of the leaf axils has a small dark bulbil which can be potted up and grown on like a seedling. ***var. splendens*** 🏆 has larger flowers of a more fiery orange and is the form in commerce. var. *flaviflorum* is an attractive form with yellow flowers but is rather prone to virus. Height: 1.7m.

Lilium lancifolium.

L. leichtlinii

This tall tiger lily from Japan has up to eight clear yellow turk's cap flowers lightly spotted with maroon. It is easy in any soil in part shade but will gradually dwindle if the position is too dry. It is perfect for brightening a dark corner. Height: 1.7m.

Lilium 'White American'.

L. longiflorum
(Easter Lily)

This strongly scented lily is very distinct, producing a cluster of long, narrow white trumpet flowers at the top of a sturdy stem in late summer. It comes from the cliffs of southern Japan and Taiwan and is not hardy but makes an excellent pot plant and has long been grown as a cut flower. The dwarf form **'White American'** has the same sized flowers but is fully hardy, even when grown in a container with no protection. It is one of the best late-flowering lilies for pots, flowering freely and increasing rapidly. My ten bulbs turned into sixty in a few years of benign neglect. Height: 40cm.

L. martagon 🏆

The classic turk's cap lily from Europe is easy to grow in part shade. It has whorls of leaves up the stem which is topped in early to midsummer by an open raceme of up to fifty small reflexed flowers in shades of purple. These vary quite markedly in colour from almost plum purple to pale lilacs with a variable amount of spotting. When growing well it will form extensive colonies and self-seed around the garden, although a period of drought in spring can cause it to abort its flowers and go into premature dormancy. Bulbs may easily take two seasons to settle down and start flowering but once established they resent disturbance. We once moved a very old and free-flowering clump, carefully replanting the huge bulbs in what we thought was an ideal situation only for them to turn up their toes and disappear. They will tolerate a wide range of soils but prefer to be in part shade. In some gardens they will even naturalize in grass. ***var. album*** 🏆 has similar spikes of pure white flowers and is just as easy (if not easier) to grow. It is particularly useful to lighten a dark corner or to flower above *Helleborus orientalis* or hosta leaves; it also blends beautifully with the spikes of white willowherb *(Epilobium angustifolium)*, which appear at the same time. Height: 1–1.5m.

Lilium martagon v. *album*.

L. monodelphum

The stately golden lily of the Caucasus is one of the most rewarding of garden plants. In early summer it produces a bold spike of between ten and thirty large, creamy-yellow, nodding trumpet-shaped flowers with recurved tips in early summer. These are rather variable in tone and some clones are lightly spotted. Although it is rarely offered commercially, with patience it is easily raised from seed. It is lime tolerant and likes quite heavy soils in part shade where it can be left undisturbed. Height: 1.5m. *L. szovitsianum* is very similar.

L. nepalense

This lily produces large, pale green trumpet-shaped flowers with an intense dark maroon centre in midsummer. The flowers nod and those I have seen in the wild are fully reflexed into a turk's cap shape but in cultivation they tend to be more trumpet-shaped with just the tips recurving. This is one of those frustrating bulbs that can be very difficult to satisfy. It comes from the foothills of the Himalayas in Nepal where I found it growing in apple orchards. It requires an acid soil and

Lilium nepalense.

is virtually impossible to grow in a pot as the shoots are stoloniform, preferring to travel underground some distance before emerging, frequently out of the drainage hole! To confuse matters even more it is also stoloniferous, the new shoots and their embryonic bulbs also preferring to emerge from the base of the pot. We found it grew best under a north wall or when planted under the shelter of a dwarf rhododendron. The shoots could then emerge safely in any direction. It requires copious amounts of water but when growing well they quickly form quite a sizeable colony. It is reputedly not fully hardy but bulbs have survived hard frosts here. Height: 70cm.

L. pardalinum 🏆
(Leopard or Panther Lily)

This is a vigorous clump-forming North American lily that flowers in midsummer. It is easily grown in a moist soil in part shade and is lime tolerant. The tall stems have dense whorls of leaves and produce an

Lilium pumilum.

open spike of up to ten rounded turk's cap flowers. These have intense red-orange tips and a distinct pale orange or yellow centre covered in purple dots. When growing well with plenty of moisture they can achieve 2m or more but on my dry light soil they struggle to reach 60cm and, instead of a handsome spike of ten flowers, I am lucky to have any. var. *giganteum* is an exceptionally vigorous variety. Height: up to 2m.

Lilium pardalinum.

L. pumilum 🏆
(L. tenuifolium)

This small elegant Asian lily flowers in midsummer and requires an acid soil and plenty of moisture. It has narrow leaves and produces a slender spike of 2–10 small, brilliant scarlet turk's cap flowers that really glisten like sealing wax. I remember seeing it glowing in the scrub across a potato field in China. Although it is regularly available and fully hardy it can be difficult to keep going. Height: 60cm.

L. pyrenaicum 🏆

This Pyrenean lily could not be described as being one of the more showy species but it is easy to grow and has become naturalized in the cooler parts of Britain, where it spreads by seed, even growing in light grass. The stiff stems are covered in tightly packed narrow leaves and are topped by a raceme of up to twelve rather small and somewhat insignificant yellow turk's cap flowers in early summer. These are flecked or spotted with maroon in the centre. The flowers have an unpleasant aroma but this is not really noticeable in the garden. They are easily raised from seed. Height: 75cm.

Lilium pyrenaicum.

Lilium regale.

L. regale 🏆

The story of this, probably the best known of all lilies, is worth repeating. It was not discovered until 1903 when E.H. Wilson was exploring the precipitous valley of the Min River in north Sichuan, China. To his amazement he saw 'thousands, aye tens of thousands' of this spectacular lily growing out of every rock crevice and filling the air in the evening 'with delicious perfume exhaled from every bloom'. Sadly, my visit was too late to see them in flower but the stems with their heavy seed pods were in evidence squashed into the narrow crevices high above our heads and growing in old oil drums outside local houses. In 1910 Wilson was able to make a collection of some 6,000 bulbs which, having survived their six-month journey half way across the globe, happily settled into their new home on the east coast of America. Virtually all the bulbs grown today have their origins in this collection.

In midsummer *L. regale* produces a stiff stem with narrow leaves and an umbel of five to ten large trumpet flowers. These are evenly spaced around the top of a stiff stem rather like a loudspeaker system. The flowers are a glistening white with a yellow throat and are purple flushed outside. Some forms are especially floriferous and umbels of twenty flowers or more have been recorded although to my mind these congested heads are rather unattractive (a case of 'less is more'). It is easy and tolerant of many soil conditions, although it prefers more sun than many and may dwindle on light acid soils. It is suitable for large pots, although the bulbs may need supporting and to be replaced regularly. It grows happily in light shade between shrubs and we grow it through *Dicentra formosa* under our pergola. It grows quickly and freely from seed. Height: 1.2m.

L. speciosum

This vigorous scented lily from east China and Japan is one of the last to flower in late summer or early autumn and has long been grown in Europe where it had the title 'Queen of Lilies'. In 1837 Lindley wrote glowingly about 'the deep rose-colour of its flowers, which seem all rugged with rubies and garnets, and sparkling with crystal points'. However, the rather wiry stem, covered in short leaves, is inclined to fall over and needs to be discreetly supported if the flowers are to be seen to advantage. The stem is topped by a raceme of large deep pink turk's cap flowers. The centre of the flower is covered in deep pink spots. It requires a cool acid soil in part shade with plenty of moisture and is an excellent and long-lived bulb for containers. **var. album** has large, pure white flowers. Height: 1–1.5m.

L. superbum 🏆
(Swamp Lily)

This is another of the vigorous North American clump-forming lilies for a moist soil in part shade. Unlike *L. pardalinum* it requires an acid soil and is later flowering, which means that a constant supply of moisture is even more important. The maroon-spotted turk's cap flowers are bright orange flushed with red and are carried in a stiff spike of up to thirty flowers. Height: up to 2m, when growing well.

Lilium superbum.

The hybrids

As already discussed, the availability of individual varieties tends to be ephemeral so the ones listed below are only an indication of the range available in each group. Some of the best places to see and buy lilies are the large flower shows. As lily-breeding develops so more unusual varieties are produced using hybrids rather than species and the boundaries between the groups is becoming blurred.

Asiatic hybrids (Division I)

These are the stalwarts of the cut-flower trade and are derived from a large number of species including *L. bulbiferum*, *L. amabile*, *L. lancifolium* and *L. davidii*. They are characterized by rather open, cup-shaped, unscented flowers. These usually face upwards (Ia) but can face outwards (Ib) or down (Ic). These are among the easiest of all lilies to grow and have no specific soil requirements. They are very variable in height and many dwarf varieties have been bred especially for pot culture. They are available in a wide range of colours and in the garden flower in early to midsummer.

'Fireking' (I).

'Destiny'(I).

'Red Carpet' is one of a range of dwarf pot lilies (I).

'Apollo' 🏆 (I).

'Netty's Pride' (I).

A new group of lilies, developed in eastern Europe, has recently come onto the market. These are very distinct and will certainly add drama to your pots or borders. They have the traditional cup shaped flower but all have a bold central band of dark marks or spots.

'Netty's Pride' is one of the new breed of lilies which have the most amazing black-maroon centres to the white flowers; **'Lion Heart'** is deep gold with an almost black-brown centre to the petals.

'Lion Heart' (I).

'Mrs Backhouse' (II).

Martagon hybrids (Division II)

These cultivars are derived from *L. martagon* and *L. hansonii* and all have the classic small, turk's cap flower. They are best grown in light shade where they flower in early summer. **'Mrs Backhouse'** is an old cultivar, but there are new ones appearing.

Candidum hybrids (Division III)

These are derived from *L. candidum* with other European species and are rarely encountered. **L. × testaceum** 🏆 is the best known of these hybrids with pale apricot nodding turk's cap flowers but it is now rarely seen, many of the stocks having succumbed to virus. Height: 1.5m.

American hybrids (Division IV)

These are derived from a range of American species such as *L. canadense*, *L. pardalinum* and *L. superbum*. They usually have turk's cap flowers and many are clump forming. They are only rarely encountered. They flower in midsummer.

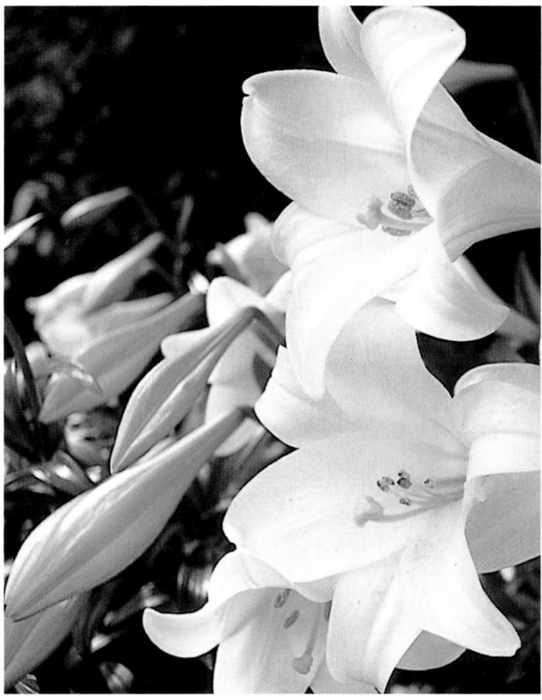

'White American' (V).

Longiflorum hybrids (Division V)

These are derived from *L. longiflorum* with other species such as *L. formosanum*. They have scented, trumpet-shaped flowers. Most of them are not hardy and are mainly produced for the cut flower trade. **'White American'** is a good dwarf form for pots. They flower mid-to late summer.

Trumpet and Aurelian hybrids (Division VI)

These cultivars are derived from *L. regale*. They have clusters of large, trumpet-shaped scented flowers and although they are lime tolerant they will grow equally well on acid soils. They are among the most versatile lilies, being long lived and easily grown. They are stem rooting and should be planted with at least 15cm of soil above the bulb. These lilies are tall enough to incorporate into the middle of a traditional herbaceous border but are just as happy among shrubs; alternatively they can be grown in large pots. They grow best in part shade. The group is further subdivided according to the shape of the flower. They produce their flowers in midsummer.

'African Queen' 🏆 (VI).

'Pink Perfection Group' 🏆 (VI).

Oriental hybrids (Division VII)

These late-flowering lilies are derived from Asiatic species such as *L. speciosum* and *L. auratum* and one of their main attractions is their strong fragrance. The shape and height of the flower is very variable and depends upon their parentage. Those derived from *L. speciosum* have recurved turk's cap flowers whilst others have flat, saucer-shaped flowers. This group includes some of the best known varieties for pot cultivation such as 'Star Gazer' and 'Casa Blanca'.

Recently, pollen-free double varieties have become available. These may be excellent cut flowers but I am not certain that their rather muddled appearance adds anything to the garden. All require an acid soil and flower in late summer. **'Cesar'** is a vigorous, scented and long lived lily with large pale pink flowers. **'Casa Blanca'** 🏆 is probably the best known of this group with 15cm flat white flowers. It is excellent in large pots where it is very long lived, making a dramatic display in late summer. Height: 1–1.5m. The compact **'Star Gazer'** was bred for pot culture and is very vigorous and long lived. The sturdy stems carry up to five large, open, upward-facing flowers of white heavily suffused with a rich, almost strident pink and with a light dusting of darker pink spots. Height: 70cm–1m. **'Miss Lucy'** is one of the newer double-flowered oriental lilies.

'Cesar' (VII).

'Casa Blanca' (VII).

'Star Gazer' (VII).

'Miss Lucy' (VII).

'Black Beauty' (VIII) in the garden.

Other hybrids (Division VIII)

This is the usual catch-all division for everything else and is the fastest growing section with new crosses appearing all the time. These are bred for vigour and make excellent garden plants, being healthy and vigorous. Some look just like oriental hybrids but because the other parent is an American species they cannot be included in that section. **'Black Beauty'** looks just like a giant *L. speciosum* but is lime tolerant and very vigorous although it may need some support. It has up to twenty deep pink recurved scented flowers on 1.8m stems. Unwanted and neglected sales pots quickly recovered in a shrub bed here and the display keeps improving every year.

The most distinctive of this division are the so-called 'Orienpets' or 'OT' which are the result of crossing oriental cultivars with trumpet cultivars. They tend to have large, rather waxy flowers and many have inherited the best characteristics of both groups, being both scented and lime tolerant.

Another new group is the tree lilies such as **'Palmyra'** and **'Big Brother'** which can reach a staggering 2.2m with huge flowers to match. Again, they are lime tolerant.

'Nymph' (OT).

'Robina' (OT).

'Palmyra' (tree lily).

'Frio' (OT).

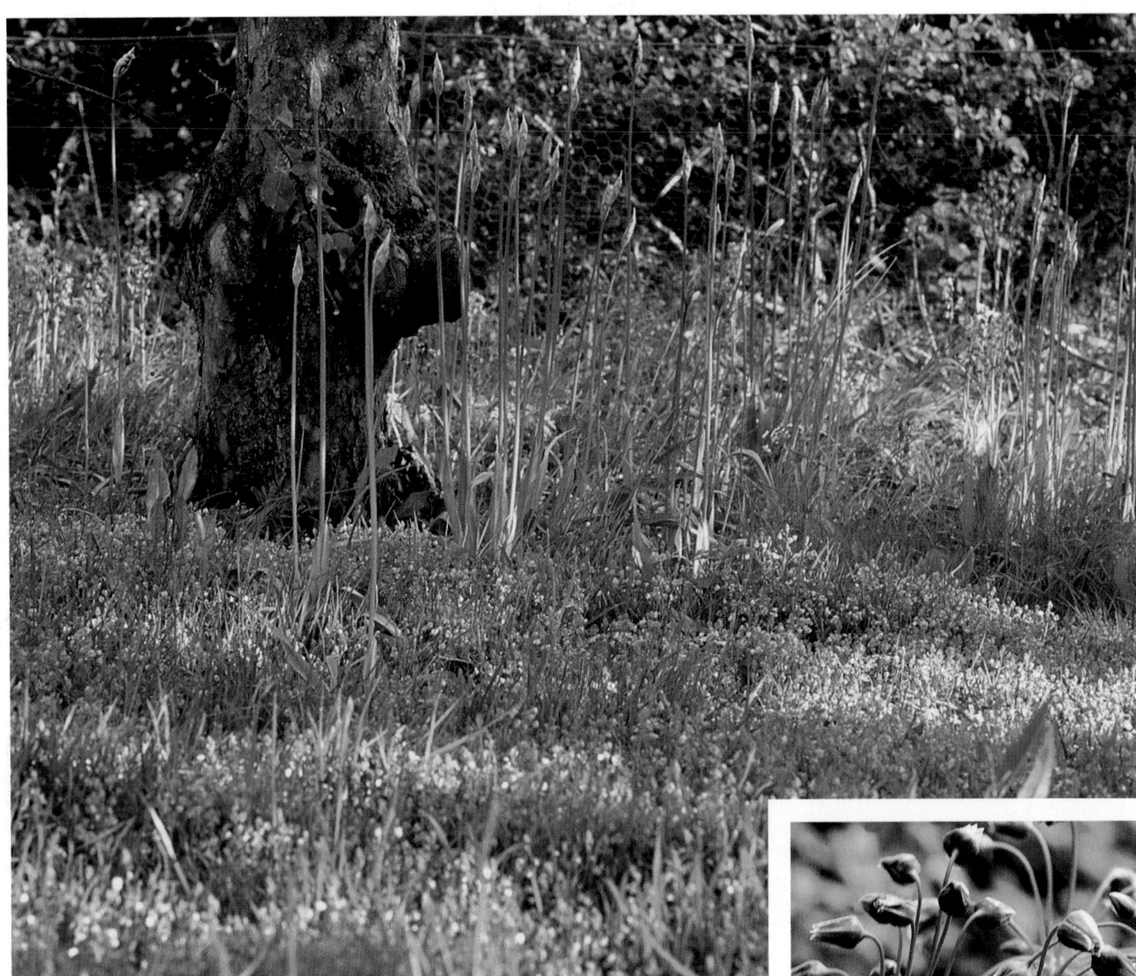

Nectaroscordum siculum naturalized with bluebells.

Nectaroscordum

Bulb catalogues often list these under allium although they are a separate genus. They require a sunny, well-drained soil.

N. siculum
(Allium siculum)

These early summer-flowering relatives of alliums come from southern Europe and have stem-clasping leaves which are very pungent. The flowers are held in a loose cluster on the top of a stout stem. The upright buds open into pendulous bell-shaped flowers of greenish-white, more or less marked with pinkish-brown. Unlike the round seed heads of many alliums these stand stiffly erect rather like the spears of a Roman soldier and if your soil is dry and sunny then they too might be planning an invasion. The assiduous removal of the seed heads before they fully ripen will check this often over-exuberant increase. Small clumps should be grown towards the front of the border where their unusual shape can be appreciated. They are particularly fine rising above hostas or similar bold foliage plants and although they love dry, sunny soils they are surprisingly effective here

Nectaroscordum tripedale.

grown in grass under apple trees where they flower as the companion bluebells fade. Height: 1.2m. Subsp. *bulgaricum* from southeast Europe and Turkey is very similar.

N. tripedale (1.2m) and *N. meliophyllum* (1.6m)

These are very beautiful and frustrating species with similar rounded heads of nodding clear pink flowers. They are very difficult to establish, slow to increase and virtually impossible to raise from seed but are fully hardy once persuaded to grow, slowly clumping up.

Nothoscordum

This South American allium relative is included only so that it can be avoided at all costs. *N. inodorum*, sometimes encountered under its highly misleading old name *Allium fragrans*, is a pernicious weed, seeding freely in any well-drained soil and especially under glass. It has clusters of long basal leaves and small heads of brown-backed white flowers. These can appear at any time in the summer and produce prodigious amounts of seed. Unfortunately the bulb also produces clusters of tiny offsets, which easily become detached when attempting to dig the thug out. It is easily identified by its lack of onion smell. Height: 45cm.

Nomocharis in Yunnan, China.

Nomacharis

These beautiful lily relatives come from the mountains of west China and north India and require a similar cool, moist climate. In warm or dry areas they quickly disappear. They require a humus-rich acid soil in part shade, and grow well with dwarf rhododendrons. They all have similar flat white or pink flowers with darker pink spots and whorls of narrow leaves up the stem. They are easily raised from seed but are prone to slug damage.

ORCHIDS

Cypripedium

The lady's slipper orchids have a reputation for being difficult but given a fertile, humus-rich soil in part shade with plenty of moisture available when they are growing, these exotic plants are relatively easy, just slow, which is reflected in their cost. They are raised by micropropagation and prefer a neutral to alkaline soil. All have a fat balloon-like pouch, the slipper of its common name, instead of an orchid's usual lip, with three narrow petals arranged above it. There is often a strong contrast in colour between these and the pouch. The pleated oval leaves are arranged up the stem. Cypripediums are very slow to increase, only gradually forming a clump, and care should be taken not to allow more vigorous neighbours to swamp them. They resent disturbance and it is best not to attempt propagation, and buy a new plant. Height: 45cm.

Cypripedium reginae.

Dactylorhiza

The northern European terrestrial orchids are relatively easy to grow in soil that is not too dry. They are only rarely offered for sale as they are very slow to increase, most of the commercially available ones being painstakingly raised by seed or micropropagation. In the garden they can be propagated by careful division of the clump-forming species in the spring; others will produce self-sown seedlings, often in unexpected places. Height: 20–30cm.

Epipactis
(Chatterbox Orchid)

This North American rhizomatous orchid has a quiet charm and is easy to grow in any soil, in sun or part shade, that is damp. It spreads to form quite extensive patches with small hooded green and maroon flowers. The common name comes from its trembling bottom orange lip. Height: 40cm.

Dactylorhiza foliosa.

Cypripedium calceolus.

Dactylorhiza maculata.

Epipactis gigantea.

Ornithogalum

The summer-flowering members of this large and extremely variable family of bulbs have basal leaves and a slender spike of flowers. In the wild they grow in a variety of habitats in South Africa, Europe, the Middle East and southwest Asia. They include the well-known Chincherinchee *(O. thyrsoides)*, but only a few are hardy or garden-worthy.

O. arabicum is one of the showiest of the genus with large, pure white flowers clustered at the top of a 45cm stem in early summer. I have seen it flowering profusely in the sand dunes behind a Spanish resort and it requires a similar dry, frost-free position. It grows well in the beds of our unheated tunnels. The brilliant orange *O. dubium* is frequently encountered as a flowering pot plant but this South African is not hardy and is best treated as an annual and used to brighten the front of a sunny border. Height: 25cm.

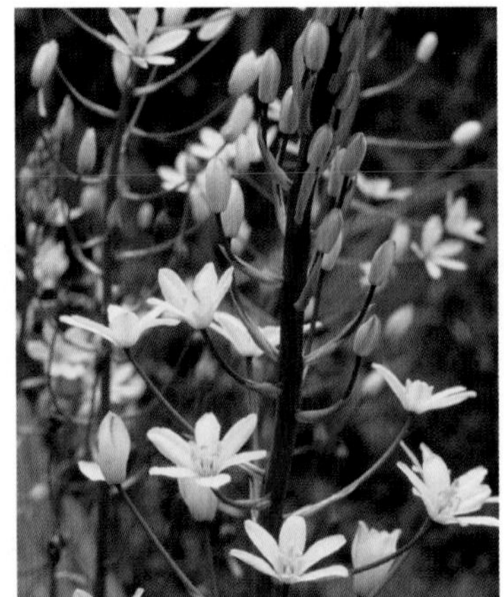

Ornithogalum magnum.

O. magnum

This handsome bulb comes from the Caucasus and is probably the showiest of a very similar group of bulbs that have their starry white flowers arranged in a tall spike. They flower in late spring or early summer. It is easily grown in a sunny position and produces a handsome 1m spike of glistening white flowers. The earlier-flowering ***O. narbonense*** from Turkey is similar but smaller in all its parts. Height: 60cm.
O. pyramidale from the Balkans has a similar spike of white flowers.

Ornithogalum arabicum.

Oxalis

Oxalis seem to fall into two camps – miffy or invasive – so most will be left out of this guide. However, the variety below is well behaved and will grow in any sunny, well-drained soil. We have well established clumps of *O. tetraphylla* on a dry rock garden under a lime tree where it flowers profusely for many weeks in early summer. It is hardy to -5°C or considerably lower if it is dry.
O. tetraphylla (O. deppei), a clump-forming bulb from Mexico, is sometimes called the 'lucky clover' and has similar four-lobed leaves and clusters of showy yellow-centered pink flowers. The leaves of 'Iron Cross' have a dark purple band at the base. Height: 15cm.

Oxalis tetraphylla.

Triteleia

These summer-flowering corms are closely related to *Brodiaea*, and *T. laxa* is better known as a cut flower under this older name. Although they are natives of California these species are reliably perennial in a well-drained soil in full sun where they will increase to form substantial patches. Like many bulbs from areas with limited rainfall they produce their slender leaves early in the season with the flowers following later. The long-lasting tubular flowers are held in a lax umbel at the top of a leafless stem. As each individual flower head is rather sparse and the individual flowers open in succession the corms are best planted close together to give a bolder display.

Tritleia 'Queen Fabiola'

Cultivation

The corms are planted about 10cm deep in a well-drained soil in full sun in autumn or spring. They are the perfect companions for lavenders or other sun lovers and are ideal in a gravel garden where they will increase to form sizeable clumps. Propagate by offsets removed after the flowers fade.

Triteleia hyacinthina.

T. hyacinthina

This corm has compact heads of white or delicate blue, rather open flowers in late spring or early summer. It is the first of the triteleia to flower and requires a well-drained soil in full sun. It is well established on the rock garden at the RHS Wisley garden. Height: 50cm.

T. ixioides 'Starlight'

This early summer-flowering triteleia is slightly more vulnerable to harsh winters than the others but will survive frost provided the ground is not wet. It has an open umbel of up to twenty-five showy sulphur-yellow flowers with a curious small perianth tube like a daffodil rather than the open tubular flowers of the other species. It is long lasting in flower, the colour only gradually fading, and is useful for a sunny rock garden or against a sunny wall. The thin basal leaves are never an embarrassment. **'Splendens'** is golden yellow. Height: 40cm.

T. laxa

This is the plant incorrectly known to florists as brodiaea. It is a showy corm with large, rather open umbels of narrow tubular flowers in shades of blue. It is usually sold in named forms and the bulbs should be massed to maximize their impact. The thin basal leaves appear early in the spring and are fading by the time the flowers appear in midsummer. They are excellent for any very dry sunny border and can be left undisturbed for many years. They are ideal for those difficult, dry borders against a house or wall. I grow clumps of them in the gravel of our sunny terrace where they are adjacent to lavenders. Height: 75cm. An upsurge in interest in these easy and rewarding corms has resulted in many new cultivars. **'Corrina'** has deep purple-blue flowers; **'Queen Fabiola'** (or more correctly **'Koningen Fabiola'**) is free flowering with good clear blue flowers; **'Rudy'** is a striking selection where the large white flowers have a deep blue stripe down the centre of each petal; **'4u'** has pinkish flowers; **'White Sweep'** and **'Silver Queen'** are two new pure white cultivars. All make excellent and long-lasting cut flowers.

Triteleia ixiodes 'Starlight'.

Triteleia laxa 'Rudy'.

Tritonia

This is one of those plants that give botanists a bad press. For many years it was erroneously lumped under Montbretia, then it joined *Crocosmia* before finally moving to the sun-loving *Tritonia*.

T. disticha rubrolucens (Montbretia *or Crocosmia rubra)*

This late summer-flowering South African bulb has distinct flat dark red corms reminiscent of a gladiolus. It is clump forming and the clusters of fine, narrow leaves give rise to wiry branched stems with a terminal spike of small salmon pink tubular flowers. It is easily grown in the front of any sunny border but it does have an annoying tendency to flop over if it is shaded by over-vigorous neighbours. It has a reputation for being slightly tender but our large stock has grown outside in the open without damage for many years. Like many summer-flowering bulbs, good winter drainage seems to be the key to success. Height: 1m.

Tritonia disticha rubrolucens.

Tulbaghia violacea.

Tulbaghia

Although these rhizomatous South African bulbs are not fully hardy they make excellent plants for containers. They produce clumps of roots rather like chives. These can be propagated by cutting them up in early spring. The variety below is suitable for growing outside in sheltered gardens, although newly divided plants should be protected from frost.

T. violacea

In mild districts this species can be grown outside in a well-drained soil in full sun where it will form quite sizeable clumps. There is a huge planting of it near the glasshouse in Edinburgh Botanic Garden where it thrives with other South African bulbs. Otherwise they should be grown in a container which can be given winter protection. They look particularly attractive in shallow pans. Although the narrow grey leaves smell of garlic if bruised, the small umbels of lilac flowers are lightly scented. These are carried on slender leafless stems and appear in succession at any time throughout the summer. Var. *pallida* has pale lilac, almost white flowers. Height: 70cm. **'Silver Lace'** has cream striped leaves and is less hardy. Height: 45cm.

Zantedeschia

Known colloquially as the arum lily, these have a large tuberous rhizome and are grown for their brightly coloured spathes. They have lance or arrow-shaped leaves and are summer dormant. They come from East and South Africa and are not fully hardy.

Z. aethiopica

The arum lily is a plant of swamps and can be grown as a pond-side plant where the water protects it from severe frost. In the open garden it does best in a deep, moist soil in full sun, and they make handsome pot plants for a conservatory. Height: 60cm. **'Crowborough'** has exceptionally large spathes of glistening white and yellow that open flat; **'Green Goddess'** has green spathes with a white centre; **'Kiwi Blush'** is a delicate pink.

Zantedeschia 'Crowborough'.

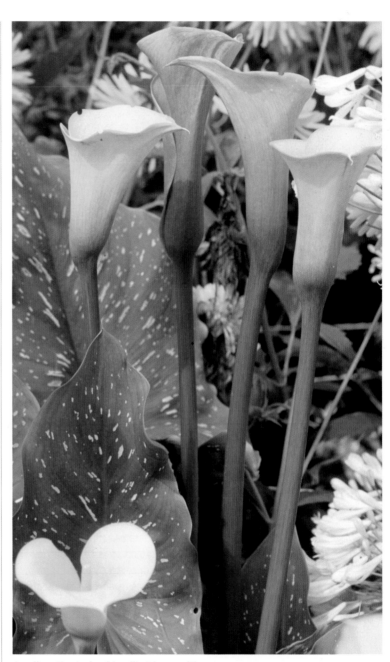

A yellow *Zantedeschia elliottiana* cultivar.

Z. elliottiana

This clump-forming tuber has upright, heart-shaped leaves covered with white spots and slender upright spathes that remain furled. There are many named cultivars with colours ranging from white and yellow to deep plum but many of the commercial stocks are mixed so it is best to choose a plant when it is in flower. They flower in late summer and add an exotic touch to a border. They benefit from a winter mulch in the open garden. Height: 60–90cm.

PLANTING TABLE

A guide to choosing bulbs to suit particular places

SUNNY BORDERS					
	Flowering time	**Height in cm**	**Planting depth in cm**	**Distance apart in cm**	**Planting season**
AUTUMN					
Colchicum	Aug – October	10 – 20	10	10	Summer
Crocus (autumn-flowering)	Aug/Sept	17	10	5	Summer
Schizostylis (Hesperanthus)	Sept/Nov	60	5	5	Spring or in flower
Tritonia and Crocosmia	Aug/Sept	60	10	5	Spring
WINTER/EARLY SPRING					
Anemone (blanda)	Feb/March	8	8	8	Autumn
Crocus	Feb/March	8	10	5 – 8	Autumn
Eranthis (Winter aconite)	Feb/March	8	10	5 – 8	Autumn or Spring
Galanthus (Snowdrops)	Feb/March	10 –25	10	5 – 8	Autumn or Spring
Iris (Reticulata)	Feb/March	15	10	5	Autumn
Scilla	Feb	10	10	8	Autumn
SPRING					
Chionodoxa	March	12	10	5	Autumn
Fritillaria 1 imperialis (Crown Imperial)	April	70	20	20	Autumn
2 smaller species	Mar/April	8 – 30	10	10	Autumn
Hyacinthus – (bedding Hyacinths)	Mar/April	25	15	10	Autumn
Ipheion	Feb – April	12	10	5	Autumn
Iris (Juno)	April	30 – 45	10	10	Autumn
Muscari (Grape hyacinths)	Mar/April	12 – 20	10	5	Autumn
Narcissus (Daffodil)	Mar – May	20 – 45	15	10	Autumn
Scilla	April – May	20 – 37	10	7	Autumn
Tulip	Mar – May	15 – 60	20	10	Autumn
SUMMER					
Allium	May – August	20 – 90	15	5 - 15	Autumn
Camassia	May/June	60	15	10	Autumn

Planting times

Spring planting – may be dormant bulbs or bulbs in growth

Summer planting – August for autumn-flowering bulbs

Crinum	July/August	75	At soil level	1m	Spring
Crocosmia	July – Sept	60 – 90	10	5	Spring or in flower
Galtonia	July/August	40 – 75	10	15	Spring
Gladiolus	July – Sept	45cm – 1m	12	10 – 15	Autumn or Spring
Iris (florist)	May/June	40 – 60	10	10 – 15	Autumn
Lilium	June – Sept	50cm – 2m	20	20	Autumn or Spring
SHADY BORDERS					
AUTUMN					
Colchicum	Aug – October	10 – 20	10	10	Summer
Crocus	Sept/October	7 – 17	10	7	Summer
Cyclamen	August – Nov	5 – 10	3	10 – 20	Autumn or Spring
Galanthus	Oct/Nov	10	10	5	Autumn or Spring
WINTER					
Anemone	Feb/March	7	7	7	Autumn
Crocus	Dec – Feb	7 – 10	10	5	Autumn
Cyclamen	Jan/Feb	10	3	10	Autumn or Spring
Eranthis (Winter aconite)	Feb/March	7	10	7	Autumn
Galanthus (Snowdrop)	Jan – March	10 – 30	10	5	Autumn or Spring
Iris (Reticulata)	Jan/Feb	15	10	5	Autumn
Scilla	Feb	12	7	5	Autumn
SPRING					
Anemone	Mar/April	15	5	7	Autumn
Arisarum (Mouse plant)	May	7	15	5	Autumn
Arum	May	30	15	10	Autumn
Corydalis	March/April	7 – 15	15	10	Autumn
Chionodoxa	March	12	10	5	Autumn
Cyclamen	April	10	10	10	Autumn or Spring
Erythronium (Dogs tooth violet)	March/April	7 – 25	15	10	Autumn
Fritillaria	April/May	20 – 60	15	10	Autumn
Hyacinthoides (Bluebell)	April/May	30	10	10	Autumn or Spring
Leucojum (Snowflake)	Feb – April	30 – 55	15	10	Autumn

SHADY BORDERS

	Flowering time	Height in cm	Planting depth in cm	Distance apart in cm	Planting season
SPRING *(continued)*					
Narcissus (Daffodil)	March – May	25 – 55	15	10	Autumn
Ornithogalum	April/May	30	15	5	Autumn
Scilla	March – May	15 – 30	15	10	Autumn
Trillium	April/May	25 – 45	10	10	Winter
Tulip	April	35	15	10	Autumn
SUMMER					
Cardiocrinum	July	1.8 – 2.5m	5	40	Spring
Crocosmia	July – Sept	60 – 75	15	10	Spring
Lilium	May – Sept	60cm – 2m	20	20	Autumn or Spring

BULBS IN GRASS

	Flowering time	Height in cm	Planting depth in cm	Distance apart in cm	Planting season
AUTUMN					
Colchicum	Sept/Oct	10 – 20	10	10	Summer
Crocus	Sept – Nov	15	10	7	Summer
Cyclamen	Aug – Oct	10	3	20	Autumn or Spring
WINTER					
Anemone	Feb/March	7	7	7	Autumn
Crocus	Dec – March	7 – 10	10	5	Autumn
Eranthis (Winter aconite)	Feb	7	10	7	Autumn or Spring
Galanthus (Snowdrop)	Dec – March	10 – 20	10	5	Autumn or Spring
SPRING					
Anemone	Feb/March	7	7	5	Autumn
Chionodoxa	March	12	10	5	Autumn
Crocus	March	10	10	5	Autumn
Fritillaria	March/April	20	8	5	Autumn
Hyacinthoides (Bluebell)	April/May	30	10	10	Autumn or Spring
Leucojum	April	25	15	10	Autumn
Muscari (Grape hyacinth)	March/April	10 – 45	10	7	Autumn
Narcissus (Daffodil)	March – May	10 – 45	10	7	Autumn
Scilla	March	10 – 15	8	5	Autumn
Tulip	April	35	15	10	Autumn

BULBS IN GRASS

	Flowering time	Height in cm	Planting depth in cm	Distance apart in cm	Planting season
SUMMER					
Allium	June	25	10	5 – 15	Autumn
Camassia	May/June	60 – 90	10	10	Autumn
Iris (English)	June/July	50	15	10	Autumn
Ornithogalum	May/ccJune	10 – 35	10	5	Autumn
Lilium	June	1m	20	20	Winter

BULBS FOR SPECIAL PLACES

	Flowering time	Height in cm	Planting depth in cm	Distance apart in cm	Planting season
ROCK GARDENS, RAISED BEDS, TROUGHS					
Acis	Aug/Sept	15	5	5	Spring
Allium	June – August	15	8	5	Autumn or Spring
Anemone	March – May	10	8	5	Autumn
Chionodoxa	March	12	10	5	Autumn
Crocus	Sept – Feb	5 – 15	10	5	Autumn
Fritillaria	April	20 – 30	10	5	Autumn
Iris (Reticulata & Juno)	Feb – April	10 – 25	12	10	Autumn
Muscari (Grape hyacinths)	March – May	12 – 25	10	5	Autumn
Narcissus (Daffodil)	Feb – April	10 – 30	10	5	Autumn
Oxalis	April/May	10	5	5	Autumn
Puschkinia	April	10	7	5	Autumn
Scilla	Feb/March	10	10	5	Autumn
Tulip	March – May	7 – 30	10	10	Autumn
SHELTERED BORDERS, AGAINST A WALL, ETC.					
Amaryllis	Sept – Nov	45	5	10	Spring
Crinum	August/Sept	90	Half in soil	1m	Spring
Eucomis (Pineapple flower)	July – Sept	20 – 90	10	15	Spring
Nerine	Sept/Oct	60	5	10	Spring
Sternbergia	Sept/Oct	12	10	5	Summer

Planting times

Spring planting – may be dormant bulbs or bulbs in growth

Summer planting – August for autumn-flowering bulbs

A

B

C

D

E